Hidden Channels of the Mind

Hidden Channels of the Mind

LOUISA E. RHINE

FOREWORD BY J. B. RHINE

William Morrow and Company NEW YORK

This book is dedicated to all those unnamed individuals who made this study possible: to those who were puzzled enough and cared enough to write down their experiences. Whether or not their accounts appear herein, they make up the representative numbers that give this study its validity.

I wish to express my gratitude to those who helped me write this book: my husband, J. B. Rhine, whose continuing interest and counsel were invaluable; and all the others who read, criticized, encouraged, and typed: Sally Rhine Feather, Frances M. Greene, Dorothy Pope, Rena Ratte, Dorothy Bullock, Peggy Murphy, and Sarah Bilberry.

Foreword

This is a *timely* book. The new study of man called parapsychology needs it—and right now. Parapsychology is a branch of science that deals with a range of mental abilities commonly called "psychic," and is best known for its concern with extrasensory perception, or ESP. Research in ESP has been going on steadily, especially so over the last twenty-five years, and in spite of the many difficulties and the small number of workers, some discoveries have been made that are revolutionary.

Why are they revolutionary? Because they show that man is not as simple as the textbooks say. To have a power such as ESP he has to be a much more complicated being, living in a far more intricate universe than conventional science has claimed. This complexity shows that much more still remains to be discovered about him. The gap between a man and an "electronic brain" is enormously widened.

Discoveries, if really new, are not readily accepted; they upset too many old habits and theories. The evidence for ESP does just that. As Arthur Koestler explains in *The Sleepwalkers,* ESP runs counter to current scientific theories about man; theories, that interpret man in terms of purely physical and chemical (or mechanistic) processes. The facts about ESP do not fit the physical theory of man and those who hold to that theory are likely to reject the disturbing facts at first. In time, of course, fact will triumph, and any conflicting theory be rejected; but it could take a long, long time.

Where does this book come in? It should shorten that time. It makes the whole subject vivid to the reader by presenting it in terms of actual human experiences. It is true, as is repeatedly affirmed here, such experiences do *not* themselves make final evidence for the occurrence of ESP—that comes from the laboratory research to which they have led. The experiences in this book make the data from the laboratory more understandable by demonstrating them, as it were, in action and in life. For many people, this demonstration makes the scientific evidence more convincing. A knowledge of this spontaneous material should help to bring a broader, richer meaning into the discoveries therein reported.

This book is well-timed for another reason. In the research field itself the need for new insights and inspiration is perennial. A fresh look at these natural occurrences may suggest new lines of research activity and better ways of working at them. Though already well acquainted with the research field, the inquiring mind may find fresh glimpses of it in examining the spontaneous workings of the abilities that produced these cases. Parapsychology is especially in need of these suggestive insights today in approaching the more difficult stages it has now reached.

This book is not, however, written primarily for research workers. It is intended, rather, for the untold thousands of persons who have had parapsychical (or psychic) experiences. They have long had questions for which they could find no answers. This book should answer many of these questions as far as the advance of knowledge within the field permits, for no one has given more study to such experiences than the author.

There is yet another side to this matter of timeliness. The very propriety of a case study in this field has depended on the results of experimental work. Such a book could hardly have been presented by a proper research scientist much before now. As the author points out, it had to await a certain stage in the developing research on ESP. As those who are familiar with the quality, extent, and methods of the researches of various workers around the world know, positive headway has been made. Now that the occurrence of ESP has been shown to be a fact, it is not only safe but eminently proper to turn to these spontaneous occurrences for fresh guiding hints on the nature of the ability and the way it operates.

The rich and little-exploited hoard of natural phenomena has been largely wasted through the centuries, because no place in science was found for it to be stored and processed and utilized. It ought no longer to be left in the inaccessible records of personal memory, family archives and casual literary selection. The kind of collection the author has been making at the Parapsychology Laboratory of Duke University should help to ensure a new respect for such experiences and stimulate the recording of still more valuable raw material for scientific study.

As a final point, I would say that almost no one else but this author could have written this book. Few persons, I am sure, would have been willing to devote the long years of patient labor she has given to the original study and emerging classifications of the thousands of case reports which make up the research that is basic to this presentation. In addition, the job of converting the research findings into a form sufficiently readable for the general public would have stalled a less determined person.

In all fairness, too, I think it should be said that the entire case research program in which she has been engaged for more than ten years was a diversion from her primary interest in the experimental side of parapsychology. Trained originally in the laboratories of plant microchemistry and physiology (at the University of Chicago, where she obtained her Ph.D.), her inclinations have been strongly and realistically experimental. Only the urgent need for re-examination of case material led her to accept the project—at first reluctantly and then with gathering enthusiasm. Her scientific reports of the last decade in the Journal of Parapsychology (of which she is one of the editors) have in consequence dealt with her studies made on the spontaneous material which had accumulated at the Parapsychology Laboratory at Duke University.

As the husband of the author I can, I think, appropriately add a further word. It is to give still another reason why the appearance of this book is appropriate. Like the "channels" of which she writes, the author herself has been a little too much "hidden," as it were, in proportion to her part in parapsychological research at the Laboratory and to the contributions she has made to whatever has come to be associated with the family name. This particular book will in no adequate way represent that large unacknowledged share, but at least it is something definitely and appropriately bylined as her own; let us say it is a step to which there should now be sequels.

J. B. RHINE

Hidden Channels of the Mind

Beyond the Senses

This book is about a very real kind of human experience, but one which is usually ignored or scoffed at, its meaning denied or debated. It is the kind of occurrence in which knowledge seems to come without the use of the senses. People generally keep in touch with the world around them by sight, hearing, touch, taste, smell. But occasionally a person says he became aware of something when none of these channels operated, and then the argument begins. How did he know or *did he actually know?* Such debatable occurrences could be instances of extrasensory perception, or ESP. They are the subject matter of this book.

To most people experiences of this kind are not familiar everyday occurrences. If they were, they would not raise questions, or start arguments. Familiar daily events are usually accepted without question, whether or not they are explainable. But familiarity is deceptive. It can dull the edge of wonder, and pass for understanding. For instance, everyone knows the size, shape and color of an orange because his senses bring the information. But how? What process changes the impression of chemical molecules into a psychological concept? No one, except a few specialized research workers, bothers to wonder about such a familiar process, or considers it remarkable.

In contrast, suppose a man dreams of a complex scene and then finds that scene exactly duplicated by one he comes upon next day; or suppose a mother "sees" her soldier son just as a catastrophe befalls him; or she knows without being told in any way the day her wandering boy will come home. Most people shrug off such accounts as just a guess, a coincidence that some little ordinary added fact would explain away. They find it incredible that the person could actually have *known*. And this skepticism is from the very same people who never question many baffling and equally unexplained phenomena of daily life, just because they are familiar.

Simple unfamiliarity, then, may explain much of the skepticism of the ordinary person. But the suspicions of the scientist have a long historical background. In ancient Greece the idea was formulated and considered to be a law of nature, that *nothing gets into the mind except by way of the senses*. This idea and many other notions about the world and man, in that day, were far from being the tested and tried scientific conclusions we respect and depend on today. They were in no way proven, but were merely statements of belief, belief based on observations of what happens to most people most of the time. Then, ages later, as modern scientific method developed, it was felt necessary to close the door on all types of untested beliefs and claims. No one tested the idea that the mind might have hidden channels, that reach beyond the senses. The door was already closed to that possibility. The idea that knowledge of the external world must come in only by the senses was so firm an assumption that no one had ever attempted to *prove* it, either. But few people, then or now, have thought of that. Even today this assumption seems an obvious truth, just as, no doubt, the one that said the earth is flat once did. That one broke down when the globe was circumnavigated. The question here is, is this one too unsound?

In practically every age people have reported happenings that one could call instances of knowing without the senses. Such occurrences have sometimes been given a religious interpretation, but in the main they have been discounted by the world in general. And, important as they could be as hints of the larger nature of man, they have remained almost entirely unclaimed by science, almost completely ignored in every area of scholarship except that of the relatively small and few societies of psychical research. In these societies, over the last century or so, they were noticed and studies along two rather separate lines were made.

One of these lines was concerned directly with the experiences themselves, the other with experimentation suggested by them. In the 1880's the English Society of Psychical Research collected a large number of case reports with the aim of proving that telepathy occurs; that one person can acquire the thought or mental content of another without the use of the senses. In order to make the experiences that seemed to bear on this absolutely reliable, only those accounts were considered for which factual proof of authenticity, almost as stringent as in a court of law, could be produced. Naturally such proof was often unobtainable. As a result many experiences, and in the nature of the case many *kinds* of experiences, had to be excluded. The collections that did result were inadvertently, therefore, made up of selected material, a fact that escaped notice then. In the intervening decades up to the present other attempts, too, were made to prove a point by strictly checked and authenticated personal experiences, whether the point was the occurrence of telepathy or the survival of the spirit after death.

The aim of these attempts has never been achieved. In none of them did the evidence prove sufficiently convincing for a final decision. It was impossible to so substantiate and verify this kind of material that it would give final *proof* of anything. But, even so, the study of actual experiences today can have a value for the student of ESP, because of the other line of study already mentioned, that of experimentation. The beginning of this line goes back to the 1870's, even before the Society for Psychic Research was organized. Unexplainable occurrences that suggested thought transference stirred up many thoughtful men—pushed a few of them to consider whether these might not be induced. Could these occurrences be made to register under conditions that would be more exact than those which nature produced unaided?

The first such experiments in both France and England began in connection with the practice of hypnosis. Investigators exploring the possibilities of hypnosis had come upon occasions when the hypnotized person showed bits of knowledge he seemed to have picked up from the mind of the hypnotist. Perhaps the hypnotist paused to take a pinch of snuff and the hypnotized subject sneezed, or the hypnotist had a localized pain and the subject seemed to get one similarly. It was sensible to follow up such effects with suitable tests. The attempts to make such tests, through a sort of trial-and-error process, led to better designs of experiments and more careful controls and safeguards.

The long story of the development of the experimental side of the movement that makes up the young science of parapsychology, as it is now called, is not the subject matter of this presentation. It would take too long to review it here. In addition to the original research reports (most of those of the past twenty-five years appear in the *Journal of Parapsychology*) numerous books covering the experimental work of the field are available. Reference to some of this research is given at the end of this volume. To sum up, however: through the stimulating activities of the societies for psychical research, the subject was kept alive through many decades until in the twenties and thirties of this century, experimental research gradually found its way into occasional psychology departments in the U.S. and elsewhere. At Duke University in the early thirties and under the sponsorship of Prof. William McDougall, J. B. Rhine was enabled to initiate a program of research in this field. It led to the establishment of the Duke Parapsychology Laboratory.

In this and other laboratories, and in this and other countries, mostly in collegiate institutions, a backlog of experimental findings has now accumulated which clearly shows that information can upon occasion get into the mind by channels less obvious than the senses, by extrasensory channels. The old dogma, saying it can not, was therefore incorrect.

The ability to know without the senses has been called a form of *psi* ability. The Greek letter psi, like the algebraic X, has no connotations that later, when more research has been done, might be proven wrong. The short and convenient abbreviation of extrasensory perception, ESP, is almost but not quite synonomous, as will be clear later.

The investigation of the field of parapsychology is still in its early stages, the psi ability still far from being understood. Much more research must go on before it can be explained. Some have surmised that it is a remnant of the early heritage of the race, an ability that may have come down to us from our pre-human forbears. In a day when danger lurked behind each bush and curve in the pathway, an extrasensory way of knowing would presumably have been an important asset to any animal or man who could exercise it. Convenient and even plausible as that conjecture may be, it is not proven. But certain other facts about ESP are established. Its main types—telepathy, clairvoyance and precognition (to be defined later)—have been distinguished, and a great deal learned about the nature of the process of extrasensory perception, and of the conditions under which it best occurs. Even though the tendency of a larger part of the scientific world has been to label the results of this research "incredible" and unworthy of consideration, the results nonetheless exist.

The point of this excursion into a discussion of the experimental work on ESP is that it is only because of this research, now taken seriously by informed students of the field, that it has become profitable to turn again to a consideration of personal experiences like those which follow. It was because of the results of this experimentation that a project of studying them, in spite of their inherent weaknesses, began at the Duke Parapsychology Laboratory in 1948.

The idea behind the study, however, was not the earlier one of thereby finding proof of something. Why was so primitive and laborious a type of study instituted at a research laboratory? It was partly in a search for clues, for new insights by which to guide the framing of experiments, that attention was turned to personal experiences. They could well be nature's own way of presenting the phenomena. But besides that, another reason for the study was to get a more rounded, full-bodied conception of the effects trapped so laboriously in the laboratory. After all, one can see so little of a natural process where the conditions must necessarily be restricted and artificial. An experiment has to be, to a degree, a distortion of nature, for all aspects of the setting must be so controlled that only one explanation for the effect secured is possible. One then needs to watch nature's way, even when experimenting. It is almost like an artist watching his scene with intermittent glances, even as he applies the paint to canvas.

It is also true that raw experimental data need to be observed against the richer background of the natural situations in which they occur. Although in parapsychology, as in any science, nothing final can be proven by case studies without controlled experiments, still something can be gained by noting the way the established law or fact fits into the processes of the natural world. If an effect which had no counterpart in nature were discovered in the laboratory, it would be an anomaly, difficult indeed to account for.

In this particular field of parapsychology another reason exists for studying personal cases. The people who have experienced ESP need to understand what has gone on. Their need, though largely an unexpressed one, was evidenced at the Parapsychology Laboratory as soon as results of research were publicized. Immediately people began to write to the laboratory to tell of personal experiences that puzzled them. They needed a bit of advice or information; asked how and why "this" could have happened—was it perchance related to the mental effects being studied at the laboratory?

By 1948 many such reports and inquiries had accumulated. An entirely amorphous and unorganized collection, the letters came, it appeared, from the "high" and the lowly, the rich and the poor, the obviously well educated and those who, often by their own account, had little formal schooling. But of whatever background, it seemed that, just as a patient might tell his doctor his symptoms as clearly and factually as he could, so these people were trying to give a careful account of the events that had puzzled them. Their motives and intentions, in fact, seemed curiously uniform considering the diversity of individual backgrounds and kinds of experience.

Although many individuals seemed hesitant and even a bit apologetic to be writing about a personal matter and admitting that such an inexplicable thing should have happened to them (many said in effect, "If someone else had told this to me I wouldn't have believed it"), perhaps the most frequently expressed motive for writing, in literally thousands of letters, was, "I hope this will help in your researches."

Their feeling about contributing to the research deserves special comment. It shows that many people will overcome their inherent reticence, take the time and make the effort to help *find out the truth* —a widespread urge to push back the border of the unknown that has no doubt contributed to the progress science has made in all fields. Perhaps it is particularly strong in people whose own experience gives them a personal interest in research in parapsychology, for they have reasons to be aware of its neglect and to be convinced of the importance of finding the explanations.

In studying the mass of material that was available, and which happily still continues to accumulate, the first thing was to separate those experiences that could have involved ESP from those that could not. Possible ESP experiences were taken to be those that bring concrete information not supplied either directly or indirectly by the senses. The accounts must therefore state explicitly what the experience was like, and also, just as clearly, the real happening and attendant circumstances. With these items to evaluate, one had a basis for deciding the likelihood that new information had been acquired and whether or not a sensory channel could have operated. The information, however, could be a complete idea, or only a fragment of one. The person would not necessarily have to recognize it as true at the time. The impression he received—the "message," one can conveniently call it—had only to check with reality.

If these conditions were fulfilled the experience could be tentatively accepted at face value, without the laborious effort at authentication and confirmation formerly considered necessary. As already observed, the earlier objective was to prove something. Now we recognized that proof could never be based on this kind of material, anyway. The attitude was, of course, no longer one of incredulity that this kind of knowing can occur. The objective was to get suggestions as to *how* it occurs. For that, one would need, not a collection of selected experiences limited to the kinds for which documentation could be procured, but one as fully representative as possible of all that goes on in this area of the human mind.

The problem of the errors of human testimony was present, of course, but could be handled sufficiently well for the present purpose without affidavit. The method of handling it depended on a principle somewhat like that of motion pictures. By the succession of numbers of closely similar items, meanings stand out which the individual pictures alone do not show. One could proceed here on the assumption that if ESP occurs in nature, it does so more than once. If it is a human ability, even an uncommon one, then by observing carefully the times when with some likelihood it is operating, the true aspects should add up, and the mistakes of individual memory, observation, etc., should, in effect, cancel out. By this method of treatment, a validity based on numbers could be given the material.

As it turned out, nearly half of the letters citing personal experiences which were received at the Parapsychology Laboratory told of one or more occurrences that filled the requirements. They were instances in which, as reported, true information was received and for which no sensory origin was indicated. They could have been, and under the circumstances seemed to have been, the result of psi. (When referring to them later, the cumbersome "could have been" will be omitted. It should always be understood, however, because, after all, no one could actually prove whether ESP did or did not play a part in any individual instance.)

This kind of experience is the one, then, to which one must turn when trying to study the way psi works in nature. The collection at Duke now includes thousands of accounts and they are the material on which the research basic to this book is founded and from which its examples are drawn.

Many similarities show up among these experiences, even though they come from people so widely different and unconnected. More than that, through the patterns of similarities one can glimpse in the background a rationale that could hardly be the result of only a series of mistakes of testimony, over-interpretation, imagination, coincidence and all that. Instead it could be the visible sign of a reality still almost unrecognized by the eye of science; the result of channels of information long unsuspected and still largely hidden from observation, but showing through sufficiently for the alert to notice and evaluate.

To convey these hints and glimpses as nearly at first hand as possible, the experiences themselves should tell the story. But as already said, the impression of validity these accounts give is one created by *numbers* of similar items. A single experience of any given kind is likely to be unconvincing. A hundred or a thousand like it, however, are not brushed off so easily. Unfortunately, however, this effect created by *numbers* cannot be fully reproduced here, for only single examples, not dozens or hundreds, can be used to illustrate a point. It will soon be apparent, however, that many of the examples would illustrate more points than one. And so, perhaps, something of the cumulative effect on the reader, which larger numbers would give, will still eventually be produced as they are marshalled according to the patterns and classifications into which they seem to fall.

The examples cited will be given to a large extent in the individuals' own words, in order to convey as much as possible the fact that these are actual experiences. They are selected for brevity, simplicity and illustrative value, but are not necessarily the "best" of all similar ones available. Sometimes the one selected was only the most convenient. When hundreds represent the same characteristic, it would scarcely be possible to decide that a single one was best.

As these various kinds of experiences become familiar, ideas about the human mind are suggested. But one must remember that they are only suggested, not proven by this material. Such ideas are not and must not be taken as conclusions. They must be tested, preferably under the controlled conditions of laboratory research before the true and false in them can be conclusively distinguished. That will come at a later stage.

This stage—the observation of individual cases no matter how large the number, in which ideas beyond the terra firma of experimentally established fact emerge—is only like a scouting expedition into new territory. It can give an outline of the terrain and show its major aspects and characteristics, but one must leave verification to other more careful and painstaking methods, for scouting expeditions can bring back erroneous, as well as correct impressions. Their great value lies in the fact that they can give long-range views and impressions not obtainable at the time in any other way. Some of those glimpsed here are of that nature.

$\cdot 2$

Types of Extrasensory Perception

One of the first things to notice about ESP experiences is that the information they bring may come from very different *kinds* of sources. In some instances, people seem to receive information from another person's thought; in others, from a distant or hidden thing; in a third, from an event that has not yet happened. These three different kinds of sources distinguish the different types of ESP which have long been classified in parapsychology as telepathy, clairvoyance and precognition.

Thousands of experiences fall into each of these categories and all sorts of conditions and varying effects can be observed in them. Guessing the symbols on cards (which has been a predominant laboratory technique) is a one-dimensional situation, but experiences from life are multi-dimensional, as can only be suggested by the examples in each category or type that follow.

FROM OTHER MINDS

The wife of a petty officer of the U. S. Navy had an unusual experience one night in 1924. Her husband had recently been transferred to duty on a vessel with a special mission, one which made communication with those at home difficult and infrequent. She, with their two-year-old son and her husband's mother, was still living at the base in Florida. It had been several weeks since she had had word from her husband and she had no idea of his whereabouts. Then, as she says,

"During the early hours of the morning of May fifteenth I awakened suddenly from sound sleep with the strange feeling that my husband was in the room; and, although the room was actually in pre-dawn darkness, it appeared to me as daylight, and I saw my husband come through the door, come to my bedside, smile, pass on into the next room where our little son lay in his crib, then return to my bedside. Then he vanished and the room became dark.

"I realized I had only seen a 'vision' but was somewhat comforted as it seemed to have brought me a message that all was well with my husband and that no doubt he was thinking of us at home, and I soon went back to sleep. At daylight, however, I wakened somewhat earlier than was my usual habit at that time, still with the sense of sweetness of the experience, and arose to go to the next room and tell my husband's mother about it.

"At that moment, my husband, in the flesh, came into the room in uniform exactly as I'd seen him in the vision. Upon comparing notes, it developed that at the very moment when I'd seen him by telepathy he had been on the train coming from New Orleans where his ship was in port, and since he thought he would arrive at home before I would awake, he was going over in his mind a plan to do just what I'd seen: to go to my bedside, then to the next room to look at his son in the crib before returning to my bedside to waken me. We were both quite delighted with the knowledge that his thoughts had been conveyed to me so exactly that the experience seemed real to me."

Telepathy, or, to be redundant, "mental telepathy," is an expression familiar to practically everyone. In the dictionary it is defined as "the apparent communication of thought from one person to another otherwise than through the channels of sense."

Experiences involving another person's thought are not necessarily the most striking of ESP experiences. Neither are they the most frequently reported. But they long ago captured the stage of popular imagination, probably because of the close rapport they seem to indicate between individuals. Scientifically as well as popularly, telepathy was the first type of psi to get attention, largely because it seems to show a meeting of minds that goes beyond the laws of matter and suggests a spiritual aspect in humanity. But its popular usage is also a loose one. Any experience that suggests ESP is likely to be called telepathy, although it may in reality be one of the other types instead, for clairvoyance and precognition are still somewhat technical terms, and not so often used outside of parapsychological circles.

The expression of telepathy is not always, by any means, one so fully visualized as in the dream or dreamlike experience related above. Quite different indeed was the experience of a woman in New Jersey. She was tossing, sleepless and restless, in her bed one night in 1947. "I hadn't been asleep for several nights and this was in the middle of another sleepless night," she recalls. "Due to a series of unhappy events concerning my family and myself, and to my run-down state of health, I just couldn't see any sense in my life or any sense in going on. With my thoughts seething round and round in endless circles, I began to think of ways and means to end it all, when suddenly, as clearly as if she were in the room, I heard the voice of a dear friend say:

"'Don't do that, Marion!'

"I was so utterly dumbfounded that it jolted me right out of my senseless state of mind. She lived in Florida and I was in New Jersey at the time. She was an older woman who had taken a great liking to me, for I resembled, she thought, her only daughter who had died some time before.

"To hear her speak to me in the dead of night when I knew she was over a thousand miles away was quite a disturbing experience. Yet—I began to think it was all due to my overwrought nerves, until next day I received an air mail, special delivery letter from her saying she had been wakened in the middle of the night by an urgent sense that I needed help. She said she had arisen and prayed for me until dawn.

"Her letter was proof to me that somehow she had been aroused from her sleep by my great need and she had reached me over all those miles to comfort and protect me. It was one of the most beautiful and mysterious experiences I have ever had."

Both the above experiences were between two closely knit individuals, who were separated by appreciable distance. Both were dramatic, and highly meaningful to each person. At the opposite extreme in all but unexpectedness are many other experiences somewhat like that of a New York school teacher who writes:

"I had just 'come to' after my operation. My new private nurse stood in the doorway and introduced herself. Chatting a bit, she told me she had a little daughter, Maureen, sixteen months old.

"I then made some remark which escapes me about, 'Your son, Peter!' to which she responded, 'What makes you say, "Your son, Peter?"' 'Why, you just told me about him.' Her answer to this, 'I didn't. I told you about my daughter, Maureen. I couldn't have. I have no son called Peter or any other name.'

"Then she came close to the bed and said, 'But I am expecting a baby in October (this was May) and if it is a boy my husband and I have already decided to name him Peter. I'll have something to tell him tonight!'

"I never did hear about the birth, but to me that is incidental. The point is that I read her mind."

The point here is that the two were strangers who happened to be in the same room, and the subject matter was quite unimportant, at least to the person who had the experience.

Sometimes, too, instead of an idea, almost pure emotion seems to be transferred. An episode from my own experience could illustrate that.

One night I was awakened from a nightmarish dream by a loud cry from my three-year-old daughter sleeping in an adjoining room. The dream had left me trembling and covered with perspiration, for in it I was being pursued up the road to the house by some looming indescribable creature and I was making a last desperate rush to get inside the door before it overtook me, when my daughter's cry brought me back to reality.

"I'm scared, Mama, I'm scared," she sobbed.

"But why? What scared you?"

She hesitated and said finally, "I guess it was a bear."

In this instance, fear was the outstanding item: hers seemed like a contagion of my own. The nameless creature, the "bear," only an invention to explain the fear, a rationalization.

From these few examples one can get at least a hint of some of the variations in telepathic experiences. One cannot fail to note how few common characteristics they have. Sometimes the people involved are far apart, sometimes near; in many they are closely linked emotionally, in others practically strangers. In some experiences the subject matter is of the greatest significance to the individual, in others scarcely any. The fact that the other person's thought was reflected is about the only common feature one can observe.

In each of these experiences, the situation can perhaps most simply be described as suggesting the occurrence of a simple mental contact. Or, one could call it a "mind-to-mind" contact, with apologies to the psychologists, who hesitate to use the word mind because it is one which cannot as yet be precisely defined. But whatever one calls this "contact," in whatever terms it is described, apparently sometimes, under some conditions, for certain individuals, these brief flashes of direct communication occur.

What kind of a phenomenon is this which occurs in ordinary life, and yet has remained so long debated and denied? Why is it that centuries passed before anyone, even those who were trying to figure out the nature of man and his place in the universe, took this phenomenon seriously enough to start a systematic investigation of it?

These questions have no answers, either here, where telepathic experiences are only being introduced, or later, when we will consider their puzzle at more length. Similar questions are raised too by the other types of ESP: clairvoyance, to which we turn attention next, and precognition, which follows that.

FROM MINDLESS OBJECTS

In those experiences that fall into the second type of ESP, the information comes from an order of reality entirely different from that of thought. In clairvoyant perception, the knowledge received is about quite impersonal things or events unknown to anyone.

Take, for instance, the experience of a young couple in New York City. They had gone to a theater, in which, at the time, round or oval cushions designed to hold men's hats were attached to the floor under each seat. After the theater, this couple stopped at a candy store for an ice cream soda. Suddenly, with a cry of dismay, the young woman saw that the stone, a sky-blue opal, was missing from her ring.

"It was a matrix stone and black on the underside," she says. "My husband had never examined my ring. We had never talked about it, and I know he did not know it was black underneath. The stone is fairly large, an oval one. A quarter would cover its smaller diameter but would leave half-moons at each end. I was heartbroken at the loss, and my husband was very sorry to see that I cared so much.

"Well, the next morning before breakfast he said he was going out for a short time. When I asked what for, he said he would tell me when he came back. In about three-quarters of an hour he came back and placed my opal before me on the breakfast table.

"He said, 'I had a dream. I saw a large, round, black thing and lying next to it a small, round, black thing; and I thought of those hat cushions in the theater. Something inside of me said, 'Go there,' and I did. I had our seat checks; a cleaning woman let me in; and there, *as in my dream,* the two black things were side by side. I picked up the small black object and was greatly surprised to see that it was blue on top and black underneath. I did not know it had a black back.'"

The word clairvoyance, used when *things* appear to be known about directly, is even older than the word telepathy. Its usage, at least in this country, has never been as common as that of telepathy. The difference arose partly, no doubt, because clairvoyance did not seem to have the same far-reaching significance as telepathy. It did not so obviously give the suggestion of a mental ability to transcend matter and physical law. In fact, historically, those who were interested in telepathy because it seemed to argue for man's extraphysical nature were even opposed to the idea of clairvoyance because they (mistakenly) felt it suggested an affinity to material objects instead. Clairvoyance, however, unlike telepathy, has been the basis of an ancient practice, or series of practices, among which the most prominent are fortune telling, divination and seership.

One of the more famous among modern seers was the eighteenth-century Swedish scientist and religious leader, Emmanuel Swedenborg, who interpreted his ability in accordance with his religious background and belief. He thought friendly spirits told him of events which occurred beyond the range of his senses. Stories are on record of some of his clairvoyant impressions. Once when he was seated at dinner, he turned to his host and said a fire had broken out at the latter's distant factory. A messenger was sent immediately to investigate and returned to report that Swedenborg's impression was correct.

Today, even though we still cannot explain how clairvoyance operates, or can operate, we know it is a natural endowment of the human mind. We also know it is not one limited to a few special wise men. Ordinary people, with no other particular claim to distinction, may also show this ability. A woman in Oregon, one day, while washing dishes, took off her engagement and wedding rings, as was her custom, and laid them on a shelf near the sink.

"It was a warm day and remained warm into evening," she relates, "so we decided to have a wiener roast outside. I got busy with preparations for that and forgot all about my rings. Later, after the children were in bed, I thought about my rings and went to get them. They were gone. I felt faint. My husband helped me look. We looked through all the garbage. I took everything off the shelf where I had put them. We even looked under the dining-room and living-room rugs. I swept every inch of the kitchen and no rings. It was getting late by this time and my husband was tired, so he went to bed. He wanted me to stop looking and get some rest but I told him I couldn't sleep until I found my rings.

"This doesn't seem possible but it happened! I was standing at the kitchen sink, trying to hold back my tears, when suddenly something told me to look in the ice-cube tray. I rushed to the refrigerator, pulled out the ice tray and there were my rings, frozen in a cube of ice. I was so happy I rushed back to tell my husband. We started talking it over and he remembered coming into the house in the dark and without turning on the lights he opened the refrigerator, pulled out the ice-cube tray for ice and reached for some glasses into the cupboard where my rings were. Then he filled the ice tray with water again and put it back in the refrigerator. He had never replaced a tray of ice before and hasn't since. Just that one time he replaced the ice tray. He didn't know my rings were on that shelf. I remember at the time I received the message or whatever it was, I had a funny sensation. What made me look in that ice tray?"

The distance between the person and the object is another circumstance that varies in the experiences. The person and thing may be far apart, and still, even in small details, the object may be revealed with clearness suggestive of actual sight at close range. It may even reveal an object the person has never seen.

An amateur geologist from a western state dreamed, he says, "of a large, beautiful, agate-encrusted, crystal geode lying in shallow water quite near the shoreline in the W—— River which flows something like fifteen miles southeast of the city. The exact location, shoreline, a long gravel bar, everything just as plain as though I were seeing it as it is, was clearly shown. When we arose on the following Sunday morning I told my wife of my dream experience and suggested we take our lunch and drive to the scene of my dream. We had only lived in this city approximately six months at the time and I was unfamiliar with the particular location but inquired along the way a couple of times describing landmarks, etc., in detail; and within a half-hour after we parked our car, we walked up to the big, beautiful geode lying exactly where I'd seen it in my dream. Later I was offered three hundred dollars cash for it but did not care to sell."

If one tries to describe experiences like these as we did those of telepathy they would have to be spoken of as "mind-to-object" contacts, or in a case like the one of the geologist, as a "mind-to-the-entire-landscape" relationship. But it is difficult to make such an idea seem real. Even the phrase "mind-to-mind" in telepathy does not give a clear concept of what must go on in an experience of that kind. But it is at least possible to imagine that two minds might somehow "get in touch." However far-fetched such imagining really is, it has at least the semblance of an explanation. One could argue in telepathy cases that human interests and emotions must somehow have played a part, that a state of interpersonal rapport was created. But one does not speak of rapport with an object. A world of difference separates thoughts from things. Thoughts are not material. Those of another person can never be known by one's sense perception unless the other person converts them into speech, writing or overt gesture of some kind. *Things*, on the other hand, are material, and we can easily sense them, provided barriers are removed and the distance is not too great.

In ESP, however, both thoughts and things are apprehended, and probably with equal ease. It is true that telepathy is reported more frequently than clairvoyance. While this possibly could mean that the latter is more difficult, it may well mean only that people are more interested in the thoughts of others than in things. This idea is more likely correct, because laboratory experiments showed no difference in "ease" between telepathy and clairvoyance, and also because many ESP experiences seem to be a combination of both.

The examples of clairvoyance used above and those of telepathy in the previous section were picked out because they are respectively clear-cut examples of each type. However, in perhaps the majority of instances, other people's thoughts and inanimate things are *both* involved. One cannot be certain that either one alone was the basis of the experience. Take, for instance, the experience of a California grandmother who awoke one night from a very frightening and very vivid and realistic dream. In it she thought she saw her baby grandson struggling and smothering in his blankets. His movements were getting weaker and weaker. It was almost the end. She awoke. It was 3:45 A.M. The young folks lived across town. Should she call them?

As she says, "After all, it was only a dream. I thought, If I call and wake them they'll think I'm crazy. But if I don't and anything happens—." So she phoned and got a surprised son-in-law on the wire.

"What on earth are you calling for at this hour?" he cried.

"Go to the baby at once," she said. "He's smothering."

"Yes, he was. We're up. We heard him."

In addition to everyone's relief about the baby, she said they marveled at the fact that even across town and in a dream she had known of the danger. Even without seeing or hearing, she had gotten an exact impression not only of the person involved, the baby, but of the kind of danger he was in. But did her dream come from the situation as an impersonal event, from the minds of the baby's parents, or from the baby himself?

Cases like this in which the person apparently all but "sees" a scene or event as it takes place may very well be entirely clairvoyant experiences, too, just like those in which an object is visualized when there was no human thought about it to complicate the situation. But when people are present and thinking about the event, one cannot be sure. It could also be that the ESP impression is based on a combination of thought *and* thing.

The distinction is not important, perhaps, to the people who have such experiences. Those in the case above were mainly concerned about the safety of the child. But in trying to understand the mental processes that go on in ESP, if the source of the experience is thus indeterminate, one cannot say it was either an instance of "pure" telepathy or of "pure" clairvoyance.

If the majority of ESP experiences are thus indeterminate, so too, one must recognize, are the majority of life situations. The topics that interest and concern us all are mostly combination affairs. They are made up of objects, events and people's thoughts. ESP experiences modeled on them would almost have to be indeterminate in a strict sense, just as this one is. Nature does not have to make the nice separation of thought from thing we try to make in thus separating telepathy and clairvoyance. Although these experiences are indeterminate, they are nevertheless instances of ESP and can be called general ESP, or GESP.

FROM THE FUTURE

Science has crossed many seemingly impassable barriers. But the one that separates the present from the future has seemed so obviously impenetrable as to discourage almost entirely attempts to cross it. And yet in this third type of ESP experiences—the precognitive—that boundary seems nonexistent.

A woman in Georgia says, "We are living in a log cabin in a small woodland just off 'Main Street' some two hundred yards, while our home is being remodeled. Our cabin is reached by a long lane, but the view from our porch to the street is unobstructed.

"On a Friday afternoon recently I was alone in the cabin. I was standing at a table in front of an open window when I glanced up and out of the window upon hearing the noise of an approaching car. There was a shiny black sedan on the top of a little incline which leads down and then up again to the cabin. Very near the cabin it was. I knew there was one person on the front seat beside the driver. It was a woman in a white blouse. I could see the full sleeves and the tight cuffs of the woman's blouse. From the position of her arms I knew that the woman was sitting squared around on the seat with her back turned to the driver, gazing intently at the cabin. I could not see her head. The car seemed strange to me. I could not tell who they were. I quickly dashed across the cabin's one room to the bathroom. Its windows were open, right onto the drive. I looked into the mirror and saw that it was too late to do anything about my appearance, even to apply any more lipstick. I dashed out onto the porch—and there was no car in sight.

"I could see the long length of the lane. No car and no dust, and it was very dusty at that time. I immediately was aware that after the initial sound of the wheels which caused me to look up, there had been no further noise, not even noise of brakes. The car couldn't possibly have gotten away in the short time I was in the bathroom without a great deal of noise and terrific speed. There was a little navigating to do around pine trees, and my car was in the way too. Believe me, I worried about my ghostly black sedan all weekend, and told the story to all who would listen—and to some of those who wouldn't!

"But on Sunday afternoon I was again alone in the cabin. Same scene, same time, two days later, same character, except a more nervous character. Every noise I would hear I would jump and look over my shoulder. Finally I did hear it—a car was coming. I looked out and at the same place in the drive was the same car of my vision. The same white sleeves hanging out. The woman squared about in the seat. I went tearing out babbling, 'Are you a ghost?' to the great astonishment of my very solid friends from the city who had been planning for several months to drive down to see us some Sunday afternoon. They had never been to our cabin before and that was the reason for the intent gazing of the woman. Her blouse was identical with the vision."

Could an experience like that come from an *existing* thought or thing? No, the idea of the visit may have been in the minds of the guests, for all one can tell, but no one knew beforehand just the position of the people in the car or the way they would look to the woman in the cabin. That view was not in existence when she "saw" it. The experience seems therefore to have been a replica of an event that *had not happened.*

Perhaps no type of ESP experience seems more incredible to most people than this type which involves the future. If incredibility offers any choice, then precognition is likely to seem more wildly improbable than knowing directly about a distant thing, as in clairvoyance, or about another person's present but hidden thought, as in telepathy. Yet experiences that thus seem to involve the future not only occur, but, however unexpected the fact may be, they are reported more frequently than any other type of ESP.

In a way, this kind of ESP is similar to clairvoyance, which also is concerned with things or events, even though only with those *in the present*. The name precognition, by which this type of ESP is known in parapsychology, means practically the same thing as does the older and more familiar word, prophecy.

The idea of prophecy is ancient. It is probably as old as civilization. But, like clairvoyance, it was thought in the past to be exercised only by a few especially gifted individuals, never that the ordinary man-in-the-street had prophetic abilities.

Prophets have in the main been associated with religious thought and writings as well as with religious rites. But in secular writings, too, prophetic pronouncements have been handed down for generations. Among such, probably the sayings of Nostradamus are the most frequently mentioned, and even today some people think his prophecies have relevance to present-day world events. Whether or not such meaning is actually to be ascribed to them or whether it is "read in," is and will likely remain undecided. To date, at least, no reliably objective check has been conceived. The status of older world prophecy, that of Nostradamus or any other, has not been raised to the level of certainty demanded by today's scientific standards.

In 1927 a volume on the subject of precognition, called *An Experiment with Time*, was published in England by J. W. Dunne. It included an account of a number of the author's own dreams which had come true. He had recorded all his recallable dreams over a period of time, and had also kept a daily record of the main events of his personal life. Checking the accounts of the dreams with the diary, he found many dreams that, as he says, were evidently rubbish, but a few were interspersed which were so closely similar to later events that they seemed to have been previews of them.

From this personal experience the author attempted to formulate a theory too complicated to go into here, but highly speculative and quite different from Swedenborg's religious ideas in explanation of his own experiences. Dunne's theory, which is primarily a philosophical reconsideration of the nature of time, has stimulated thought on the topic of precognition; the account of his dreams has turned the attention of many people to their own, and thus helped to hasten the day when the phenomenon of precognition at last is receiving a degree of attention.

The fact is that the idea of prophecy is one that long has been completely relegated to past ages. It is one that appears so entirely improbable as a present-day occurrence that, like the idea of ESP itself, it has come to seem incredible. Besides, to many people it is an unwelcome idea because of the questions it raises. For instance: if one has a precognitive dream, is he doomed then to fulfill it? Would this mean he has no freedom of will? Is his destiny irrevocably "fixed?" These questions and others are raised by the idea of precognition. But in approaching any new and revolutionary idea, one should first examine the facts before stumbling over their possible implications.

One fact is that many people, like this woman in Georgia, who are not heaven-ordained leaders but just ordinary individuals, have experiences which at face value do suggest that a future event was foreseen. What sorts of events? One finds that they vary widely, but the most arresting cases, like the one above, are concerned with personal rather than world affairs, and, as in that instance, they are often marked by the inclusion of small details.

Charles Dickens, from an account in his biography, dreamed of a visitor whom he would meet at tea the next day, heard her introduced, heard her name, which was strange to him. The next day he met the lady just as dreamed. History records no significance to the meeting. And so, Dickens and hundreds of others appear to have "lived beforehand" quite trivial experiences which in real life were only enacted hours later.

The impression of the woman mentioned above, as it happens, came true in a few days. The time interval may be shorter or longer. A woman from Massachusetts had a dream that came true about three months later. As she says, it did not foretell death or an accident, "but something so screwy it didn't seem possible.

"In this vivid dream it seemed that my mother and I were sleeping together (something that we never did. We had separate households about five miles apart). Mother was wakened during the night by the baby whimpering and lit a cigarette. While holding the flaming match she saw a bedbug scurry up the wall. She exclaimed, 'Good Lord, look!' and her hand automatically went out and she held the lighted match under the bug. She lit another match and looked at the mattress we were lying on and found more of the insects. Using a flashlight so as not to arouse the baby, she and I picked the bugs off the mattress and dropped them into an ashtray which held lighted match sticks. We approached the baby's crib with the flashlight and arrived in time to see a bug scurry across the cheek of my very young daughter. Horrified, we put on the overhead light and spent the rest of the night looking for the common bedbug.

"About three months later my husband went out of town for the weekend. My father had recently gotten a new job working nights, so knowing that both my mother and I were alone I called her, invited her for the evening and to sleep overnight. Something I never did before or since. We retired around eleven and slept. During the night we were awakened by the baby whimpering. While making soothing noises from the bed to calm the baby, my mother lit a cigarette and—you know the rest.

"I can't explain the dream, but I can the bugs.

"My husband and I had had a week's vacation at an old farmhouse in New Hampshire. There was a bed for us, but we had to bring the baby's crib with us. I found out later, after my house was overrun, that the farmhouse had had bedbugs for years, and that we had probably carried them home to our house in the baby's crib without even knowing. Let me tell you, after my mother and I actually found those things (and I still shudder) we spent the next day dragging mattresses out on the lawn, spraying and more spraying. It took a little while but we finally got them all out of the house and have never had anything resembling them since.

"But how do you explain such a dream in the first place? We still laugh over it."

The question of how such a dream can be explained *is* baffling "in the first place." But the first step, of course, is the recognition that such precognitive experiences do occur. Those who felt content to think of the grand-scale Old Testament prophecies as miraculous, and not subject to scientific explanation, could hardly feel that a miraculous rather than a scientific explanation should be demanded in the case of the foreseeing of an infestation of bedbugs.

Yet that case, in its comparatively unimportant and personal character, is typical of ESP experiences that come in this third group, the precognitive type of ESP. As already said, these experiences are not mainly concerned with the fate of peoples, of governments, wars or the rumors of wars, but instead have to do with the ordinary doings of ordinary people. Neither are they cryptic, or symbolic. They require no labored interpretations. Instead, they are predominantly realistic, true to small detail. They are in fact mostly so personal, so mundane as to make incongruous the older supernatural explanations. They call for explanation in terms of this world, instead.

Precognitive ESP experiences do not usually cover the grand sweeps of time—decades or centuries—often involved in traditional prophecy. Many are fulfilled within minutes, hours or days. The time element, however, geared it would seem to the day-to-day life of men rather than to the destiny of man, is elastic and varies from case to case. Sometimes the interval between the experience and the fulfillment may be years. A man in New York dreamed he was driving his car (even though at the time he did not own a car) down the street of his parents' home. It was night, and there was snow on the ground, although it was not winter when he had the dream. He thought he drove up to his parents' home, and as he was getting out of the car he saw his father come and sit down by the window. As he recalls, "I went into the house and saw several people sitting in the living room. I didn't recognize any of them. My father said 'Hello' to me and motioned me into my mother's bedroom. I went in where she lay dead. That was the end of my dream.

"*Ten years* later I was notified one night that my mother had died very suddenly. I got into the car which I now owned and drove to my parents' home and it was night and snow was on the ground. As I was getting out of the car I saw my father come and sit by the window. I went into the house and several people were sitting in the living room, relatives and friends whom I recognized. My father said 'Hello' and motioned me into my mother's bedroom, where she lay dead."

A question that comes up when considering precognitive cases is whether they always involve some occurrence the person will himself later experience. Sometimes they do not.

A woman whose understandably unsigned letter is the only such to be given in this book, says that when she was a girl in college she phoned her mother one weekend that instead of coming home as planned she would have to stay and finish an experiment on Saturday afternoon.

"Then," she says, "Saturday evening on my way back to the dorm a man I shall call Bill asked me if I would go with him on a picnic the fraternity he belonged to was having the next day. It was at a lake some fifty miles away. I had dated Bill occasionally before and said I would go. I thought no more of the matter until about ten o'clock the next morning when Mother phoned me. She was upset, I could tell, and asked me please not to leave the dorm that day but to stay there in my own room, saying she would explain when I came home the following weekend. I comforted her by saying I would and promptly upon hanging up the phone began gathering things I would need for the picnic, including my bathing suit. But I was a little worried over the phone call, as my mother is not an excitable woman and it was not like her to worry about me.

"Bill arrived in his car about then and we drove to the lake. We were the only couple to go in swimming that day and when we came out we did not go immediately to the bath houses to get into our dry clothes, as it was a warm day and the bath houses were on the far end of the park, a drive of about three miles. Along toward sunset, though, we drove to the bath houses and changed. The drive back led through two stretches of forest where there were no picnickers and it was here that it happened. To make a long story short—I can think of no way to soften the word—I was raped. It is to be remembered that Bill was not a roughhouse type. He came from a well-to-do family, was president of his fraternity and was well liked on the campus. I was too shocked and ashamed to mention it to anyone and to this day no one knows, though it got around the small campus that Bill and I had had a fuss and weren't dating any more.

"The following weekend I went home, and as soon as we were alone Mother asked me if I had stayed in the dorm Sunday. Recalling her phone call, I assured her that I had, not wanting to remember the happening of that day. I asked her why she had made the request, and she laughed and said she just wanted to be sure I had studied, but after some persuasion she told me the truth. She had had a dream Saturday night in which she saw me at the lake with a boy who met Bill's description very well, and she told me about the rest of the dream, which was practically word for word what happened on the way back from the bath house. Mother said she knew it was silly, but that the dream was so vivid that it had upset her. I successfully concealed my shock and comforted her as best I could, assuring her that no such thing had happened.

"I am very happily married now and have a son of my own, so for necessity I want my name to remain secret. I do hope that this may be of some use to you as it is not easy for me to remember this incident."

The dreamer, the mother in that case, never even found out that the dream came true. But if it is not necessary that the person eventually find out about the event he foresaw, one may well ask what happens if he dies beforehand. In other words, can precognition go beyond the person's lifetime?

Sometimes it seems to do so. Sometimes, although such cases are rare, it seems as if an ESP experience may have been based on the person's own death or funeral. But usually the circumstances are such that one cannot be certain.

In New Zealand, a woman was watching at the bedside of her hopelessly ill husband. The night before he died he asked her why she was crying. She said she was not crying but was about to prepare him a drink. He looked at her in surprise and saw it was true. He said he could not understand it and wondered why "those people" were walking about, and who had died.

She assured him nobody was dead. He seemed unconvinced, and said they better get in touch with S——. She could not distinguish the word, but thought it sounded like 'Sims.' He continued that they had a place at Newmarket, a nearby suburb. He said no more, and died soon after.

His wife called the doctor, who came quickly with two nurses. Then a friend arrived, so that four women and the doctor were moving about the room where so shortly before her husband had thought he saw people walking about.

The undertaker who was called was named Sibuns and came from Newmarket, the nearby suburb. It was then the wife recalled her husband's words, that they better get in touch with S——.

Even rarer than experiences that seem to concern a person's own death or funeral are the occasional ones that seem to go well beyond the person's own lifetime for their fulfillment. One such comes from a dreamer's granddaughter, a woman now living in Iowa. She writes that in 1918, when she was only a child about thirteen years old, her grandmother was very upset one morning about a dream she had had the night before. Her grandmother did not ordinarily believe in dreams but this one was not mixed up and "fuzzy" like most of her dreams, she said, but very clear and distinct.

"In it," recalls the granddaughter, "Grandmother had seen a black horse with a white face charge me, striking me down. It was in the orchard just north of our Iowa farmhouse. But we had no horses running loose and did not own a black one with white face.

"Grandmother died in 1934. We moved away, came back, and in 1947 I took in livestock for summer grazing, among others two black mares, one with a white face. They belonged to a bachelor and were unused to women. They usually snorted and ran when I approached. But I was never afraid of horses and Grandmother's dream had faded.

"One morning when I went into the orchard, the white-faced one snorted, then began to circle me, wide-eyed. I yelled, swung my arm, grabbed a broken branch. She squealed and rushed. I jerked off a rubber, threw it in her face. That stopped her for a moment. I whacked her with the branch which broke in several pieces but scared her long enough. I reached the gate somehow, got through it and back into the house.

"And then I remembered. Here in this kitchen Grandmother had sat, shaken, almost sick, describing her dream to us, and only a rubber and a broken bough had kept that long-ago dream from coming true. Maybe it was just a coincidence, but—"

Maybe it was just a conicdence. But if it was more, it was a precognitive experience that came true long after the end of the life of the dreamer.

Another thing about it is significant too, if it was a precognitive experience. The dream did not *quite* come true. The girl did escape. She was not trodden down by the white-faced mare. Such an experience could have a bearing on the question, already mentioned, of whether a precognized event can be avoided. This question deserves a special discussion later. Here it is enough to show that ordinary people have experiences which seem to indicate they do somehow get information about events still in the future, and possibly even beyond their own lifetime.

As a postscript to the discussion of experiences that involve the future, one might ask: Does the past return at the call of ESP? Oddly enough, the answer to that is very difficult, although at first thought it might seem easy. As we know very well, the past often comes back to all of us as memories and in dreams. The question is, are any of these occurrences due to ESP of the past?

A woman now living in Georgia had a dream when a freshman in college which was so vivid that she somehow could not forget it, even though in a way it was not particularly spectacular. She was not herself a character in the dream, but seemed to be a spectator from a little distance.

"The dream," she says, "centered around a large house, a very beautiful one which seemed to be of light color but was not of boards. Also, for such a nice house it was very close to the sidewalk and surrounded by a high wrought-iron fence. A lawn party was taking place and on one side were grouped adults and on another side, young people. Among the young people was my steady beau and with him a dark-haired boy who would not turn around so I could see his face. The whole thing seemed to be taking place at night, and yet it was as bright as daytime. All the while, a man in a dark suit and wearing a brown hat kept walking back and forth on the sidewalk, watching the party. I awoke suddenly and sat up in bed, saying, 'I know that house must be in W— (a nearby town)—it is in W— I know it is.' The next day I told my beau about the dream and he became very excited. Finally when I had finished he told me all this had taken place three years ago and he had almost forgotten about it.

"He took me to see the house in W— and it was as in my dream, only now I could see the outside was of cream-colored plaster. He explained that the friend with him was John, whom we both knew, and that the lawn had been lighted by spotlights the night of the party. However, he could not remember seeing any man, such as in my dream, go walking past the house. A year later I happened to meet the girl who lived there and she also verified my dream, and a year after that I met the man who kept walking past in the dream —who is now my husband. At the time of the party and at the time of the dream, he was living in another town, but when we met, he was living in the house across the street from my dream house."

Although all such experiences (they are, however, comparatively infrequent) seem to concern a past occurrence directly, they may not have that origin after all. The ESP that seems to have been involved could have been ESP *of the present.* In this instance, it could have been a case of telepathy, in others of clairvoyance, or of general or indeterminate ESP, GESP. For the details which could be checked and shown to be correct, existed as memories in the minds of those who had a part in the event.

And so, because verification must always depend on a memory or an objective record of some kind, one cannot be sure that ESP of the past occurs. It has been much easier to show that ESP goes into the future. Because of this difficulty, retrocognition, as ESP of the past should be called, is not, strictly speaking, part of the definition of this third type of ESP, precognition. If it should ever be established as a reality, a name would have to be found to include both ESP of the future and of the past.

Just as the line marking off telepathy and clairvoyance is not clear and sharp, the one which separates precognition from clairvoyance is also indistinct. A foreseen future event may involve illness, pregnancy, a place, or person existing but still unknown to the person having the experience. In such cases one cannot say whether clairvoyance or precognition or a combination of the two was involved.

A woman in Chicago a few years ago got word from her son, who was working in Louisiana, that he had fallen in love and would be married in November. His letter was short, and he did not describe his bride. He said only that they would come home at Christmas and he was sure his mother would love her as he did.

The mother says, "Of course I was curious about her, since he had given not the least hint of her appearance or personality.

"About three weeks before Christmas I had a very vivid dream. I heard a rap at the door and upon opening it I saw my son, his arm around a very beautiful young lady, plump, with large baby-blue eyes and long blond hair in braids around her head. My son said, 'Well, Mom, here she is.'

"I anxiously awaited their arrival, and when they came the dream came true. She looked exactly as in my dream."

In such intertwining of present and future items in many ESP experiences, one notes again, as in the combinations of telepathic and clairvoyant elements, that nature is not so particular about her boundaries as man-made classifications try to be. In these combinations of types of ESP, it often looks as if difficulty in classification comes not only because insufficient information is secured in the experience, but also because reality itself is not so divisible as we tend to think, but is made up of both present and future or of telepathic and clairvoyant elements at once.

Nearly all experiences that fall into the definition of psi come in one or another of these three groups: the telepathic, the clairvoyant, or the precognitive. Those were the divisions of ESP found in the laboratory, and those seem to be the main types of ESP as expressed in nature. On this account one can say that in a way the two lines of evidence, the spontaneous and the experimental, intertwine and support each other.

One can even take this idea a bit farther. When the experiences are sorted into these ESP types, a few cases still remain, and even these, it develops, have a possible prototype in the research. The reason these few leftovers do not fit the ESP category is that the information they bring does not come primarily as an idea, but as a *physical effect* of some kind. That, then, must be translated into an idea. These occurrences classify as possible psi effects, although not as instances of ESP, and because of them the terms ESP and psi are not quite synonymous. The latter term is broader and includes both this physical kind of effect, as well as the ideational, or cognitive ESP.

The discussion of these leftover physical experiences and of the research which seems possibly to give them support will be deferred until much later in this book, when the place particularly appropriate for them is reached.

· 3

The Forms of ESP Experience

One cannot read about or hear about many ESP experiences without realizing that they appear in consciousness in a variety of ways. Of course, some are dreams and some are not, but even beyond that rather obvious line of distinction, the dreams have their differences, and so do the various waking experiences. The background of experimental work in parapsychology does not help much in trying to make sense of this hodgepodge. Practically all experiments have been conducted in the rather limited environment of a laboratory, in which dreams certainly are not usually featured. But in life occurrences the range of condition is less restricted, and a variety of ways or forms of experience can well be expected here. As it turns out, however, the number of actually different forms is not unlimited. Once one begins to look for basic similarities, it is not too difficult to see, beneath the surface variations, lines of similarity and of order. Among these, it is possible to analyze the various forms into only four that appear to be significantly different: realistic, unrealistic, hallucinatory and intuitive.

REALISTIC

Almost the first thing one notices about the way ESP experiences come into consciousness is that many of them take a decidedly pictorial form. Such true and realistic detail may be given that the accounts sound almost like a description of a photograph—a photograph of the event. This realistic form stands out above the others, both because it is reported the most frequently, and because the similarity of the experience to the event is so striking.

Some years ago, a woman in West Virginia had such an experience. Her father had decided to move to Utah, where he had bought a tract of land which none of them had ever seen. She and her husband had decided to go West too.

In this dream of hers while she was still in West Virginia, she was in Utah and looking from a distance at the town nearest her father's land. She could see it in the evening sunlight spread out over the flat land, sunshine glistening brightly on the rooftops. But all around it, as far as she could see, was a picture of only gray desolation. The desert stretched away miles and miles, barren and lonely, with nothing but emptiness. As she looked at it, a feeling of heartbreak came over her which wakened her to the realization that it was "just a dream," although it had been a remarkably vivid one.

They went to Utah. But she and her husband were terribly disappointed. They were not prepared for the change. As she says, they were not of "the stuff of pioneers," and soon grew homesick for the wooded hills of West Virginia. So before long they loaded the trunks on the wagon and her father drove them to the town where they could catch a stage out. As they neared it and were driving across a high mesa, they suddenly came to the edge where the road went down.

And there was the dream! It seemed to be the scene exactly. The town in the distance spread out over the flat land; the sunshine glistening on the rooftops, on the desert surrounding it. She felt she must have seen it before; the dream and the reality, she thought, were identical.

Most realistic ESP experiences are dreams, but exceptions occur. The case of the woman who thought she saw a car full of guests arriving a few days before they did so is one example, as is that of a farmer's wife who, washing dishes one cold day, "in her mind's eye," saw her youngest son fall into a lake which was a quarter of a mile behind the house and out of view beyond the orchard. She could not possibly have seen the place really, yet it was as if she saw her husband wade in to pull the boy out, carry him to the house with water dripping from his clothes, and then bring him to the kitchen range and rub him dry with towels.

She finished the dishes and started to knead the bread, still worried over her "vision." Just then she looked out the window and her husband was coming into the yard, the dripping boy in his arms. As her hands were covered with bread dough, her husband undressed the child and rubbed him dry and warm. She said the "vision" passed before her eyes "like a motion picture."

With detail thus included, a waking experience like this seems no different from similar dream experiences. Some people do have daydreams which differ little from "night" dreams, which perhaps can account for the waking experiences that take the characteristically dreamlike form.

One fairly general thing about this true and detailed pictorial kind of experience is that the scene or picture appears as if taken from a specific viewpoint. The woman in Utah, for instance, recognized the scene of her dream only when in actuality she was able to see the land from a specific viewpoint.

It is interesting to note that sometimes the edge or limit of that viewpoint cuts off part of the picture, even excluding an important item of information. One summer several industrialists went for a fishing trip into the wilds of Canada. Among them was the district manager of a sheet and tin plate company. For about two weeks they had been in the deep woods, cut off from all news sources.

The night before they were to return home, the district manager had a dream, so clear, so vivid, he could not sleep afterward. In it, he writes, "one of our locomotive cranes that was unloading a car of scrap iron, together with the car, was on the track near the bank of a river alongside the water tower which served the locomotives. For some unaccountable reason, as the huge magnet swung around with a heavy load of scrap, it suddenly toppled over the river bank. The operator, whom I called by name, jumped clear of the crane and landed below it as it came bounding, tumbling and bouncing down the river bank, and he finally disappeared from view as the crane came to rest twenty feet below at the water's edge. I particularly noted the number of the crane and the number and positions of the railroad cars, and was able to tell how the crane operator was dressed. Furthermore, I noticed the approximate damage done to the crane. I did not know, however, what had finally happened to the operator. He had disappeared under or behind the crane after it had come to rest. In other words, I was observing the accident from somewhere in or across the river.

"Upon my return to the mill the following day, the first man I met was the master mechanic. He told me to come with him to the machine shop to inspect the crane of my dream, to talk with the operator who had emerged from the accident without a scratch. The operator explained his lack of injury by the fact that the crane had fallen over in front of him as he made his last jump and as it made its last bounce. The record showed the smallest detail to be as I had dreamed it, with one exception. The exception was that the accident had happened two hours after the dream."

It is too soon to make a conjecture as to the reason that some experiences should be so faithfully pictorial. At least one can see that this realistic form is not governed entirely by the person's conscious interest, for if it were, in a case like this one, the person would "know" what happened to the operator, just as definitely as he "knew" the number of the crane.

The pictorial or realistic form is not only common among ESP experiences, but it is easy to recognize because of its accurate detail. The details make it unlikely that such an experience will be passed off as sheer coincidence.

UNREALISTIC

Just as truth can be conveyed by fiction as well as by factual description, many ESP messages are expressed through *un*realism rather than realism. "In January, 1945," writes a woman from San Francisco, "I dreamed that my young son, an only child, who was overseas in combat duty in the South and Southwest Pacific theatre, came to me while I was busy in the kitchen and handed me his uniform which was sodden, soaking, and dripping wet. He had a most distressed expression on his young face, and, feeling disturbed and confused, but saying nothing, I mechanically began to wring the water from the uniform, the navy-blue dye clouding the water in the process and increasing the disturbed and confused, bewildered feeling.

"Billie, standing next to me, took the uniform from my hands and dropping it into the laundry tub, turned me around and took me in his arms, saying, 'Isn't this terrible! Oh, Mom—it's all so terrible!'

"Although he had never given me any cause for concern when it came to getting into any mischief of any major degree in the 'growing-up' process of his nineteen years, I thought—in the dream —that he might have gotten into some sort of difficulty that he thought would therefore be distressing to me for he said, 'This is the one thing, Mother, that I had so hoped you would never have to hear!' So I said to him, as I had at times when he was growing up, 'Billie, dear, remember? There is nothing so terrible that we can't sit down together and talk it out.'

"We went into the living room and when I sat down in the chair he sat down in my lap, put his arms around my neck and his head on my shoulder—sobbing—but quietly. I held him in my arms and suddenly he was a little infant again and I was rocking him as I had in his babyhood! As his sobbing ceased, I awakened abruptly, but the dream remained with me most vividly.

"That was on a Monday night. The following Sunday afternoon a chaplain from the Thirteenth Naval Base in Long Beach, California (I was living in southern California at that time) came to me with the message that something had happened to Bill's ship, the USS S——, a long list of those missing—and his name was among them. It was later established that all those listed as missing—two hundred fifty lads—were killed, having been blown into shattered unidentifiable bits at the time the ship, laden with tons of ammunition, depth charges and bombs, was torpedoed by the enemy at Lunga Beach, Guadalcanal, on that very night of January twentieth when I had dreamed so vividly of Billie in the dream here recorded."

Did that dream tell the truth? Scarcely a detail was real, from the first scene of wringing out the sodden, fading uniform to the boy's transformation in his mother's arms to the infant he used to be. Yet the dream, in its deeper meaning, was quite true. While entirely different in form from the realistically true dreams we have just been considering, this one carried the sense of tragedy indirectly and by dream fantasy and dramatization. In it one can see the mixture of the ESP information and the mother's memories of her son as a baby. On the whole, the fantasy was a fairly complicated one, but often when memory is not involved, the tendency of the dreaming mind to dramatize a situation may stand out even more clearly.

In North Carolina, in 1945, the waitress in a café had as a patron a handsome young man who began to pay attention to her. He said he was a salesman from Boston, single, and asked her to go to a movie with him.

After several dates, she began to fall in love with him, and soon they talked of marriage. One evening he said he would have to make a quick business trip back to Boston, but would return in a week and they would then set the date. The night after he left she had a dream. A sad, frail woman with dark brown hair and in the last stages of pregnancy appeared to her, and said she was the man's wife.

The next day the waitress learned, from someone who had overheard a telephone conversation, that it was not a business trip to Boston that had recalled her friend, but a call from his wife who was about to have a baby.

The man returned in a week, and when confronted with the story that had been revealed by the telephone conversation, admitted his duplicity, and that the description of the woman in the dream fitted his wife.

Though nearly all unrealistic experiences are dreams, occasionally the unrealistic tendency is shown when a person is awake. Just how different day dreams really are from night dreams seems again to be the question. For example, in Cincinnati one afternoon a few years ago, a young woman was washing the luncheon dishes. Her husband was out of town on a business trip.

Suddenly, looking out the window she saw, as if in a daze, a vision "of the Grim Reaper," running madly across the sloping lawn. It was gone in a flash, but left her cold, shaken and terror-stricken. She knew something terrible had happened.

She had expected her husband about 3:00 P.M., but he did not come. By seven she was walking the floor with a perfect case of jitters, when the phone rang. It was a call from the hospital to say her husband was hurt and unconscious. It turned out that about the time of her unusual experience his car had been struck by another traveling very fast, and he was crushed against the windshield. He was injured badly, but lived.

In the religiously inclined, the imagery of this kind of fantasy often plays on religious concepts. In a Minnesota hospital a woman had had a major operation. As she regained consciousness she was aware of someone in another room groaning and crying constantly. The nurse said everything possible was being done for the patient across the hall and that he would be all right. But this woman was much concerned and prayed that he would be relieved.

"It was long after midnight" she writes, "the nurse finally went for a sedative so that I might sleep. She went out the door, closing it quietly behind her."

Certainly the distinction that a weak or ill person in bed may make between sleep and waking cannot be taken as a very reliable one; but in this instance the patient was not aware of going to sleep. She was facing the door. In a few minutes she noticed it opening. She first thought it was the nurse but she says, "as I watched I saw the figure of Christ. He was dressed in flowing white robes as I have seen him in pictures. He walked slowly and quietly to my bedside. I thought He had come for me, but laying His hand on my pillow He smiled and said, 'I have come for him. Everything is all right.'

"Then as quietly as He came, He went out, closing the door behind Him. Somehow it didn't seem at all queer. I turned my head and saw by the clock it was two-forty A.M."

The next morning the patient said to the nurse, "The man across the hall died last night, didn't he?"

"Yes, but how did you know?"

She told her of the night's experience and finally, after overcoming the nurse's objection to giving out information about another patient, learned that he had died at two-forty A.M.

The idea of Christ coming for the dying is, of course, symbolic, and in a way the dream that incorporates such concepts can be called symbolic; but still the meaning of the dream is clear enough not to need interpretation.

Completely cryptic or symbolic dreams, however, are familiar, even legendary. Stories involving them abound in all epochs of history. Their veiled and mysterious quality has given them a lure and interest far surpassing that of the plainer realistic dream. To the clear eye of science, however, their connection with the reality they are supposed to symbolize is often as unconvincing as it is unproved. Often the meaning can too easily be merely "read in."

In many experiences of this kind, no indication is given of the specific person, time or place which are presumably concerned. Naturally, the next appropriate event the person hears of is taken as the fulfillment of the experience without any proof of a connection between it and the dream. An elderly man in Texas says that for twenty years he has had occasional repetitions of the same dream, which is, "I have lost a tooth. It is out, gone. I can feel it missing with my tongue. But, I have all my teeth and all are good. After each such dream in a week or two weeks, I learn of the death of a close friend or relative."

Obviously such a dream would *have* to "come true," since unfortunately, sooner or later, news of the death of a friend or relative will almost certainly come. To be classed as an ESP experience with reasonable reliability, such a dream would have to include some specific item linking it to a definite event.

It may be because of today's more critical attitude on such matters that really symbolic dreams are reported—at least as evidence of ESP —much less often than are the more prosaic realistic type in which the multiplicity of matching detail makes the possibility of coincidence seem remote.

And yet, in certain cases, one can trace in a person's ESP dreams the development of what might be thought of as "personalized" symbolism. Sometimes one can chart the way in which a dream symbol, muddy water, let us say, or a white stallion, or an avenue of trees might have developed into an omen of crisis, usually that of death. It is not necessary that the first of the series of dreams be based on ESP. That one could be an ordinary dream fantasy; but if it comes at a critical and significant time, it appears possible that it could be "stamped in" unconsciously so that later, when a comparable crisis occurs, even if it is one which can only be known through an ESP impression, the same fantasy might be repeated and thus create a symbolic ESP dream.

On a hot July afternoon in South Carolina, a girl, then twelve years old, whose mother was very ill, was sent by the nurse out to play. She went out in the yard and fell asleep in the swing.

"I dreamed I saw my mother," she says. "She was walking down a beautiful avenue of trees—going away from me. I ran as fast as I could and realized that I could never catch up with her; then I called her. She turned and put up her hand and said to me, 'Go back, my daughter, your father needs you.'

"I immediately waked up and went into the house. My father met me in the hall and took me in his arms and said, 'Daughter, I need you. Your mother just left us.' When I told him that I had seen my mother, walking fast down this avenue of trees I had never seen before, he said, 'She must have given you her last farewell.' This dream has remained with me throughout these many years, because in my sleep I have had visions of the same avenue of trees on three other occasions.

"In the first of these my younger brother was ill in a hospital in another state. I was ill and could not be with him, but my father and brothers were by his bedside when he passed away. I dreamed the night he passed away that he too was walking down this same avenue of trees that I had seen in my dream some twelve or thirteen years before, and I tried to catch up with him and he told me not to come on but to go back. When my father brought my brother's body home for burial, I told him about the dream and the hour. He said that my brother had passed away a few minutes before the hour I had awakened.

"Then in January, 1947, my husband and I had had friends in for a game of bridge. Afterward we retired and both went to sleep. I had this same dream—this time it was my husband who was walking so fast. I ran and ran and called and called for him to stop—he, too, as in these two other dreams, put up his hand and said, 'Our precious children need you—go back.' I was frightened and turning in my sleep, put my arms around him, awakening him. The first thing he said was, 'I am so sick, please call the doctor.' He died in a few minutes.

"Then, on Good Friday, 1934, my daughters and a friend of theirs went to a dance. Before their return I dreamed that my eldest daughter and this girlfriend of hers both suffered fatal accidents in front of my home, and the same avenue of trees came into the dream. When my daughters returned home around one o'clock I told them of my dream and my relief that they had returned safely. The next evening, the Saturday before Easter, my daughters had a dance in my home. The girlfriend was killed within a block of our house on her way to her home, and the accident was just as I had dreamed it."

It sometimes appears that a personal symbol may develop in some such way. But even so, the danger of assuming a connection where none exists is obvious. The development of a true dream symbol of ESP significance probably occurs very rarely. Many dreams assumed to be meaningful are probably only the result of a repeated but non-ESP dream, which the dreamer associates with the next death he hears of. The reason for the repetition is usually something psychological and has nothing to do with ESP.

Just why should some experiences be symbolic whether or not ESP is involved? Answers have been given to this question, but none of them can be considered as established or even applicable to all cases. A common assumption is that an unrealistic dream with its more hidden meaning is a gentler way of breaking bad news, but in ESP at least the number of dreams bringing bad news in the stark and undisguised realistic form seems to be many times greater than that of symbolic or even only slightly unrealistic dreams. Whatever the full explanation may be, the point here is that dreams which show a tendency to fantasy rather than to literal representation can be considered a distinct form of ESP experience, and one which is in sharp contrast to the realistic.

In the majority of cases the realistic and the unrealistic forms seem to be fairly distinct, so that a dream is either one kind or the other. Occasionally, however, a combination of both may be observed. One example of this would be if the dreamer had an unrealistic impression of going on a trip or visit during which he "sees" a scene in true and realistic detail.

A woman in California dreamed she went to visit her mother's friend who lived in Austin, Texas. She had never been in Texas, and had had no recent word from the friend. In the dream she says, "I entered a large square old southern house with a center hall and stairway and rooms on each side. No one met me and I started up the stairs. The woodwork was dark and gleaming and I would swear there wasn't a grain of dust in the house. I glanced into the rooms as I passed and got the impression of space and graciousness and a few pieces of fine old furniture. There were no curtains anywhere. Everything was in the most exquisite order. As I went upstairs a feeling of tranquility and happiness began to permeate my usually troubled spirit. I came to a closed door, opened it and entered. This room was in what I felt was a state of emergency disorder. Clothes were thrown on a chair. A queer-looking cot, which I was sure didn't belong, was set in the middle of the floor. On it lay my friend. She greeted me cordially and I sat down beside her. We chatted and visited happily for a long time. At last I had to go.

"I had enjoyed it all in my dream but when I awoke the next morning and thought it over I grew uneasy about my friend. That low, queer-looking cot had had very much the shape of a coffin, and I remembered she hadn't raised her head from the bed. I knew something was wrong. I sat down at once and wrote her every bit of my dream as I freshly remembered it, including my impressions of the house, and asked her if she were sick.

"It was weeks before I got an answer. She had been taken violently ill the night I had had my dream. She and her husband were accustomed to sleeping on cots on the sleeping porch, but they had brought her inside. She had had a close call but was recovering. She thought my description of her house very strange. I had described it exactly, and many of her friends had spoken of the peaceful atmosphere. As for the curtains she added, 'I hate the things. I never have one in my house.' She had married rather late in life and had formerly been a teacher in a boarding school, so I had never been in a home of hers or had any idea of her way of housekeeping."

Combinations of realistic and unrealistic elements in one dream, are, however, exceptional. Apparently the unconscious "dream maker" usually does not mix his ways of expression any more than do the conscious writers of prose and poetry.

HALLUCINATORY

Many ESP experiences occur just as the person is waking. In some of these it is not easy to say for sure he is awake, and yet his experience does not appear to be a typical dream. It may be more vivid, more nearly like the sense experience which comes when one is awake. Who has not, for that matter, had a non-ESP dream so vivid it carried over into wakefulness and seemed more real than reality? With some, this impression of realness may linger for an appreciable time, so that the figures in the dream may at least temporarily seem to have been actually seen or heard. Certain ESP experiences are of this kind. Because the person thinks he is using his senses, they are more than just dreams.

One of the paratroopers of World War II who made the D-Day jump was a Pennsylvania boy named Jack. On two succeeding nights after the invasion his mother had vivid dreams about him, but on the third, one of these different, borderline experiences. In the first dream he was lying in a long ditch with other soldiers, and although trying hard to get out, did not succeed. The dream the second night was similar, except that all the boys but Jack seemed to be covered with blood. Jack seemed to be protected by the others.

On the third night, she thought she wakened, sat up in bed and saw Jack smiling at her, telling her not to worry, because he was all right.

She told her husband of each experience and he made a record of the dates. They were notified that Jack was a prisoner in a German camp, but for a long time heard nothing from him directly. Nine months later he came home. His father asked him about those nights of his mother's dreams. He said he had been hiding in a deep ditch, trying to keep from getting hit while the German planes were strafing them. He told about trying to get out when the planes were at a distance or flying away from the ditch. On the second night, while he and the others were in the ditch, most of the boys were killed or badly wounded from the strafing, others had found refuge in the ditch, and he was mostly on the bottom. On the third night, he escaped from the ditch and was taken prisoner with the rest.

Experiences that, momentarily at least, seem like actual seeing or hearing are occasionally repeated another night, and when that occurs, the sense of reality wears off and is less convincing as the person comes to realize the hallucinatory effect. During the war a woman in New Jersey, whose husband was overseas, had a series of such borderline experiences. She dreamed her husband was calling her, knocking at the door and saying, "Come to me, Ronnie. I'm all right. See!"

She jumped up, thinking she saw him, but no one was there. It was all a dream. But it went on morning after morning. Each time, she says, "I would reach toward his image to touch him, but he would disappear. I hadn't received any mail for a long time because he had been on the front lines, but I kept on praying he'd be all right.

"Finally when I heard him call I refused to get up. I put a pillow over my head. Then a knock came at my door. It was a telegram from the War Department. He had been found seriously wounded.

"When he came home I found that he had been unconscious much of the time during which I had heard him; and he had called over and over, 'Ronnie, come to me. I'm all right. See!' "

More often than not, however, this kind of experience does not occur a second time. Since there is only a first time, the novelty of the effect remains and to the person the relation it bears to a dream is likely to be less obvious. Often, not remembering a preceding dream or perhaps having had none, the person takes the experience to be a "vision," and consequently it seems more memorable and significant than any dream could be. Such experiences, of course, *are* more than dreams, because momentarily the individual is convinced his senses are actually functioning.

A woman in Wisconsin had gone to bed early after a tiring day and had been asleep for about two hours, when, as she says, "I awoke from a terrible nightmare. I saw my husband standing in the bedroom door, his face all bloody and beaten up, clothing covered with blood and he was saying, 'Don't be alarmed, Mother. I just had a little accident.' I jumped out of bed, turned on the light and there was no one there. So I looked at the clock and the time was nearly ten-thirty P.M. I went back to bed; around midnight I was awakened again, and there standing in the bedroom door was my husband, face all beaten up, clothing all bloody, looking just like I had seen him two hours before and he said, 'Don't be alarmed, Mother. I've just had a little accident.' I said, 'What time did this happen?' He said, 'Around ten-thirty P.M.'

"Two brothers had beaten him up about an old grudge."

Although such an experience gives the impression of being quite other than a dream and the absent person seems within sensory range, its actual difference from a dream seems to lie in the conviction the person has that his senses were functioning. That conviction makes the real difference between these experiences and the day dreams in the previous section. The woman who saw the "Grim Reaper" while awake, and others like her, knew they were day dreaming and not really using their eyes. But those mentioned above were wide awake, and for a moment or more thought they were actually *seeing*, not dreaming, something which was not there.

When ESP is not involved and when someone thinks he sees something that is not there, psychologists say he has a hallucination. In earlier days, dreams were considered to be one kind of hallucination, because they picture something that is not there. Today the term *hallucination* is used only if the person is awake and at least momentarily thinks his sense organs are actually involved. The word hallucination, as now used, covers all kinds of waking experiences which involve the senses when nothing is present to excite them. Ordinary hallucinations usually occur to persons who are drugged or ill or in delirium. Any hallucination, whether coming from an abnormal mental state or even from a strong emotion, as in certain religious experiences, is characterized by the (mistaken) impression that the object perceived is present to the senses.

Hallucinatory experiences such as the cases above also occur, however, and are different from all ordinary hallucinations. They are evidently the result of the psi ability, and can be referred to as psi experiences, or as ESP hallucinations. They perhaps should have a name of their own, because they are so different from the others. But, until new expressions have been coined, we must make the best of the old terminology.

Psi hallucinations are different from ordinary hallucinatory experience for several reasons. The most important one is that the thing that seems to be there *does have reality of some kind*, even if only as a thought in someone's mind. It is real in the broad meaning of the term, and though the senses can not reach it, extrasensory perception can. And so, in contrast to all other hallucinations, this kind—the psi hallucination—is, in a way, true, and not just an experience without any factual basis. But in order to be certain which kind one is dealing with, it is necessary for the target or basis to be something that can be checked and proven to have reality. The woman in an earlier case who thought Christ came into her hospital room had no evidence, beyond her own belief, of that identity, or that any personage was actually present. That imagery could have been the result of dream dramatization only.

Psi hallucinations are different from other hallucinations in that they usually are experienced by perfectly normal people who are not in abnormal mental states caused by drugs or illness. As suggested, however, they do frequently occur to those just awaking and, therefore, the question of dream versus hallucination often is difficult to decide. But not always. Sometimes there is no doubt that the person having an ESP hallucination is fully awake. His experience may be either visual, like those above, or auditory if he only hears something relating to the distant person. During the Korean War, a mother and son had "joint" experiences, both of which were hallucinatory, the mother's occurring just as she awoke, the son's when he was wide awake. The mother tells how at the time she thought her son was en route to Korea. In reality, it turned out, he was in Manila. She explained that earlier, when still in training, he would occasionally drive home unannounced for the weekend. He would arrive late at night, stand in the doorway of his parents' bedroom and whisper, "I'm home, Mom." She continues, "On the night of which I write we were sleeping, when suddenly I awoke and saw him standing there, looking at me. I arose quickly and said, 'Dick, how wonderful! We thought you were on the other side of the world.' As I said this, he turned and walked before me into the living room, where he just faded away! My husband followed me and said, 'What's the matter? There is no one here. It was only a dream.'

"I just couldn't believe it. I felt a great sense of depression and heaviness. I scarcely slept the rest of the night."

When her son returned a few months later and they compared details, he said, "I was almost killed on shore patrol in Manila." He then went on to tell how his buddy had been knifed and how he himself barely escaped. He said, "Just as it happened I saw you and heard you say, 'Dick, how wonderful.'" As nearly as they could tell, the time of the two experiences was the same.

Hallucinatory experiences in which someone "hears" the human voice are the most frequently reported kind of psi hallucination, but not the most well known. Popularly, the visual type of hallucinatory experience is much better known than the auditory, because many visual hallucinations involve the human figure.

Other kinds of pseudo-sensory experiences besides the visual and auditory ones are represented in psi hallucinations. Occasionally it may be the sense of smell; occasionally more generalized physiological effects, even that of pain or general bodily discomfort. Such experiences are often of the telepathic type. It seems as if the person *projects* in his own organism either a replica of the sensations being felt by the distant person or his own interpretation of what those sensations are.

"In 1951 my mother was gravely ill of cancer," writes a woman from Philadelphia. "Her death was expected at any time. On a certain morning in August, I had just finished my breakfast coffee when I had an unbearable pain in my chest in the heart region. I had never had any pain or trouble of that kind in the past, but I was sure I was dying of a heart attack.

"I massaged my chest, trying to lessen the pain, and worrying that my two young children would be frightened if I died. After several agonizing minutes the pain receded, and in maybe fifteen minutes it was completely gone.

"A little later the phone rang. My sister asked me to get a taxi and come at once to my mother's home about twenty minutes' drive away. I thought it meant that my mother was dying, and rushed out almost at once. But when I got to my mother's home my sister told me my *father* had just died of a heart attack, and they were trying to keep it from my mother.

"On retracing, I found that the pain I had had in my chest coincided very closely with the time my father had his attack. And even the conditions were the same. We were both finishing our cups of coffee and had the chest pains at the same moment by the clock. I had had no idea my father was not perfectly well."

One characteristic that marks *non-psi* hallucinatory experience is that it is "private." No one else shares the hallucinations of the ill or drugged, any more than anyone shares his dreams. ESP hallucinations are usually private too, even when other people are present who would be in a position to share them. But very occasionally, several persons are reported to share the experience. A woman from Ohio says that in the summer of 1912 her husband, whom we will call Martin Jones, gave her three theater tickets. She says, "I took my daughter, who was about twelve years old at the time, and a neighbor boy, also about twelve.

"When we came home that night, around twelve o'clock, we came up a long flight of steps leading from one street to another, there was a big electric light at the top of the steps, that lit up the steps pretty well. It was a bright moonlight night and we were just taking our time. When we reached the last flight, I looked up and saw my husband walking along at the top of the steps and looking down at us. I did not say a word to the children, but the boy spoke up and said, 'There is Mr. Jones.' I felt a little tired from climbing the steps and I did not answer, so my daughter spoke up (thinking I did not hear the boy). She said, 'Mom, there is Papa.' I said, 'I see him. I guess the baby is getting cross and he wants me to hurry.' Well, we came up to the top of the steps, and while we were looking at him he just was no longer there!

"Not one of us spoke a word, we felt suddenly afraid, and we came silently along the street. My daughter and I waited for the neighbor boy to gain entrance to his home, and we hurried into our house. My mother met us at the door, and I said, 'Where is Mart?' and she said he was in the next room asleep on the couch. I went in and lying on the couch, sound asleep, was my husband. I awakened him and asked him if he had been dreaming. He said not that he knew of. He was dressed just as we had seen him on the street. He always wore suspenders, but he did not have them on. He had worn no suspenders when we had seen him at the top of the steps."

Are experiences like the above simply illusions caused by some natural shadow or light effect; are they instances of mistaken identity; or are they really cases when a hallucination is shared by several people? If the latter, could they be the result of telepathy between the several persons, or is something actually "there" to be seen? One cannot answer these questions yet. For one thing, such experiences are very rare. Without more conclusive evidence than is yet available one can only leave the questions open and say, if these effects are what they seem at face value to be, then another difference between psi and ordinary hallucinations must be added to those already mentioned. No one else sees the snakes that torment the sufferers from delirium tremens, nor the heavenly figures a particular religious mystic may entertain. If psi hallucinations *are* ever shared, then they are a different kind and not the entirely private affairs of non-psi hallucinatory experience.

The question whether the person seen in such experiences could in some unusual but real sense be there has been a much debated one, and has seemed to have special importance because of certain instances in which he is someone dead. This is the case of shared and, the much more common, unshared experiences.

In 1944, Norman, an American soldier, was stationed on the island of Guam. He had been well acquainted with another soldier named Pete. Later Pete was killed, and this Norman knew. Some three weeks afterward, Norman had driven several staff officers on an observation tour back of the front lines. While he had waited for them, one of the Marines at the outpost told him of a shortcut to take on the way back.

About dusk he came to the turning-off place. But when he had turned into it and gone only a truck's length or so, he saw Pete about fifty feet ahead in the middle of the road, his hand raised as if to signal a stop. He thought Pete meant, "You better go back the way you came."

Norman backed the truck out, taking care as he did so not to hit a truckful of Marines waiting to take the shortcut. None of the officers noticed and so Norman gave no explanation. But it was after he was back on the other road that the full realization hit him that Pete had been dead for a couple of weeks (a realization it would seem a fully awake person would have had instantly).

Next morning, when the casualty reports came in, Norman learned that the truckful of Marines waiting for him to back out had been blown up by a mine about two miles up the shortcut. Every man had been killed.

The inference to be drawn from such experiences obviously gives them special importance—the inference being, of course, that the deceased one is in some way still existing, and that he knows of the danger and gives the warning. The question of what if anything the dead have to do with such hallucinations, or any ESP experience in which they appear, however, belongs in a chapter of its own. Later we will come to the consideration of the question of whether communications can be received from the dead. Here we are interested only in trying to see how and why such a phenomenon can happen.

Fortunately, instances are on record, too, in which the person seen is not dead or asleep at the time, but alive and wide awake and able to give testimony.

In 1947 a young American girl who had earlier been in Germany and had driven a certain road frequently with a friend in the Army of Occupation, was visiting her friend's mother in England. It was a certain Wednesday afternoon and she says:

"I was on edge all afternoon and kept telling his mother something had happened to Allen. A day or two later I had a letter from him, asking if I had been to Germany and what clothes I had worn on Wednesday.

"It seems that he and two other soldiers that day were taking a prisoner to jail about fifteen miles away. They had to drive along this certain road where we had driven together before. It was wooded on one side, with laneways cutting through, not visible from the road. Suddenly a girl stepped in front of their car, waving her hands to stop them.

"Just then a trailer broke away from its truck and crashed down the lane. Had they gone on, they would have collided and probably been killed. I know this sounds fantastic but *the girl was me*. And the clothes I wore on Wednesday were the same as those she had on. Allen told me I stood in front of the car, urgently waving my arms to stop them. The German driver, who didn't know me, pulled up. He was giving off about 'silly women.' The two companions, who did know me personally, both recognized me, Gerry calling out, 'Look at Pat,' and Allen saying, 'I thought she was in England.'

"The girl disappeared as suddenly as she appeared. Gerry and Allen got out to see where I had gone to. They said I was so real they actually searched the woods.

"I was at Gerry's wedding a few months later, and he confirmed Allen's story word for word."

In such cases the point is clear that the person seen had very little, if anything, to do with the experience. Even if as in this case the girl in England was worrying about the man in Germany, she was unaware of his specific danger and had no idea of actually being in his vicinity.

As we know, the persons who have these experiences could have received the information by ESP. Whether it was only an incidental item like the lack of a pair of suspenders or an impending danger like a mined road ahead, the information would be accessible by clairvoyance. The apparent *seeing* of the figures could have been the projection of them by an unconscious dramatization process.

Why should an ESP impression occasionally take this hallucinatory form? It is the least frequent form of ESP, a fact that suggests that only a few individuals are so constituted that they can easily fall into the mental state necessary; a state which, like that of Norman's, seems to have some of the characteristics of dreaming, in spite of the fact that the person is ostensibly awake. The psychology of individual differences of this kind needs further study before the question can be answered satisfactorily.

INTUITIVE

All the ESP experiences that are neither dreams nor hallucinations are of one basic form, more like that commonly known as an intuition than anything else. Most typically, it is a sudden "just knowing," as in the case of the woman who found her wedding rings in the ice cube tray. But sometimes, instead of getting the idea, the person only feels the emotion appropriate to it. Or in cases in which action would be called for, he may compulsively do something without knowing why.

Of course, practically everyone has an intuition now and then, a supposition or hunch that something has happened or will happen, even though he may not know just how or why he thinks it. Most such impressions can be traced to such factors as unconscious inference from known facts, from observation, memory, etc. But mixed in with ordinary hunches and intuitions are others in which no sensory source, however indirect, seems to supply the information. The majority of ESP experiences that occur when people are awake are of this kind. They are not instances when someone infers or supposes or fears that some distant event quite beyond the reach of his senses has happened. They are instances when he seems to know it directly.

In 1907, a college student (who is a man in Seattle now) was on vacation at his home in Iowa when he witnessed an experience of his mother's, which he says was so unforgettable that in all the years since it still stands out. He explains:

"My parents had been divorced in 1905. To my mother it was a matter of shame and sorrow—divorce being deemed a defeat. While both parents had frequently written to me off in school, they had not corresponded with each other. When with one of them, I never mentioned the other—I had early learned not to do so.

"Seated chatting with my mother that day, I saw her face take on a sudden expression of astonishment—possibly agony. I exclaimed, 'Mother, what's wrong?'

"She replied, 'Your father is getting married.'

"I laughed. 'Impossible. He would have told me. I had a letter from him only a few days before I came here.'

"But no assurance from me could change her complete conviction that at that moment my father was remarrying. In contrast, I continued to be convinced that he would have advised me in advance, my relation to him being very close and our letters very intimate.

"However, in due course I received a letter from my father telling me of his marriage. The marriage had taken place in New York on the evening of the day my mother and I were visiting in Iowa."

One distinguishing feature of this form is what one could call its lack of outline. In contrast to the others, it includes no imagery. Dreams, whether realistic or unrealistic, leave something of a mental picture in memory. Hallucinations have the vividness of sense experience. But ESP intuitions have none of this. The experience conveys an idea or impression of which the person simply becomes aware, without any obvious reason for knowing and without any rational connection with the thoughts it may have interrupted.

This form of ESP experience is a particularly difficult one to make convincing to other people. Coming as it does without a recognizable "lead" and including no confirmatory detail or outline, such an intuition repeated to a second person is quite unlikely to impress him. Even the person himself may often later, on reflection, lose his conviction and question the validity of the intuition.

During World War II a California widow had two sons in service, and in 1944 the third, Harold, as soon as he was seventeen, joined the Merchant Marine. After the war ended he stayed on "to see the world." But, boylike, he was careless about writing and his letters stopped coming. His worried mother finally called the steamship lines and found he was still in service.

One day in May that year her other sons and their families were going to their cabin on the Sacramento River for the weekend. They wanted her to go, too. But she got a strange feeling that she must not leave the house.

"I knew Harold was coming Sunday and someone must be home to greet him. My sons knew I had not heard from him. They acted as if they thought I was losing my mind. They went on their way.

"On Saturday I managed to keep busy. On Sunday morning I put the house in order and sat down to wait for Harold. At last it was four-thirty and I began to feel a little let down, when I heard someone come running upstairs, two at a time—and in came Harold!

"I said, 'Well, it's about time. I've been waiting all afternoon for you.'

"He looked so puzzled. 'How did you know I was coming? I didn't write.' I said, 'Oh, I just knew it.'

"I was very happy to say, 'I told you so,' to the family when they came home that evening; but I believe to this day they think I knew something I wouldn't tell them."

In most cases an intuitive experience concerns not a future event but one that is happening at the same time, as in the case above, in which the woman knew when her ex-husband was remarrying. Even the one concerning the mother's awareness of her son's impending return may have been the same, for her son no doubt knew he would be home, and his mother's experience could therefore have been an instance of telepathy. But occasionally the circumstances are such that an intuition seems definitely to concern a future event.

A man in New York recalls an experience of his during World War I. He says:

"I was in France in 1918 with the Sixth Marine Regiment—with the Seventy-fourth Company, to be specific. I had seen the worst kind of bloody service during June, July and August, and had been hearing many men tell of a hunch that their numbers were up. In each case these fellows were unfortunately right about their 'hunches.' I was prone to take such hunches seriously.

"About September 12, 1918, I was one of the few left in my com-

pany who were of the original personnel to go into battle. I was completely exhausted and feverish. I had gotten gassed earlier but had
determined to stick it out. In this state I was of little use, and to help
things out I 'knew' that unless we were relieved next morning I was
in for a 'hit.' I tried to shrug it off but it just wouldn't shrug. When
we were ordered forward the next night I was not resigned to my
fate, but like a rat in a corner, I tried to push it off with all my will.
Finally, when I couldn't shake the foreboding, I began to hope that
I would not be crippled in such a way that I would be useless and a
burden (it did not occur to me that I might be killed). In my mind,
I rejected wounds in this and that part of my body, until, at last, I
settled for a flesh-wound in back of my left shoulder.

"In the gray of the morning of September 14, 1918, we awoke to
the realization that the company had been moved into a salient
where there was little natural cover. The Germans were no better off
than we, except that they were dug in and therefore were in a much
better position to inflict damage from their unexposed positions. We
were practically face to face with them. I commanded a 'Suicide Section' and was instructed to move it into a position on a small knoll.
When I looked at the spot I 'knew' that this was the place where I
was to be wounded! We got settled. A German machine gun was
spraying my position till I could hear the air waves ringing on my
helmet. While I was hugging the earth, a shell glanced over my
body, barely missing hitting me directly. It burst just beyond my feet
and into the faces of several of my gunners. I felt a hot searing pain
in my left shoulder. I wriggled back off the knoll and noticed that I
had a flesh wound in the rear of the left shoulder! Actually, the
wound was caused by a piece of shrapnel rather than a shell fragment, but not by a machine-gun bullet. I am convinced that my
wound was 'in the cards' and that it could not have been avoided.
Maybe it was God's way of granting me a rest when my poor body
and mind were about to the limit of their endurance."

One gets the suggestion that in situations when none of the sensory processes on which the individual habitually relies can possibly
operate, when neither normal observation, memory or any kind of
shrewd reasoning are possible, and when even anxiety or expectation
could be no guide, intuitive ESP may come in as if a last resort. At
least at such times the intuition stands out so one can recognize it.
Of course, intuitive ESP could occur at other times, too, when no
one is aware of it. Quite possibly it reinforces memory, inference,

judgment, and gives them added point and validity. But if it does so, who would know? Only when the situation somehow throws the extraneous nature of the material into relief is the occurrence likely to be suspected to be one involving ESP.

Intuitive ESP experiences, although frequently reported, are somewhat less frequently reported than dreams. This may be because of the difficulty people have in convincing themselves that more than coincidence is involved. Realistic ESP dreams, with their wealth of corroborative detail, are naturally less likely to seem coincidental either to those who hear of such experiences or to those who undergo them.

With the two kinds of dreams (realistic and unrealistic), hallucinations and intuition, the list of basically different forms of ESP is complete. In them is run the gamut of mental states, from sleep to clear wakefulness.

One reason for the initial impression given by the cases that their forms are so different is that the line of sleep versus waking runs zigzag between them, with dreamlike experiences, both realistic and unrealistic, occasionally occurring in the waking state. Another reason is that occasionally combinations of two forms occur in one experience. Also, in each of the three types—telepathy, clairvoyance, or precognition—any of the forms from realistic dream to intuition may be employed, in endless variation according to circumstance and individual reaction.

Once the nature of this variation is recognized, the initial confused and baffling aspect of ESP experiences fades away and one can see that they come in quite natural and even familiar ways. For after all, everyone has dreams and intuitions, whether or not the burden of any of them is supplied by ESP. And everyone has at least heard of hallucinatory experience, whether or not he has known it personally, or realized that it, too, could be a vehicle of expression for information coming in by hidden channels. These are *normal, ordinary* and *familiar* forms of mental life. Once this fact is accepted, another quickly emerges, namely: *ESP has no distinctive form of its own.*

4

The Difficulty of Recognition

The fact that ESP has no distinctive form of its own creates a problem. How can an individual tell an ESP dream or intuition from an ordinary one? At least, before he has objective corroboration for the information it brings, how can he tell that this one is "different"?

The answer, of course, is that he can't. The problem of identifying an ESP experience at the time it occurs is a real one, not only for the individual, but for the scientist as well. However, although no reliable method of distinguishing is yet available, the quest for one is not entirely hopeless. For one thing, it is a help as well as a hindrance that the forms of ESP experiences are not unknowns, but old acquaintances. Psychologists know a great deal about the mental processes of dreams and intuitions.

The only thing that makes ESP experiences different is, after all, the way the information is obtained. They are unique only because it comes by channels other than the senses. Granted, however, that it somehow does arrive, the rest of the process is not so unfamiliar. One can trace it to a degree and thereby get an idea of both the difficulty and the hope of learning to identify an ESP experience even before events have corroborated it.

One can best begin this tracing with incomplete cases, those with messages limited or fragmentary in the meaning they convey. In the most extremely incomplete of these, a person takes specific action at the time of some distant crisis without any rational excuse whatever. He goes, he does, as it were, from an inner compulsion. And then the action turns out to be the one he would have taken had he known the reason why.

A salesman in Arkansas, whose home was in St. Louis, went to bed one night tired out and expecting a good night's rest. It did not work out that way, however. Instead of sleeping, he found himself wider awake by the minute. Finally, as he says: "At about three o'clock I began to have a peculiar urge to return to St. Louis, an urge such as I had never before experienced. It seemed as if, regardless of plan or reason, I simply must return to St. Louis. The more I thought of it, the more I tried to call it foolish, the stronger became the urge. Then I remembered that about four o'clock the train to St. Louis came through. At that, my urge became unbearable and a short time later I was aboard the train. I went directly to my home in the suburbs of St. Louis, and my brother met me in the yard saying, 'I am glad you got my telegram.' 'What telegram?' I asked. 'I didn't get any telegram. What has happened?' 'Well,' said my brother, 'Papa died just an hour ago.'"

In the past, experiences like this had no rationale. They could only be called "an odd coincidence." Now, however, it makes sense to consider them in terms of ESP as well as psychological processes already familiar. To begin with some familiar aspects of ordinary mental life, we are all aware of a stream of conscious impressions running on constantly during waking hours and, even if in a somewhat interrupted fashion, in sleep as well. We know that knowledge of the world coming from any and all the senses, whether one is awake or dreaming, floats, as it were, in this stream or, it might be better to say, makes up the stream. When one is awake even his haphazard thoughts are more restricted, guided and organized than when dreaming. This means that material from the deeper, unconscious levels of mind, whether involving ESP or not, must be organized and restricted, if it is to cross the threshold of consciousness when the person is awake. As one would expect then, the material of intuitive ESP experience (waking experience) is characteristically less free, voluminous or detailed than that of dreams, for after all the transition into consciousness is in effect an obstacle, a barrier to be crossed.

The degree of difficulty the transition involves varies, of course, with persons, times and situations. And so sometimes, and for some individuals, one sees more information emerging than for others. In some of the intuitive cases given earlier, the individuals got messages which lacked detail but yet brought complete and rational ideas: "My ex-husband is re-marrying"; "My son will be here on Sunday"; "I will be wounded in the shoulder." On the other hand, in instances like that of the salesman from St. Louis, it would seem that even though no rational idea of the crisis could cross the threshold of consciousness, the urge to action did so.

In other cases, it seems as if a bit more information gets into consciousness; the person may at least act as if he knew *who* was involved. A woman in Brooklyn had, what seemed to her, an inexplicable urge to telephone a friend. Even though she was very tired, and, as she says, "did not feel like talking to anyone, and it was after ten P.M. when normally I never phoned after nine o'clock, still finally the compulsion won. The phone rang a long time before my friend answered, and when she did her voice was thick, and she sounded sort of choked and far away.

"I yelled, 'Are you all right?' She said hoarsely she thought so, but was very tired and had lain down and must have fallen asleep. I felt foolish for having disturbed her but—in spite of all the rules—I felt compelled to keep her on the phone. I asked her a question about some anthropological data in which we are both interested. I begged her to answer just this one question before she hung up, though I really had no need for the information at the time at all. She hesitated, then said she'd have to go into another room for a reference book. She was gone some time, but then returned and in a voice overcome with emotion, said, 'My God, Ruthie, your call saved my life.'

"It had been cold that evening, and she had shut the windows and turned on the gas oven for heat. Her husband was away and not to return till late. She had gone to lie down, and forgotten to turn off the oven. The burners were faulty and fumes were escaping, oxygen being used up.

"The insistent ringing of the phone had finally gotten through, but she was sure she'd answered the first ring. And so, if I had not felt compelled to call, and then gone on to ask the question which made her go to the other room for an answer, she'd never have noticed the forgotten oven—she'd have slept not for a little while—but forever."

Such cases in which no actual idea was secured seem more reasonably to be instances of ESP because of many others in which a partial idea *is* received. A woman in Texas was expecting the arrival by car of her mother and two young sons who had been in Indiana. It was a long trip, but the night before her mother had called to say they would arrive about noon the next day. "I was not worried about them," she says. "I felt relaxed and glad they would soon be back. The next morning about eleven o'clock, I was sitting in an easy chair with my feet on an ottoman, when I suddenly jumped as if I had been struck; and I threw my arms around my body and called out to my husband that something had happened—I said something awful has happened—it must be Mother and the boys. Of course, I was very agitated for the next twenty minutes, and then the phone rang. I said, 'That's it.'

"Well, it was a man who said that there had been an accident and my mother and the boys were all right—not hurt. Another car had a blowout and sideswiped my mother's car, and she was going about seventy miles an hour. It took the whole side of the car, and she did not apply the brakes but rode it out, so to speak, and that way avoided overturning. A truck driver who was following them complimented my mother on her handling of the car, for he said it looked to him as if several people were going to be killed. The people in the other car were not hurt either. I think I jumped and had that terrible feeling at the exact time they were hit. I never have felt so lucky as I did that day when my mother and the boys arrived safe and sound."

"Something awful has happened." That first impression, incomplete as to who and what were involved in that particular case, still brought the information of a crisis, a sufficient basis for the following rationalization, "It must be Mother and the boys."

It is interesting to note here, more or less incidentally, that the crisis which may seem to be the reason for an intuitive experience is not always in the present. Occasionally it appears that future crises too are thus incompletely registered. In a town in Wisconsin, on June 5, 1936, a girl was on her way home from work. Responding to the radiance of the lovely day she varied her usual route, absorbed in the beauty of a special street on which the sun shimmered through the trees arched overhead. It took her past the home of Mrs. D. But just as she was passing, she recalls, "Suddenly the sun became a dull disc in the sky shedding a gray pall over all. My body became leaden. I felt terrible. From her porch Mrs. D. called, 'Why, Rosemary, why look so sad on such a beautiful day?'

"I answered dazedly, 'I don't know. I don't know. Just a moment ago I was so happy.'

"This ashen feeling persisted all the evening. At home it was a gala celebration for the wedding anniversary of my parents. Besides that, a brother and sister and friends arrived from college to attend the alumni dance to be held in town that evening. Strangely, I, who loved to dance, refused several invitations to the dance and stayed at home.

"My sister, Frances, seventeen, was leaving for the dance looking like an angel. I cried out in panic, 'Don't ride in that car, Frances. Ride in this one!' The latter was a new Buick which still had to be driven at thirty-five m.p.h.

"At two-thirty the following morning Frances was killed in the first car. The group had transferred because the Buick was too slow."

Another indication of difficulty at the threshold is given by the occasional instance when emotional effects seem to be interfered with or unusual. Usually, as may already have been observed, the emotion the person feels as part of an ESP experience is appropriate to the situation. But not always. Reference was made earlier to the kind of experience illustrated by my small daughter's fear, which seemed to be unaccompanied by an idea. In many cases the emotion felt may be anxiety alone, unaccompanied by any information as to the reason for it. Some years ago, a New York family was spending the summer at their cottage on the ocean. It was their custom to walk the three quarters of a mile to the beach and spend the morning there.

One forenoon, when it was time for the mother to return home to prepare lunch, the younger boy and she started on ahead of the father and older son. They had only gone a little way when the mother, who just before had been gay and lively, became very subdued and depressed, so much so that the boy wondered what the matter was.

She did not know. She said she just did not feel happy, and tears began to flow. The more the boy wondered why, the more she cried, and finally she said she thought something terrible had happened at her home in Evanston.

When the others returned they found her still crying. Her husband tried to reason her out of it; said it was ridiculous that she should know about something a thousand miles away. It did no good. She went to her room, and the perturbed family could hear her still sobbing.

That afternoon a telegram came. It was from her mother in Evanston, and informed her that her younger brother had been drowned that morning while sailing his boat. His body had been found float-ing in Lake Michigan. It was assumed from a bruise on his head that the boom had struck him and knocked him overboard, perhaps knocking him unconscious. The time the New York woman had first felt unhappy coincided with the time her mother had received the news. Mother and daughter were very close.

The opposite effect—which also brings confusion in the identifica-tion of ESP experience—is that the emotional element is repressed, though factual details are provided. It is more likely to occur when the experience is a dream than in the intuitive form.

A woman in Montana dreamed that she was standing on a depot platform watching a big box—similar to the rough box in which a coffin is enclosed—being unloaded from what appeared to be a box car. It was dark, obviously night, she reflected, when she recalled the dream next day, and thought how odd and senseless it had been. But a few days later she had a telegram from a sister in San Fran-cisco saying briefly, "Dan killed. Bringing his body home." She says, "Even then I did not connect my dream with this shocking news of my brother-in-law's death. The night my sister was due to arrive at eight o'clock or so, we were all on the depot platform in the cold dark night waiting for her train to pull in. When it came, I stood and watched while trainmen and the mortician's helper lifted Dan's cof-fin from the express car. Then it hit me—I had seen all of this in my dream."

Whatever may be the reason why the ESP idea and the emotion it engenders should be thus separated, the fact that such separation seems to occur suggests that the two items are separate ones in the unconscious, and as each crosses into consciousness, it meets its in-dividual kind of difficulty.

And so, by the very imperfection of these intuitive experiences, whether ideas or emotional components are involved, one can de-duce that ESP impressions, coming from unconscious levels of mind, may or may not cross the threshold of consciousness perfectly.

In a small proportion of waking ESP experiences, as we have seen, the person has an hallucination rather than an intuition. This seems to mean that this is a person especially prone to the use of sensory imagery so that for him, more than for the average person, an incoming idea tends to be projected as sense experience.

Take for instance the auditory experience of a woman from Mon-tana. She says, "My husband and I lived on the outskirts of town.

He was a miner and when he was at work one day I went to town as usual to get the mail. I had the habit of walking down the railroad track, as it was nearer that way. On this particular day I was alone on a stretch where not a house nor a soul was in sight. The railroad was on level ground, no ditches, no shrubbery for anyone to hide in. Suddenly, I heard my name, 'Lucille.'

"I stopped, looked around, expecting to see someone. I called. No answer. It surely made me feel funny. I hurried on to town and made a quick trip back home. As the land was level, I could see our house a long way before I got there. I saw a car in front of the house and started to run, still having that uneasy feeling.

"I found that they had brought my husband home from the mine with an injured leg. When I asked him when the accident happened it coincided with the time I heard that voice. He said he thought he had called my name when the timber in the mine fell on him, but he was not sure."

But even if the man had actually called, and in many similar instances it is certain that a call so "heard" was uttered, the person could not possibly have heard the actual sound. By auditory imagery the effect was *acted out*. Visual imagery could equally well be used, and occasional reports show that it sometimes is. But, as a matter of fact, whichever the sensory mode, this method of expression is perhaps the least efficient of all, for practically all hallucinatory experience transmits only incomplete ideas. In the case above, the hearing of the call did not tell the person the nature of the crisis, nor would she necessarily have known that if instead she had had a vision of her husband. However, the incomplete idea given thus by sensory imagery seems not so directly the result of difficulty at the threshold, as in the intuitive experiences. It seems here rather to be the result of a personal proclivity to express an idea by sensory imagery, a form inherently limited as the conveyer of exact information.

Turning to ESP dreams now, the most common kind of imperfection is somewhat different. Granting here, too, that the ESP information is somehow accessible at unconscious levels, it evidently mingles with the stream of impressions coming from various other sources, and like any of them may be incorporated into a dream. But the information or content of a dream does not get directly into consciousness. It must be *remembered*. One of the greatest hazards, and consequently most frequent imperfections of ESP dreams, seems to be the matter of recall. While a surprising number seem to be recalled in detail, many are not. A woman in Chicago awoke early one morning because, so it seemed, someone had been speaking to her very urgently. But all she could remember when she woke was that someone had said, "This is it. She is gone." A terrible sense of grief and foreboding drove her crying hysterically from her bed. Her precipitate exit woke her husband. He followed her, wondering what on earth was the matter.

"I could only tell him what I remembered and that I didn't know what the matter was," she says. "At eight I asked him to phone his brothers and sisters and ask how they were. They were all right and curious about the early phone call. We did not habitually visit over the phone.

"I was still distressed when I called my mother later to arrange for an errand I was to do for her that day. She said the errand would be unnecessary, and so I planned to see her after dinner that evening. I felt relieved that I needn't trouble her with my mood. Surely it would wear off.

"After dinner Mother telephoned to say she was tired and wanted to go to bed early, and she'd rather have me come another time when my visit could be longer. Still I could not shake off my feeling of apprehension and neither could I pin it down. It continued far into the night. I could not sleep and so at four A.M. I took one and a half grains of Nembutal.

"When the phone rang early the next morning, it was my sister who, living closer, had been called when Mother had the heart attack that took her off a few days later."

But even if the dream is well recalled, it still may bring an imperfect message. Realistic dreams, the most frequently reported form of all, and the one that brings the greatest amount of information because of the detail included, may by their very mechanics omit some all-important piece of information.

A man in Washington State dreamed that he entered a familiar chapel in Seattle in which members of his and his wife's families were gathered around a closed casket. He did not know who was in it, but glancing around at the assembled group, he saw that his wife's father was missing. Thinking the father was the dead man, he started to go to his wife to console her when his father-in-law entered, came up to him and laid an arm across his shoulder. At that point the man awoke, so troubled that he told several people about the dream.

A few weeks later he got word that his brother in the Coast Guard had fallen overboard and been drowned. The body was sent to Seattle, and at the funeral the family entered the chapel from the family room. The dream scene was enacted. Standing, as in the spot of the dream, his father-in-law putting an arm across his shoulder, all was the same except this time he knew who was in the casket.

Not always, however, is the scene shown the crucial one. Instead, in many cases of realistic dreams, the single scene presented may not tell the whole story. The husband of a woman in a western state worked for a copper company. He was killed in a mine accident on February 27, 1919. On the night before he was killed she had dreamed that someone knocked. She opened the door to see her landlord standing there, a large bunch of flowers wrapped in green silk paper lying across his arms. He said nothing, just held out the flowers to her. She put out her arms, he laid the flowers across them, she turned without a word, carried them to the kitchen table—and awoke.

All the next day the dream haunted her, but she did not get the idea of funeral flowers. In the dream she had not wondered but seemed to understand.

Her husband was killed in the mine that evening. After the funeral the landlord told her that he had ordered a floral piece but it had not been delivered in time for the funeral. He felt so bad about it she told him she would like to see it when it came.

Later that day someone knocked. She went to the door. There stood the landlord with the floral piece across his arms. She was dumbfounded. It was the dream all over again! She reached out, took the flowers without a word, and carried them to the kitchen table.

By thus looking at the dream form of expression from the point of view of its imperfections, one can see that even realistic dreams are not entirely vehicles to convey information. They may also limit it. The man in the chapel could no more see into the closed casket in his dream than in reality. The scene of the reception of the funeral flowers was a complete unit in itself, though one wonders why this particular scene, instead of a more revealing one, came through.

It seems from such cases that the unconscious maker of dreams has definite laws of procedure which are followed without regard to the individual's direct interests and motives. If a desired item of information becomes embodied in a dream it will be only as clear as the dream imagery permits. Similarly, the intuitive form of experience may or may not be an effective one, depending on whether or not sufficient information arrives in consciousness to give a correct idea, or the basis for correct inference or assumption.

And so, through their imperfections especially, one can glimpse the kind of process by which ESP information appears in consciousness. Just as ordinary dreams and intuitions betray something of the unconscious matrix from which they spring, these psi expressions, too, do so. They seem to indicate a wide scope of information in the *unconscious,* and if fragments only get into consciousness, it well could be for other reasons than lack of information on an unconscious level.

Another sign that the path of ESP information to consciousness is hazardous is given by the person's reaction to his experience, whether or not he believes in it, or recognizes it as the truth. If he does not so recognize it, this too may be a kind of incompleteness.

We have recounted examples in which the person receiving ESP information was convinced his impression was correct. This reaction, however, is by no means general; it is, in fact, rather exceptional. When belief or strong conviction is shown, it seems to contradict the fact that ESP cannot be recognized by its form. One wonders how these people can be so sure.

Of course, experience does not necessarily involve ESP just because the person firmly believes it. Common sense says that conviction alone is no criterion. One knows from common observation that little reliance can be placed on the feeling that an experience, whether a bad dream or a waking hunch, is true. Many people have had such a conviction in a given situation, only to find it quite unfounded: the "foreseen" wreck did not occur; the delayed family member had a perfectly good reason for not appearing; the hunch that calamity befell him was only an expression of worry or anxiety and had nothing to do with psi. It is also common knowledge that the delusions of certain types of mental illness are hugged tight by those who entertain them with a certainty beyond any doubt or question. Yet they are delusions. This feeling of certainty, therefore, is no guarantee that the experience was one of ESP.

On the other hand, the ESP impressions of people, who "just know," and cannot be argued out of it, are instances of *conviction of the truth.* When one studies the way and occasions such conviction is felt, something of the probable cause can be glimpsed.

As we have already noted, the *amount* of information transmitted in dreams is generally much more profuse than that in intuitive experiences. Since dreams then bring more information, one might expect them to be more convincing. The opposite is true. Dream experiences only rarely carry strong conviction. Why should that be the case? Let us examine some and see what the situation is.

Of course, one can say that common sense alone would assign no credence to a dream of trivial matters. For example, one would not expect a dream like this one to be taken seriously: A Colorado man, recuperating from an operation and spending some time with his grandmother in the country, dreamed one night that she came in from gathering eggs and showed him one three times as large as usual, and longer in proportion. He mentioned the dream at breakfast and they laughed at the oddities of dreams. But later that morning, as he says, "She came in with that crazy egg!"

Sometimes, however, even important dreams are not only not believed, but forgotten. A young air cadet at Kelly Field in 1941 had for several weeks been making practice flights, taking off to the north on the north-south runway. One night he had a clear and vivid dream that the wind shifted to the northeast so they had to take off on the runway in that direction, a runway at the end of which was a huge maintenance hangar.

In the dream he saw a twin-engine aircraft take off. When about sixty feet above the runway and just in front of the big hangar, it flipped over on its back, crashed, and killed the two pilots. Although the other details were clear, he did not know who the victims were.

He *did not recall* the dream the next day until he and some companions in a GI truck were riding to the field from their barracks. Then he looked out of the truck at the wind tee, as they always did at that point, and saw the wind had shifted to the northeast. It brought back the dream, and he told it to the other cadets in the truck.

The afternoon flying section was divided into two parts, one taking off at 12:30, the other at 1:00 P.M. He and his companions were in the 1:00 P.M. section. While changing into flying clothes, they heard a crash, ran outside, and he saw that a plane had been wrecked in front of the hangar, as in his dream. Both pilots in it were killed. They were men he knew.

In spite of much detail, in spite of the importance of the messages, many such dreams are forgotten, recalled only when later events confirm them. This is true, no matter whether the event involved is of direct or indirect concern to the person, or whether the dream is realistic or unrealistic.

During World War II, the husband of a Pennsylvania woman was the pilot of a B-17. On the night of February 8, she dreamed that she and her two small children were at the seashore. Then, in the dream, she says, "A strange soldier in Air Corps uniform came to me on the beach and said, 'Here is a letter from your husband. He said I should give it to you if anything happened.' I asked this man when it happened, meaning the fact that he died, and he replied, 'The night before last.' The next morning I told my mother about the dream at breakfast and went to a calendar and looked at the dates, remarking the time mentioned in the dream would have been the sixth. After mentioning it to a girlfriend, *I thought no more of the dream* until two weeks later when I got the telegram. It said my husband had been killed in a plane crash on February sixth."

It is only rarely that a dream experience really impresses the person that it *might* be true. Even then, doubt and indecision, not conviction, usually result.

A woman in Texas dreamed about a man who was only a casual acquaintance. She thought she was begging him not to commit suicide, rather, she says, "to face life in reality. But he left me standing in his living room (one I had never seen), rushed to the bathroom, took a white powder and collapsed into the tub.

"I told my husband about the dream, also called our pastor and my two sisters. I was very disturbed. My husband insisted I call the man, but I thought he would think me a crank and refused to do it. I was troubled about it still when I received a late phone call from a friend. She said, 'Helen, have you heard about Jim? He was found dead a few minutes ago in the bathtub at home.' I was shaken. The coroner ruled it death by heart attack. He had been taking a powder, presumably baking soda.

"I can't forget the dream ever and continually live with my conscience. Possibly I could have prevented his death."

On the whole, then, we find that dreams tend to be discounted and not believed, whether about important or unimportant matters, and in spite of the fact that they may bring relatively complete information. One can scarcely escape the observation that whatever may be the basis of belief in an ESP experience, it is not directly related to the amount of information that gets into consciousness.

The idea is strengthened when we turn from dreams to waking

experiences. Scarcely any of the experiences that occur when people are awake bring the person much knowledge of detail, yet among these are the majority of cases of belief, whether the experience be hallucinatory or intuitive.

Hallucinatory ESP experiences are almost always believed to be meaningful. Perhaps this should be expected, since people are so used to relying on sense impressions. Practically all visual hallucinations are taken with the conviction that they represent a truth, even if the circumstances show that they could not be "real."

Before World War I a man in Seattle had a close friend. As he explains: "We had attended the same high school and then worked together for a number of years and so became very close. During the First World War we both entered the U. S. Army Service. My friend told me that he was sure he would be killed and never return in the flesh. Shortly afterward, he was sent into action on the German-French line. One day while I was shaving, Earl stood before me in his army uniform and looked me over for a few minutes and then disappeared. I informed my parents at the time that I had seen him and that I felt he had been killed and had returned to me. Several weeks later I found out that he had been killed in action at the time he appeared to me."

Auditory experiences, too, are almost always believed, as shown in cases already given; so are the occasionally reported olfactory ones. A California woman, one night in 1944, awoke to a very strong smell of scorching paint. She recognized it at once as the smell from her old-fashioned water heater when she forgot to turn the fire off. But the old heater was in a house six blocks away, from which she had moved months before.

The smell was so strong and bothered her so much that she got up, dressed, walked the six blocks, and called to awaken the tenant. The minute the door opened she knew she was right. The actual odor greeted her. "Did you forget to turn off the water heater?" The tenant smelled it then, too. Together they went to turn it off, found it red hot and the wall near it scorched and blistered.

In all modes of hallucinatory experiences, then, it appears that the habit of believing one's eyes, ears, even nose, is so strong that impressions of this kind—even against common sense—are readily taken to have a true bearing.

The intuitive type of experience, as we know, not only brings little if any detail, but more than any other it interrupts the stream of thought, and arrives with no rational introduction. One might think that therefore it would be received quite tentatively and be easily brushed aside by common sense. Instead, as already stated, the number of people who are convinced of the truth of intuitive messages is much larger than the number who are convinced by realistic dreams. The conviction "this is true" may come quite without any *rational* reason for belief; and sometimes, particularly if the truth is an unwelcome one, the person may try to ignore or disbelieve it.

One morning a woman in Florida was snatching a few moments of freedom in her neglected flowerbed while the baby slept, and while her little toddler, Stephen, was away for an hour with his father, who was making a business call on a celery trucker a few miles away.

Suddenly, with a stab of pain, she knew "Stephen is dead. I'm glad I didn't make him take the medicine he so much hates before he left." And then, "Oh, no! What am I thinking?" and to help get over the awful thought she went next door to talk to her father. He wondered why she was so pale—was she overworking since the baby came? She admitted perhaps she was, and a prey to morbid thoughts.

But—she soon learned her intuition was all too true. While the father's back was turned, the little boy had fallen into an irrigation ditch. All attempts to revive him, after he was found, had failed.

Yes, she knew. In spite of all her attempts at denial, she had known. She tortured herself afterward by the question: "Did he cry out to me as he was drowning—and I would not even answer? Could I, should I, have believed my intuition?"

Incidentally, the answer to that question was that she did believe it. But the thought was too awful, too unwelcome to face, so she tried as best she could to deny it. She could have had a little relief from her torturing afterthoughts if she had known that the significant part of the experience was not that she would not answer when her little boy called to her, but that, even subconsiously, she was so closely "keeping track" of him that he did not escape her vigilance though he did get beyond her physical reach. Instead of feeling she had failed him, she had in one sense, or beyond any sense, been right with him.

Sometimes when intuitive information is incomplete or practically nonexistent, a person may feel just as certain that something significant has occurred as if he knew what the occurrence was. It even seems as if some incomplete intuitive messages engender a greater sense of conviction than more complete ones.

One evening a woman in a New England village had such an experience. It was just before the rehearsal of a hundred-voice chorus. She was one of the six first sopranos and was combing her hair, getting ready to go to the church. Suddenly she knew she could not go. She could not sing that night. Something was terribly wrong somewhere, though she had no idea what. She said to her husband, "John, I can't go. I can't sing tonight. I just can't."

He tried to convince her it was just a frame of mind, but couldn't. She called the minister's wife, who said perhaps it was a cold coming on and she'd do well to stay home and rest.

"No, it's not a cold. It's not like that. I don't know what it is, but something is wrong." She was still sitting beside the phone, comb still in hand, trying to think, when the phone rang. It was her brother in Boston nine miles away, asking if their mother was at her house. He had been expecting her all day at his, but now she was so long overdue he was worried and wondered if his sister knew anything about it.

The outcome sometime later was that their mother was found dead in bed at her home where she lived alone, her bags all packed to make her visit to her son's house.

"How could I sing that night?" the daughter asks.

From these various descriptions of the *kind* of conviction felt by these people, who as it turns out seem to have had an ESP impression, it is clear that this certainty is not worked out on the basis of logic or conscious reasoning of any kind. Instead, it has the earmark of a judgment stemming from some deep, unconscious source. It seems as if at some unconscious level, the judgment "this is significant" has been made.

People like the soprano, and the woman returning from the beach when the tragedy occurred in Evanston, seem to know from this inner source that "something" significant has occurred. The intuition, thrusting into consciousness with no rational component, consists only of this judgment. In cases of greater information, such as that of Stephen's mother, an idea as well as the judgment "this is true" crosses into consciousness. But when realization catches up, and rationalization begins, doubts may grow stronger than certainty. Apparently this happens more easily if the experience is a dream.

But what then about a case like that of the "crazy egg"? Is it conscious thought of the triviality of the subject matter that makes the dreamer say the item is not worth taking seriously? Hardly. It seems more likely that on unimportant topics, too, the evaluation occurs below the threshold of consciousness, and the subject matter is there tagged as unimportant, so that consciously the question of taking it seriously never even comes up.

But then, what about cases like that of the cadet who forgot the dream of the crash that killed two of his companions; persons who are not even awakened by their dreams? Apparently for them the "significance" tag never reaches a level near enough to consciousness to leave a memory.

If such deep-level judgment does occur, and if items there are rated according to their importance, they presumably would then carry their appropriate emotional accompaniment. It could be, however, that the rating and the emotion, like the idea itself, do not necessarily cross the threshold of consciousness together, but may be separable and each have its own special hazard at the threshold.

From the kinds of incompleteness one observes, it seems that in dreams the factual side is likely to be represented more regularly than the "importance" rating. But in halucinatory and intuitive experiences, the detailed information tends to be omitted while the rating and the emotion emerge in consciousness. These are, of course, only tentative observations and general impressions which could explain the facts as observed, not tested and proven conclusions.

The discussions in this chapter have shown that for various reasons it is difficult, if not impossible, to identify ESP with certainty as it occurs. It is clear from this parade of reactions to ESP experiences that all degrees of belief in them are shown. Some messages are never even considered to be true; in contrast, others are believed —no matter how illogical such belief may seem at the moment, regardless of which form the experience happens to take, and irrespective of the amount of information that gets into consciousness.

And so, one can note the difference between strong belief in ESP experiences and that which accompanies the delusions of mental illness. In ESP experiences, the feeling is one that comes to sane and normal persons; it is simple, quick, definite, and applies to a specific event; it is over when the corroboration is made, and entirely rational if ESP is taken into account. It is thus quite different from a morbid delusion, except that no confirmation for it is at the time obtainable.

A reason for it does exist, however, accessible to extrasensory but not at the moment to sensory perception.

This strong belief, when it occurs, appears to be an element not only significant for the understanding of ESP, but also for the individual who often needs so much to be able to recognize an ESP experience.

To better understand this conviction, special attempts have been made to trap it in the laboratory. Subjects trying to identify the symbols on concealed cards in ESP tests sometimes have said they "felt" that certain of the responses they made were correct, but they were not so certain about the others. These subjects have been asked to put a check mark by the calls they were convinced were correct. Later the calls so checked were assessed separately from the unchecked ones.

The results, in tests made by various experimenters and with many subjects, have not been as revealing as had been hoped. In general, the "certain" calls were correct more often than the others, but not all of them were hits, by any means. The margin of difference in favor of the checked calls was not pronounced enough to prove that the feeling of certainty was reliable. The difference was great enough, however, to show that the subject's conviction, even under test conditions which unavoidably, it seems, tend to disturb somewhat the process of ESP, has a degree of validity.

Most of these experiments, it is true, did not concern crises, situations of emotional and personal concern to the people involved. No experiment yet devised can fully duplicate that factor. Without it, the test situations are no doubt more comparable to cases like that of the "crazy egg" than to those which carry strong conviction. The best that can be said at this stage of psi research, in view of all the above, is that no sure and certain way is yet known by which a psi experience can be recognized beforehand. The situation is one that must, for the present, depend on hindsight rather than foresight.

In experiences that do carry conviction, however, the outline of an identifying characteristic can be discerned. It must always be remembered that *feeling sure* is not enough. But when, in addition, a person who is not given unduly to anxieties or to sudden irrational whims has such a feeling about a given impression, it is good sense to note it and use it as a warning against a possible calamity, but having done that, then to forget it. It *may not* be the genuine thing and for the sake of mental and emotional adjustment such an experience must not be overemphasized. Until a firm, scientific method can be given for identifying ESP, no person can rightfully blame himself if he refuses to "live by dreams," and finds too late that he has had one which should have been taken seriously. He is no more to be blamed than are those who did not practice antisepsis before the discovery of bacteria.

5

Space and Time in ESP Experiences

ESP brings information about events whether they are occurring nearby or far away and even if they have not yet occurred. From the range of distances and time intervals that may be covered it is clear that ESP is not limited by time or space, although each experience bears witness to the interaction of this unlimited mental process with the space-time world of objects and events: the world in which direct messages from the senses are confined to the here and now.

How can such interaction occur? The full answer will doubtless be long in coming, for it involves the very nature of ESP. If, instead, the question is limited to the way space and time are treated in ESP experiences, the answer is here to read. For easier reading, each dimension is taken separately, although the two are, of course, inseparable.

SPACE

When the eyes or ears bring us a message, we feel able to judge the distance involved. But the occurrences reported by ESP may be half a world away. As we have already seen, space may simply not appear as distance to be covered. It may be as nonexistent or at least as unrestricting as in this experience that occurred one night in January, 1918. That night in South Africa an English woman watched at the bedside of her only son, a little boy of five and a half, suddenly stricken and entirely paralyzed with polio. It was only the second night of his illness; nurses had not yet been procured. It had been determined that the child had meningitis too, and the mother had been warned that, even if he recovered, his brain might be affected. As she sat there she suddenly decided she could not let him live to be a paralyzed imbecile. She arose and fetched a loaded pistol, decided that when he fell asleep she would put a bullet through his brain, and then one through her own.

At midnight he slept—but something stopped her hand. She could not do it. She put the gun away and told no one about it.

A few days later she had a frantic letter from her mother in England, who wrote asking what the trouble was. At midnight, the night of her daughter's near desperation, she said she had wakened suddenly and knew her daughter was in desperate trouble of some kind. She got on her knees and prayed that God would help her.

Incidentally, the child lived, and though physically handicapped, his intellect was unimpaired. He is now happily married and has three children.

How were the miles between those two persons treated in that experience? As if they did not exist. Neither person had any imagery of coming or going. Whatever the contact between the two, no acknowledgment whatever was made of their spatial separation.

The ignoring of space is not a characteristic solely of the intuitive form of experience. Even in realistic dreams with all their detail and regardless of whether the intervening distance be relatively short or long, the distant scene is visualized as though the dreamer and the dreamed-about were within ordinary sensory range. Rooms of adjoining buildings can be beyond the range of vision, but, as we have seen in many instances already, not beyond the range of ESP. And if the dreamed-of person is half a world away, he may still be "seen" in a realistic dream as if he were only across the room.

During World War II the fiancé of a girl in New York was stationed in England. For over a week she had not heard from him.

Then one night she saw him in a dream, as she says, "sitting at a typewriter in an office full of empty desks looking troubled and with perspiration dripping from his face. I awoke weeping and 'knowing' that he was ill. The next day I wrote him about the dream and my letter crossed in the mail with his, telling me that for several days he had been assigned to work in the office, and that on the day of my dream he had been given the task of typing top-secret troop movement orders. For this he was required to stay at his desk alone and unable to leave the office until the work was finished. He worked far into the night even though, he wrote me, he was sick with a fever. He felt he should finish the job and so told no one how badly he felt. He nearly had pneumonia."

Distances are not only covered without any indication of their length but, as a matter of fact, experiences involving relatively long ones are reported more frequently than those that cover short ones. Possibly people closer together, with more frequent contacts and communication, are less likely to develop the strong sense of separation that long distances engender. Possibly, on the other hand, the numbers are not as disparate as they seem: long-distance experiences are more spectacular and hence more likely to be reported. No count of actual cases has been made nor would one be reliable if it were. Regardless, however, of the relative numbers of short and long-distance experiences, they are obviously similar in general form and character. The scene pictured from across an ocean and the one a block away may each bring a true and detailed message and in each case without a reference to the intervening space.

In not all experiences, however, can one say that no indication whatever of the distance is shown. Sometimes an indirect reference is made that can be taken as recognition that distance intervenes.

A Russian now in the U.S.A., who formerly lived in Kharkov, U.S.S.R., recalled: "In 1930–33 many people were arrested and charged with participation in the anti-Stalin underground movement. Among the people arrested was my fiancée, Helen. We were very much in love and there was a great mutual understanding and sympathy between us. About five months after her arrest I had a dream of unusual brilliancy in which I was invisibly present in her cell where she was jailed with another girl whom I did not know. I clearly saw Helen and this girl sitting on the bed and playing some kind of chess which I could not see clearly. I saw the exact location of the beds and a small table in the cell. I also saw a window, half

closed by an iron sheet. When I climbed one of the chairs I was able
to see the top of the city cathedral, about three miles away. The jail
was located about six miles from my home. There was no communication between us during the nine months of her confinement for
the secret police, NKVD, did not allow any letters or gifts to be sent
to her, since she was not willing to sign a false confession to crimes
she never did.

"Later, being unable to break her resistance, NKVD released the
poor girl and after we met again, Helen told me about all her mis-
fortunes. During the conversation she mentioned the fact that, about
five months before, she had been transferred from solitary confinement to another cell where another girl was jailed. At this moment,
listening to her words, my dream came clearly into my mind and I
interrupted her conversation and described to her the content of my
dream, the configuration of the cell, the objects in it. She was completely astonished, for all of it was true. Helen told me also that the
game which I could not understand in my dream was the chess
game they organized, using a handmade cardboard and the chess
figures were made from the soft parts of black bread."

Since the point of reference was changed from the dreamer's actual location to his being "present in her cell," the intervening distance was in a way recognized. It is necessary, of course, for the
person to be "there," if the scene is portrayed realistically. That necessity is indirectly recognized in cases like the above.

In unrealistic experiences, whether the person be awake or
dreaming, the necessity of being within sensory range of the other
person's location is not so strict, for in this form the dream imagery
is more fluid and the event can be located as fancy dictates. It may,
so to speak, "come" to the person.

In 1912 a young Texan of twenty-two was working the night
shift at a factory some four hundred miles from the home of his
parents.

As he recalls, "At approximately eleven A.M. on a certain Friday
I was asleep at the boarding house and my mother came to me in my
dream. I saw her face very distinctly and I could tell by her expression that she was in trouble. There was nothing to indicate its specific
nature but clearly it was serious, and I awoke with a feeling of impending trouble.

"At eight o'clock that evening I received a telegram from my sister
saying, 'Mother hurt seriously. Come at once.' I was shocked but not

surprised. It was as though I had been expecting that very news.

"I arrived home too late, but found that, that Friday morning, while Father was in Denver, my mother had decided to drive the team and wagon to get my sister, who taught school six miles away. At approximately eleven A.M. the team ran away, Mother was thrown from the wagon, struck by one of the rear wheels and mortally injured, passing away about 2 A.M. the following morning."

Sometimes when the sleep-waking borderline is ill-defined, the person apparently retains the sense of his own location and visualizes the distant distant as if it had come to him. In Cincinnati a woman went downtown and told her sixteen-year-old daughter she would be back at 5:45, but by 5:45 she had not returned. Her daughter became worried. As she says: "I began to pray for her safety. I sat in a rocking chair where I could look along the side yard to the front gate.

"Suddenly, as I prayed with my eyes closed, I heard the gate click. I looked up and saw my mother walking slowly toward me. She was perfectly beautiful with a glorified beauty. She wore a white silk lace gown. When she left earlier in the day, she had worn a white linen blouse and a wool skirt. I arose and walked toward her, admiring her unearthly beauty. I was about to say, 'Where did you get that beautiful gown?' But before a word had left my lips she sidestepped off the walk and into a patch of flowers and was gone. I looked all about and called her. I became panicky and sobbed and prayed. Seated again in the rocker, I fixed my gaze on the front gate wondering. Finally, Mother came about five minutes past six. I ran along the yard and grabbed her hand and told her excitedly all that had taken place.

"She then explained to me that she had had an accident on the streetcar two blocks from home. Our city at that time had a type of car which was called summer cars, very much like sightseeing cars of today with sides open and a long running board from end to end on which the conductor walked to collect fares. Mother had been seated at the end of the bench near the running board when the car lurched around the corner unexpectedly. It was supposed to come to a stop before turning the corner. Quite unprepared for this jerk, Mother was pitched out of the car. A gentleman seated on the same bench with her grabbed her, grasping his fingers into her belt. The conductor rang an emergency bell and the motorman stopped at once. The conductor jumped off the car and ran forward to help hold

Mother up. The two men managed to hold her weight and at her instruction, let her down to the street gently in a heap and kept her from striking hard. She said her thoughts flew to me."

Then, again, the event in an unrealistic dream may be neither an actual "here" nor "there," but a place supplied by fancy, or perhaps by memory. A woman in Minnesota had a close friend who had gone to work in Oregon. Later she had a letter from him saying he was ill. She feared a spell of sickness, and knowing he was among strangers and probably with no great amount of cash, she wrote at once offering help and urging him to go to a hospital. Then, as she says: "Some two weeks passed. I was in complete ignorance of the situation. But on Thursday night, July twenty-seventh, about ten days after his letter, in what I suppose was a dream, I seemed to find myself in the old schoolhouse where he and I had met. It was utterly dark, and there seemed to be no floors in the building. The windows were empty openings in the outside wall. It was black all about me, and then I heard his voice coming out of the darkness saying, 'Don't feel too bad, Helen.'

"And then the dream was gone. On August second, I had a letter from him which had been written July twenty-seventh. All it said was, 'Just coming through a terrific siege of typhoid. If you can, send help.' It was so faintly written I could scarcely read it. Three days later a letter in a strange hand came saying he had died in the late evening of July twenty-ninth."

Occasionally an unrealistic scene, like a realistic one, is laid in the area where the action or event presumably is occurring. A woman in New York tells of a friend of hers who, during World War II, was much distressed because for a long time no word had come from her son, a soldier in the European theater. As she recalls: "My friend was crying almost day and night. It had been six months and she had not heard a word. We would tell her, 'No news is good news. Don't carry on until you hear from the government one way or another,' but she couldn't grasp it.

"On three successive nights in February, 1945, I dreamed the same dream, but a little different. On the first night I was looking for my friend's son among the dead and wounded. I was directed to a hospital and woke up. The second night I was in the hospital going from bed to bed looking for him. There were so many I couldn't finish, and woke up. The third night in the hospital I finally found him, his eyes closed, uncommunicative. I was told he was all right but had had a great shock and some nervous disorder.

"I related my dreams to my friend and said, 'Don't worry, no limbs or organs are missing. Only, he is very sick and unable to identify himself.'

"Four months after my dream he was brought to the hospital in Staten Island. His mother learned that for a long time they had been unable to identify him. His identification tags had been lost and he was completely without clothes. Months later he began to remember. Then they found out he was an officer, but among GI's, so his hospital was changed and through this change he was at last found."

The matter of who is where in ESP dreams thus seems to be a function of the dream imagery. As on the stage, the scene can be arranged now here, now there, and not necessarily according to reality. In fact, occasionally it may be changed within the space of a single episode. A Philadelphia couple had gone to California to live. One night a few years afterward the young woman had a dream which she relates as follows:

"I was back in my husband's family home and in the master bedroom and my father-in-law was sick in bed. My mother-in-law was in the room. She never cared much about me, but my father-in-law did. How I arrived there was not in the dream. But I was sitting on the side of the bed, which was an adjustable hospital bed.

"He looked at me, and although he did not speak I knew that he wanted to say, 'I want to tell you something but cannot because Mother is here.' (Meaning his wife.) He reached up and put his arms around me and sobbed. At that point I awoke; I lay there wondering why I dreamed about back home. Right then a man's voice called me, 'Florence.' I thought it was coming from outside through a window, that was at the head of my bed. The voice spoke again, 'Florence.' As I turned around to look out the window, I had the feeling as though ice water was being poured down my neck and as though every hair on my head was standing up straight. There, standing alongside my bed, was my father-in-law. I saw every feature just as though he were in the flesh. He was facing me and right beside him, standing in profile, holding Daddy's hand, was Jesus. My father-in-law looked right in my eyes and spoke my name again. He said, 'Florence, the Lord is my shepherd and we go in peace.' This vision was enveloped in a very pale blue light. Then it just seemed to dissolve and fade away. I cannot prove what I have written. But it is true, as true as I am writing this letter to you.

"The next day a telegram came saying that Dad had passed on. We did not go back East for the funeral, but in due time a letter came from my mother-in-law, giving us the details of his death. She said they had to get a hospital bed for him, just as I saw in the dream. She said when he was dying she stood beside his bed, and at the last minute he revived and said, 'The Lord is my shepherd and we go in peace.'"

In a few cases, exceptional because they are infrequent, proximity seems to have an effect, though one external to the content of the message itself. Some ordinary occurrence, near enough to the person to be apprehended by the senses, seems to "trigger" an ESP experience. A New York woman had a married son who lived a distance away but in the same town. One Saturday after he had finished work at noon, he went swimming. It was a very hot day and he told his wife beforehand he was going swimming before coming home to lunch.

His mother knew nothing of this, but was sitting in her living room with her husband's sister early that afternoon.

"As the train came into the city across the river," she recalls, "it blew its whistle. I never had it happen that way before, but when that whistle blew it seemed to tear the heart right out of me. I wanted to cry and I went all to pieces. My sister asked me what was the matter, and I told her that the way I felt, someone very close to me had died.

"Around seven o'clock that night my son's wife came and told me that Jack never came home. We went to the place where he had gone in swimming and sure enough, there was his car all locked up. Then we knew he had drowned. They found his body three days later. I had that awful feeling around the same time that he was swimming, because some of the fellows he worked with told us what time it was. They had talked with him shortly before he went swimming. He had had a heart attack."

Proximity occasionally seems to exert an influence in a still different way. In such a case, an approaching ESP "target" seems to be picked up by ESP only when its distance from the person is short. In these cases, physical nearness seems to set up an unconscious "awareness" or readiness, so that the idea of the target, whether thing or person, is easily suggested. It is as if ESP, like a searchlight scanning the horizon, is only directed to the target when distance is short. A Florida M.D., beginning his internship in a Philadelphia medical school, had had in his undergraduate days a favorite young instructor, a Dr. F. But since his internship began he had been so busy that, as he says: "I do not believe I had thought of Dr. F. during the first few months there. There was no reason for him to think of me.

"One day during the fall of that year, as I was working on the fifth-floor ward, I heard the elevator stop outside in the vestibule. I glanced casually at the glass panel of the door leading into the ward, and whom should I see getting off the elevator but my former instructor, Dr. F. I hastened to the door to greet him, wondering what he was doing in Philadelphia and particularly during the school term. My pleasure in seeing him was short-lived, however, as it turned out to be not him at all, but one of the visiting staff on his way to make the rounds.

"I returned to my work, still wondering what had made me mistake the reflection in the glass for Dr. F., and after a few minutes I left the ward and took the elevator to the main lobby. As I stepped off the elevator, Dr. F. walked in the front door. This nearly floored me, and as soon as I greeted him I asked him if he had not been up on the fifth floor. He told me that he had not, that he had just arrived in town by train and had just arrived at the hospital by cab. I told him what had happened and he offered no explanation. He had come to see about some postgraduate work, and although he did not say so, I doubt that he even knew I was in Philadelphia. The staff member whose reflection I had mistaken for Dr. F. in no way resembled the latter. I am firmly convinced that this was no case of mistaken identity."

Sometimes proximity seems to act as a suggestion on which the fantasy of an unrealistic dream may be based. An Indiana woman during World War II recalls: "My younger sister had accompanied her husband to Baltimore, where he had begun his officer's training. As far as any of us knew, he was to be stationed there for about two years. One night I was awakened out of a sound sleep by a knocking at the front door. Not being accustomed to having visitors at that time of night, and there being no one in the house but my ten-year-old son and me, I decided to investigate before turning on any light. I looked out of the window and saw that the caller was a man, and a very large one at that. I could not see his face, but there was nothing familiar-looking about him, so I decided not to answer the door. Finally he turned and walked away. I returned to bed and soon was sound asleep. As nearly as I can judge, it was about three when I first awakened.

"When I awakened next, it was broad daylight. I had tears streaming down my face, caused by a dream that Edith and Jack—my sister and her husband—had come and I had not let them in. I was heartbroken. Still under the influence of the dream, I reached for my robe and slippers, walked to the door, opened it, and there chained to the knob was a Western Union telegram. It was from Jack, saying that he had been ordered to Louisiana for maneuvers and he was bringing Edith to stay with me.

"They drove in that afternoon. His orders had come so suddenly that there had been no time to write. They had driven all night and all day to get here. The amazing thing to me was that I should connect them in any way with the messenger, as I had had a letter from them shortly before and there was nothing in it to cause me to think that they would not continue to live where they were for the rest of the two years."

In such instances, again, the *proximity* of the "target," in this instance probably the telegram, seemed to bring the situation to the "attention" of ESP.

Through these occasional effects of proximity, another hazard to ESP information is suggested in addition to those we have already noted. Very possibly, before they can cross the barriers into consciousness, ESP messages must *compete for attention* with all the other impressions of the external world the person is constantly receiving. Those items that fail in the competition are, of course, never "there" to be counted.

Instances when proximity in any of these situations seems to make an ESP target accessible are exceptions, not the rule. If ESP is a searchlight constantly scanning the personal horizon, seldom does one get a hint that it might be limited in its range to targets spatially close. Whatever the reasons may be for these occasional occurrences—whether a personal condition or a special peculiarity in each situation—they at least show one more way, even though an indirect one, in which distance, or the lack of it, can affect ESP.

In all of these cases we see the operation of ESP as "spaceless," even though it concerns an event located in space and even though it is apprehended by a person whose mental processes are geared to the appreciation of space. We also see the imagery used, or the lack of it, as a matter of the *form* the experience takes, but seldom involving anything but the indirect "here" or "there" of viewpoint.

But why should intervening distance be so largely ignored in ESP experiences? Before discussing the possible reason, it is well to take into consideration the way time is treated in ESP.

TIME

ESP messages, as we have repeatedly seen, are no more limited to events of the present than they are to nearby locations. In perhaps a majority of instances, time intervals, just like intervals of distance, are simply not indicated in the messages of ESP. Compare, for instance, two typical experiences, involving widely different time intervals: the dreams of two young women, each of whom, never having held a job before, dreamed of a future one. One was a girl in California who dreamed she was walking along the street of what she knew to be a small western town. She says, "The sidewalk was of boards and the buildings overhead extended out to form a wooden roof over it. I was carrying what seemed to be a small overnight case and I knew the name of the town was 'Tomb—'"

When the job materialized, this girl, with two companions, was traveling through several southwestern states modeling dresses. They stopped at Tombstone, Arizona, for dinner one night and she walked down wooden sidewalks, as she says, "carrying the model's inevitable make-up box which was about the size of a small overnight case," as in the dream.

The second girl, this one in Texas, dreamed she was a maid working for a couple with children, and in the dream was especially impressed with the furniture in the living room. She says: "I saw a tall ebony cupboard with satinlike finish with sprays of white flowers on each side. It was glass-enclosed at the top with locked doors. Inside the cabinet on the shelves were little green figurines resembling jade and queer little Chinese images like idols and images that looked like dragons."

Later, in a different city, she took a maid's job with a couple who had two small children. "Upon entering the home and turning around to set my suitcases in the hall, I came face to face with the black Chinese cupboard of my dream. On the ebony shelves were green figures, idols and Chinese-made dragons sitting behind glass-enclosed doors."

Characteristically, the two realistic dreams pictured details that later proved to be true. Before they did, a series of intervening events occurred, but the time necessary for them to occur was not hinted at in either instance.

The girl who went to Tombstone says: "I answered an ad for an office worker in a textile-manufacturing plant. I did not get that job but signed a contract with them to go on tour *that summer* with the manager, his wife, and three other girls. We were to go through Southern California, Arizona, and New Mexico, and it was the manager who decided to stop for dinner in Tombstone."

And the girl from Texas writes: "Years passed, and in the course of events my mother passed away and I began to work out, first at one type of job and then another. I finally moved to Houston, where I accepted a maid's job with a couple who had two children on December 26, 1952—*seventeen years* after my dream."

Each precognitive experience does fit a specific future time period, however, even if the time interval is ignored. It may be a very exact and specific moment, as in the case of a Canadian girl who had a dream one night in which, as she says: "I was in a small room with a single bare lightbulb hanging down. There were many posters or something on the wall, and in one corner was an old-fashioned desk with an old upright telephone on it. There was an old man at the desk writing and the phone rang. He answered it and said, 'Yes, Emma, one pound onions and a dozen oranges—I'll bring them home.' In this same room with me were four other girls—I couldn't tell, however, who they were. Each girl seemed nervous and so was I. One by one they went out and came back about ten minutes later. When my turn came I woke up.

Two days later I was to try my driver's test. There were three other girls who took the lessons with me. We were to go out one by one. We entered a small office which was exactly the same as the room in which I had been in my dream. The old man was filling out our forms when the telephone rang. He said the same thing I had heard him say in my dream. I was the last one to try my test and each girl had gone out one by one and had been gone about ten minutes. We were, of course, nervous. I was quite shaken, feeling that I had lived this all before."

Occasionally, a date or time interval does appear in an ESP experience; when it does it seems usually to be included as one more detail of information. A young woman in Brooklyn, married and living some distance from her parents' home, was unable to see her mother very often. A young brother came one Saturday to visit her. She asked him about their mother. He said she was, as usual, feeling fine.

"We went to sleep," she recalls, "but just in that twilight time between sleep and wakefulness I got a sudden inexplicable feeling. It was not a dream, nor was it a voice telling me something. I can hardly explain it, except to call it a sudden knowledge. It was not a ghostly warning of any kind. It didn't come in a frightening manner. But what the feeling foretold, if I had believed it, would have been something to frighten me and make me very apprehensive indeed!

"I called to my brother and woke him. Angrily, he asked me why. I told him I'd had a sudden feeling that our mother would be taken to the hospital *exactly one week from the following morning,* that is, on the eighth day from this night, and that she would be seriously sick—very, very sick. He just got angrier than ever and told me to stop talking absolute nonsense and go to sleep. There was nothing wrong with Mama and nothing bad was going to happen either! He wondered what was wrong with me to say such a stupid thing.

"Well, I thought it all pretty queer myself. This sort of thing had never happened before. My brother had convinced me I was talking nonsense. I fell asleep and I gave it no further thought.

"On Sunday morning one week later I was awakened out of a sound sleep by the ringing of the doorbell. There stood my mother. While in my house she became dreadfully sick, and it became my sad duty to call the ambulance and watch them take her away to the hospital. It was her last illness."

In occasional instances a person may have a specific future date so emphasized, either in a dream or intuition, that he feels it will be a significant time. If the date stands entirely alone with no idea whatever of the reason why it should be of particular interest to him, it very well may not be an ESP experience. Since any event that is at all outstanding which happens on that day can be taken as a fulfillment, the possibility that only coincidence was involved cannot be minimized, even if an event of world significance occurs on that day.

Because of the way time is treated in ESP, complications often arise that are caused by the person's inability to interpret his experience correctly. As this "time aspect," is generally unrecognized, few persons are aware that usually no distinction of imagery is made between past, present and future. Besides, in many cases, even if the person realized it, he might still be unable to interpret correctly an impression at the time.

One of the most common effects of all, and usually a baffling one, is that referred to by the girl above who, taking her driver's test, said, "I was quite shaken, *feeling I had lived all this before.*" Her realistic dream had been experienced as if it were then occurring. On that account, the fulfillment seemed exactly like the previous experience. In many instances, the dream may be quite forgotten, but when the actual scene unfolds, the sense of familiarity comes and the person remembers the dream. A man in Philadelphia who says he has frequently dreamed glimpses of scenes and events later viewed in reality, recalled specifically an incident when he was in an army camp in California. As he says: "One day, on a firing range, I happened to be standing outside a shack and looking down a valley. Suddenly I remembered I had seen this view before in a dream. The dream had occurred months before when I had never been west of the Rockies."

Then again, the dream may never be recalled as such, but besides the feeling of familiarity the person may know something which could scarcely be accounted for, except as an item from a dream. A girl in Minnesota had in her school days known a boy whose name was Dan Brown. She finished school and was teaching away from home, but went back for a weekend one time. As she was preparing to go to Sunday school, this conversation with her mother took place:

" 'Who is the Sunday school superintendent now?'

" 'Mrs. Brown.'

" 'Oh, is Mr. Brown married again?'

" 'Again? What do you mean?'

" 'Why, Dan's mother died a long time ago. I know she did, for I—'

"Then Mother said, 'No! She did not.' And I realized then I had ver seen Dan's mother and I did not know the place where I ought she had died. But still I could describe it to my mother and was like this: 'It was a summer night and soft rain was falling. I as in a house in a woods of small pine trees. In an unfin- ed lean-to kitchen, with window openings but no windows. A e was burning in a wood cookstove and cloths were being sterilized an iron kettle, then hung above the stove to partly dry. Dan's ter was ironing dry some, which I carefully picked up and carried rough two rooms to a bedroom where a white-haired lady lay very , and a nurse took the cloths and handed me soiled ones, which I rried to the kitchen just as Dan came in the door.'

" 'Well,' Mother said, 'You must have dreamed it, for Mrs. Brown very much alive.' 'I certainly am glad it was a dream, but I must ve dreamed it some time ago, for I surely remember it now,' I re- ied.

"I went back to my school and promptly forgot all about it. Some ne later I met Mrs. Brown and was once in the living room of her me but in no other part of the house, until later, hearing that she as very ill, I went, as was the village custom, to do what I could to lp, and was called upon to sterilize cloths and carry them to a rse.

"I had been home only a few hours in the morning when we heard at Mrs. Brown had passed away. After the funeral I remarked to other, 'I have a strange feeling that *all* of this has happened be- re,' whereupon she recalled my having told her, 'I was there en—.' " (Incidentally, this girl later married Dan Brown.)

Still more common than the situations which seem to point to a ore or less forgotten dream are those which consist only of the feel- g of familiarity—of one's having somehow lived this moment be- re—but in which apparently no impression of a preceding dream ever dredged up. "For as long as I can recall," writes a man now in alifornia, "I have experienced what I call 'flash-backs,' when for a w seconds the immediate locale and what I happen to be doing or eing seems to be happening for the second time. For a very brief riod, I have the feeling that I am reliving a previous period in hich the scene and happenings are identical to the present.

"Last fall, for instance, I had recently been appointed an auditor tached to a certain audit office. I was scheduled to start on a three- onth trip abroad with an audit team. I was preparing my passport application when it all seemed like the second time around. I told the auditor something unpleasant was about to happen, and in a few minutes we received a message that financing had been cut back —and my trip was canceled."

"Flash-backs" of this kind have been recognized in psychology under the French phrase *déjà vu*—"seen before." They have been explained in various ways—as an intuitive (forgotten) memory of some clue, as a shrewd half-conscious guess, or as a vague resemblance of the present scene to some only dimly similar past occurrence. Now that we know that many people do dream precognitively, ESP can be added to the list of possible explanations. At least, in some cases, it seems likely that a precognitive dream has preceded. One can be sure that many dreams are not only forgotten but are never even fleetingly recalled. Even so, they could leave a trace sufficient to produce the feeling of familiarity when the moment is actually lived.

Since precognitive impressions carry no time label, various confusions may easily arise. An ESP message about an event may be taken as pertaining to the future, when it is actually occurring at the time or has already occurred.

A woman in Massachusetts was in the hospital to have a baby. Three hours after the birth she awoke suddenly, as she says, "covered with perspiration and tears after having dreamed that my brother was in the hospital following a serious automobile accident. In the dream a doctor came to my husband and me and told us my brother would not live. At that point I awoke and could not sleep again for two days. I thought constantly of the dream while in the hospital and could hardly wait to see my mother to tell her about it and advise her to be more kindly toward my brother than she had in the past, because I realized from that dream what sorrow we would have if anything serious ever happened to him.

"When I was out of the hospital and got home, the first thing I did was tell my mother about the dream; and as I was telling her, the tears were streaming down her face. I said, 'Well, don't cry, it's only a dream,' and then they told me that it was true and my brother had been in a serious accident and had been in the hospital for almost a month, in and out of comas, and still was. He was suffering skull, neck and spinal injuries and was delirious most of the time, raving like a madman. They had told me nothing about it previously because I was going to have the baby and they didn't want to upset me. (We live in towns 125 miles apart.) It was one of the strangest things that ever happened to me."

Even if the event delineated has occurred in the more distant past, the person may think of it as something possibly then occurring or about to occur. In the summer of 1934, a young woman with a group of students went to the seashore on vacation. She was assigned to stay in the home of a doctor and his wife, strangers to her as she had never before been in this locality. She recalls: "As I was preparing to retire I noticed on the table beside the bed a miniature of a lovely young girl. I studied it for a moment, as I was impressed with a spiritual quality quite unusual in the beautiful face. I soon was asleep and it was early morning when I had this dream, or vision. I saw a train bearing down straight toward me. I heard the grinding of the brakes as it came to a full stop before it reached me. People came running and I stood beside the engine looking down at a young man whose lower body was pinned beneath the engine. He was calm, and I looked into his face with great sympathy and admiration for his courage.

"Suddenly I became very agitated and tried to tell people that we must hurry and get the ambulance. Then I became aware that there was someone else on the other side of the train; I just seemed to know it. I shook people's arms and tried to tell them, but no one noticed me. I was excitedly doing this when I was awakened by the doctor's wife knocking at my door. She came in, bringing me hot water, for it was a farmhouse.

"I was still agitated and was thinking that I must send a wire immediately to see if all was well at home. I asked where the nearest Western Union could be found, etc., and then started to tell her the cause of my agitation, which I could not shake off. I told her I had just seen a terrible accident, a young man killed, etc., and how very real it seemed and not like a dream.

"She became very serious and said, 'You have just described the accident in which my daughter and her sweetheart were killed near here. That is her photograph beside your bed. They found the young man first and did not know anyone else was killed until they found my daughter's body later on the other side of the tracks.'

"I asked her who usually occupied the room I was in and she said she did. Did I read *the memory of nature* or was it impressed upon me by the mother's thought, or what?"

Occasionally an experience cannot be correctly interpreted until the fulfillment, because an ESP element is combined with a memory of the past. For this reason, it may be the two can only be disentangled later. Such an experience occurred in Sweden the night of March 3, 1954, to a woman who happens to be a personal acquaintance. She had a dream about a "tram" accident which was recorded in her diary as follows:

"I had the feeling that my husband and I were flying over Stockholm. I looked down at the neighborhood of Kungsträdgården, and saw an accident happening there. I saw an ordinary blue tram like No. Four and I saw that a green train ran into it from the back, with several green carriages lying at right angles to the No. Four tram. A clumsy driver of a motorcar was the cause of the accident.

"Then in the dream I went to a policeman and told him that if he wanted a witness I was willing to give evidence that the motor driver caused the accident."

At the time of the dream a railroad crossed the tram line here, but all the carriages on this line had been in shades of brown. However, green ones were introduced soon after. On March 4, 1956, two years later, a collision between a No. Four tram and a train occurred at the crossing. In a policeman's sketch of the position of the cars after the collision, they are shown lying perpendicularly, just as in a sketch made in the diary.

A curious aspect of the dream, and the point significant in the present context, lies in the dreamer's offer to be a witness to the accident. In London between 1930 and 1932, she had been witness to an accident of which she says: "One evening after a theater, when driving my car to Hampton where we were living, I drove for a long while behind a road hog who finally turned over with his car. He was drunk and I went to a policeman, telling him that if he wanted a witness I was willing to give evidence against the man. I was later called for it." A future event and the memory of a past one apparently were combined in this dream.

From these various kinds of examples, then, one can see again that some seemingly tangled and confused ESP messages have after all a basic logic, once the timelessness of ESP is appreciated. Let us suppose that somehow in the unconscious, items from past, present and future time are, as it were, equally accessible to ESP without the intervals and seriality that separate them in conscious experience. The difficulties of trying to fit "untimed" items of information into the "timed" experience of everyday life thus become understandable.

We have seen short and long distances covered by ESP with apparently equal facility. Many more experiences are reported, however, in which a long distance is involved, than in which a long time interval intervenes. This difference in frequency could well be caused partly by the natural tendency to forget an impression that does not come true for a very long time. But other, somewhat less obvious causes, too, could add to the effect.

For one thing, ESP experiences, just like those of sense perception, are influenced by the person's interests, and his interest may be even greater in a person or event when far away. But when that person or event is one a long *time* off, his interest in it inevitably decreases. One can well suppose the number of ESP impressions he might have about them would fall off too.

That dreams, at least, are largely preoccupied with affairs of the immediate time period rather than more remote ones was attested to by the observations of two men, Mr. G. F. Dalton of England and Mr. J. C. M. Kruisinga of the Netherlands, each reporting in 1954 in the *Journal of the Society for Psychical Research,* London. They separately undertook the project of recording their dreams. Then they checked the recorded dreams against events that seemed to be much like actual later happenings, and found the number of similarities was greatest during the days immediately following the dream and fell off rapidly thereafter.

One has no way of knowing whether the dreams that seemed to resemble events of the next day were the result of ESP or just similar by chance. From most accounts, dreams that can more certainly be considered precognitive usually concern occurrences which stand out from the ordinary day's expected activity. Since the content of these men's dreams was not given in their reports, one cannot surmise whether their observations involved ESP or not. But even if it could be shown that the "coincidences" of their dreams were really due to ESP, the quick falling off in numbers would be only what should be expected. One can suppose that people most of the time would tend to let the more distant future take care of itself, just as we do such coming events as "death and taxes." We cannot give them the sustained attention demanded by the affairs of the present.

In any event, the actual operation of ESP seems to be unaffected either by distance as such, or by time as such. In laboratory tests covering long distances, the fact that the subject and the experimenter were far apart seemed, if anything, to increase the motivation to succeed, and the results were generally just as high and sometimes higher than when the two were near each other. In precognition tests, too, when time intervals were varied, the results showed no favoring of short versus longer times, if the person was equally interested in the outcome when a longer time was involved. One subject in a recent research scored considerably higher in tests covering a year of time than in others similarly made that covered only five days. The experiment reported in 1959 in the *Journal of Parapsychology* involved a long distance also (France to the U.S.). It was conducted by Miss Margaret Anderson, then of the Parapsychology Laboratory, with a subject, a young woman, who was much interested in the implications of longer-term precognition. This interest may well have been the decisive factor in the higher scores of her one-year tests, although there were other aspects of the situation, too, which could have had an effect.

Certainly, the effect of different time intervals still needs much more investigation—particularly periods of long duration. These naturally are unlikely to be favored either by subjects or experimenters, both of whom are likely to be impatient at the long delay before results can be known.

And so we see both time and space intervals as tending not to be registered in ESP experiences. Why should this be so?

It well may be mainly because ESP is expressed by minds geared to impressions coming from the senses and the senses *are* limited by space and time. In realistic dreams, for instance, one can quite easily see effects that could be the result of the mental habit of dealing with sensory impressions—in this instance, those of sight. For these dreams give the picture-like impressions of *seeing*, the indiscriminate inclusion of detail, the localization of viewpoint, the obstruction of objective barriers. Accordingly, in them one does not see around corners or behind closed doors any more than he does in actual seeing. But extrasensory perception of distances and times beyond the range of sense experience goes beyond the bounds of mental habit. With no precedent to go by, what does the unconscious maker of dreams do? He takes the easy way—he ignores these greater dimensions. However much time and distance may intervene, he sets his focus within visual range, and as if in the present. Though the "mechanics" of waking experiences are different from those of dreams, hallucinations and intuitions too are the productions of minds habituated to space and time.

And so we see the greater reach of ESP cut down to the size of the mind through which it operates and its extrasensory reaches confined to the dimensions of the senses.

6

The Range of Subject Matter

Every ESP experience brings information, a message about something in the external world. As we have seen, it may be about someone else's thought, or about a thing, or about an event still in the future. But within this all-encompassing range, each message is also a personal one coming to a particular person. One might expect that a person's ESP experiences would reflect his strongest needs for information, his deepest interests. Many of them clearly do just that. But on the other hand, many are about relatively unimportant matters. What then governs the selection of the topics? By considering the personal values of topics, an answer is suggested.

If one were to list topics according to a personal scale of values, perhaps first in importance would be the crises of persons close to one—within one's intimate circle of relatives and friends. As we have already seen, ESP experiences often concern the death of close relatives. Although this is usually unwelcome news, if it does happen, the knowledge of it is most important.

A woman in Oregon one Saturday afternoon in June, 1952, became suddenly worried about her mother who lived in Minnesota. "I became filled with a deep feeling of urgency and foreboding that something was wrong," she says. "I tried to put the idea aside, but by evening I was pacing the floor. My husband said, 'I don't think there can be anything wrong or they would call you—but you call them if it will relieve your mind.'

"I got the sister with whom my mother was living. She said Mother was a little frailer but had had a check-up and the doctor said she was in very good condition for her age. But what should have been a reassuring conversation didn't cheer me, and my feeling increased, if anything. By two o'clock the next afternoon I dashed upstairs and threw myself on the bed, giving way to uncontrollable sobs. It went on for an hour or more before I could throw it off and join the family downstairs.

"As I reached the lower step the phone rang; and, *as I expected*, it was my sister saying Mother had passed away. Automatically, I said:

"'At three o'clock our time, five o'clock there.'

"'Yes,' she answered, and added, 'If I'd had the least inkling of this when you called yesterday, I'd have told you to come.'

"What puzzles me is that I, living eighteen hundred miles away, should divine what my sister who lived right there did not."

The death of even a casual friend would also be high on the scale of importance. A woman in Kentucky had been unable to keep up all her friendly correspondence after the arrival of her second baby and felt particularly conscience-stricken from not having written to her friend, Betty, a girl suffering from tuberculosis. She says: "One early morning in April after I had been up to give the baby his bottle, I went back to bed. It seemed as though I were lying there awake when I heard the door in the lower hall open. I arose to see who it was; hanging over the banisters, I looked into the upturned face of my friend Betty. She was steadily climbing the stairs, and it was as though this was a usual thing; I felt no surprise. She reached the upper hall where I stood and put her arm about me and said:

"'I just couldn't go by without seeing those two wonderful babies you've been telling me about.' I took her into the room where they slept, and she went from one crib to the other, hanging over them and admiring them, making such remarks as, 'How can I make up my mind which is the prettiest—the blonde or the brunette?' She then said, 'I must go now,' and I took her to the head of the stairs where she told me, 'Don't bother about coming down with me. I can let myself out.' And I stood watching her as she moved down the stairs and out the door.

"Naturally, this incident, which seemed more vivid than the actual facts of the morning chores and those around me, made me feel guiltier than ever, and losing no time I wrote Betty the long-overdue letter. Usually within a week or so an answer would come—of late dictated to her nurse—but no answer came. In the rush of activity I did not dwell on Betty, so was surprised when about a month later a letter was in the mail from England. It was from Betty's father, who managed the English branch of an American company there, and in the letter he remarked on the fact that when I had written Betty of the incident involving her in my 'dream' I had given the time and the date, which he pointed out was very strange indeed since that was the exact time at which she had passed away. Needless to say, this shook me up considerably; but in time I just accepted what I believe to be a fact—that Betty stopped by to see us on her way to her 'new environment.'"

A great many experiences, too, reflect the danger or nonfatal crisis of someone close. In May, 1941, a young woman in Iowa was in the hospital, following the birth of her second child, a little girl who had been named Nancy. The first, a little boy, Dennis, was a year older. One night the mother had a nightmare and was awakened by the night nurse, who heard her screaming. In the nightmarish dream she had seen Dennis with a knife accidentally hurt a little girl with long golden curls. She thought the little girl was the baby, Nancy. Although the injury was not entirely clear, she knew it was a facial cut of some sort. She could see the blood and golden curls.

Nancy grew to have golden curls. One day *when she was four* she ran out of the house and up behind her brother, who had been cutting grass with a small knife. He turned suddenly and accidentally struck her with it in the eye. Her mother saw again the blood, the golden curls of her nightmare four years before.

The important events of these experiences and of many others in earlier cases have been serious occurrences of a tragic or near-tragic nature. But serious events that become the subject matter of ESP are not always tragic. An ESP experience may also mirror a joyous "crisis."

At the end of World War II a woman in New York State knew that her husband was a POW in Germany. "We had had no letter from him during the last few months of his imprisonment. As the war in Europe came to an end, news came almost every day of camps being liberated. My husband's camp was never mentioned and I became more and more worried about his safety. Everyone noticed how blue I was, and I felt really depressed from this constant worry.

"On the evening of April eighteenth I suddenly had the feeling that my husband was safe. Some mention was made on the radio about prisoners, but not about my husband's camp. I think the radio announcement was what started me thinking about it. At any rate, I was sure then that my husband was safe.

"The next day my employer and friends asked if I had had good news, because I looked so happy. I replied that I had had no word, but that I was sure my husband was safe. I wrote the date in the scrapbook I was keeping, and after it, 'The day I knew that Henry was liberated.' On April thirtieth a cable came from my husband in England, and when he got home he told the story of how he and a buddy had escaped from a group of prisoners being moved. They hid in the woods for several days until, on April eighteenth, they saw the British tanks coming down the road. They came out of the woods and the soldiers gave them food and saw that they were returned to England."

Among the more definitely cheerful topics covered by ESP is sometimes a piece of desired information. It is as if the person learns what he *wants* to know, just as he may learn an unwelcome fact because he *has* to learn it.

A couple in Pennsylvania, waiting vainly for years for a child of their own, had finally applied for a baby to an adoption agency. After some more long waiting, a call had come of a prospective baby for them to see. The night before they went, the woman says, "I prayed that the Heavenly Father would show us in some way whether or not the little boy we would see was the one God really intended us to have. That night in a wonderful dream I saw a head of golden curls nestled on my husband's shoulder. In the dream I didn't see the child's face, but I knew he must be around two years of age. I wondered about this, because we had hoped to get a much younger child. The next day at the Agency we were just being ushered into a room when we saw a nurse removing a cap from a head of golden curls. Before the nurse turned 'our little Jimmy' around even, so I could see his big brown eyes and rosy cheeks, I said, 'Oh, he's the one.' They were all surprised because they had wondered too if a little boy of twenty months of age would be acceptable to us, who had wanted a tiny baby. This wonderful dream come true has made my life happy and complete. I'm so thankful."

Still, one cannot help observing that the topic of a great many ESP experiences is something very serious, often tragic. The reason why is not at once obvious. It cannot be because ESP ability is limited to tragic topics, for too many joyful occasions figure in ESP experiences. If, then, it is not because of the ESP *method* of getting information, it must go back to something deeper, something in human nature itself, something that makes the dangers and tragedies of life more *newsworthy* than the joys. That such a human tendency is a real one can scarcely be denied by anyone who reads the newspapers.

On the other hand, one must also recognize that appearances are at least partly deceptive in this matter of tragedy predominating. Many ESP experiences which concern serious or threatening circumstances *turn out happily.* Take, for instance, experiences like this one of a woman in Wyoming. She had gone to the dentist one afternoon leaving the baby, two, and little boy, three, with a baby sitter. Then, she says, "As I sat in the dentist's chair, and he was filling my tooth, I suddenly felt that something was wrong at home. I wanted to run out of the office, but the dentist was working on my tooth and I couldn't. Tears began to run down my cheeks and I became emotionally upset. The dentist, of course, thought he was hurting me or that I was sick. I assured him I wasn't but please hurry and finish so I could get home as soon as possible. That was all I could tell him. *That was all I knew.*

"When I reached home, the police were just bringing my little boy home. There was an ice-cream man who passed our house each day. The girl had given the child five cents and said he could go and get ice cream. Then she left the door and went to see about something. When he didn't come right back, she went to the front yard and couldn't see him anywhere. She went to the circle, looked in the fountain and up and down the street. She didn't call my husband at work or me at the dentist's as she had been told to do if anything happened.

"The lady next door finally called the police. It seems that a woman had nearly hit him on Grant Street. So she picked him up and took him to the police station. That was all we ever knew about where he had been. He said the policeman finally gave him his ice cream, for he couldn't catch up with the ice-cream man. He had crossed several main streets. All this while I was at the dentist's."

The foregoing experiences give an idea of the range of the more serious and important kinds of events reflected by ESP. In addition, as various examples already given show, topics of a lower level of personal significance are not lacking. Some of them, too, deserve to be called crises certainly, even if not major ones.

A woman in Florida writes: "To my knowledge I have never had any cause to be jealous of my husband, but this morning I was awakened by a dream. In it I saw him standing against a wall with a woman in front of him and he had his two arms around her waist and they were talking and laughing.

"When he came home I had forgotten it for a while, when suddenly it came to my mind. I started laughing and said, 'Honey, if you were standing against a wall last night with a woman in front of you and you had your arms around her like this, just who would that woman be?'

"He started to laugh and said, 'Oh, honey, I didn't do anything wrong. That was Lois, the three to eleven waitress. She came over to me and said, "How's my sweetie?" Why, were you down there?'

"I started off to joke about my dream, but when he verified it I didn't want him to know so I said our neighbor and I had gone down for a cup of coffee and that I saw him and wouldn't go in. I am still angry about it."

Relatively minor situations which still have very definite importance to persons involved also fairly commonly become topics for ESP. In England, when transportation was still difficult after the war, a friend of mine, after a series of bus mischances, was put down one day tired and almost ill, at a bus stop some distance from home. It was at an hour her husband, who she thought was at the golf club, had no slightest reason to expect her there. But he drove up just as she alighted.

"What an extraordinary coincidence!" she exclaimed.

"Not at all. As we finished our game I felt you wanted me, so I refused the drink offered me by my opponent, saying that if I hurried I should just catch you, and I came at once. I knew you would be here."

Occasionally an experience may concern a topic too unimportant to be called even a minor crisis. Yet it may have some aspect or novelty that seems to give it an interesting angle. A girl in Wyoming had such an experience. She says:

"I saw myself sitting in a small crowded house with my neighbor friend and an unknown girl who was sitting in a rocking chair facing me. I was eating something like uncooked macaroni or spaghetti, when the strange girl said, 'That'll swell up in you.'

"About six months later our neighbor purchased a newly built but only two-room house three miles from ours; and I was visiting her, as was her niece, whom I had never seen before.

"I had bought a package of Lipton's chicken noodle soup in an envelope. I *had not known it existed* at the time of the premonition. I was fascinated by the newness of soup in an envelope, so I said, 'I think I'll taste this now.' As I sat munching the noodles, the girl leaned forward in her rocking chair. I recalled the premonition and I knew exactly what she was going to say before she said it.

" 'That'll swell up in you.' "

The fact that the new, the strange or the unfamiliar—from persons to events—do turn up in the subject matter of ESP experiences has been evident in many of the experiences recorded here. But it is one that deserves a bit of emphasis. When we come to them, the events of every tomorrow are new, of course, yet they are made up in the main of familiar elements. We know most of the people we will be concerned with, we know in general the affairs we will be occupied with, and the range of joys and sorrows we will meet. The newness will be mostly in peculiar combinations of these familiar items. But occasionally in ESP messages, something or someone comes along that is new beyond this level of ordinary familiarity. Of course, this "something" will become familiar at a future time; it is strange at the time of the experience because it is still hidden from sensory contact by the barrier of the future. Since the future is no barrier to ESP, it should not be surprising when unfamiliar items appear in ESP experiences.

The totally unfamiliar item is not necessarily limited to unimportant messages, of course. It appears also in situations in which one can easily see that strong need for the information exists. In Seattle a girl's sister-in-law had been taken ill and had died quite suddenly. As she reports it: "Mother called me and asked me if I would get in touch with my twin sister, who had recently moved to a new apartment and didn't have a telephone yet. She had told us that because there was no house phone we would have to call her landlady if we ever urgently needed her. She told us the name of the landlady, but since I had not written it down I had to go back in memory and relive the scene of her telling about it. Even then I couldn't quite remember what it was, but I was sure it was a short name beginning with 'St' and had a common meaning.

"I got out the telephone book and looked through the 'St's,' when I came to the name Stout. It rang a bell and I found one with the correct address. I called and asked for my sister. The lady who answered was very annoyed and wanted to know how I got her number. I made some poor excuse, not wanting to get my sister in trouble.

"Then my sister came to the phone and asked me the same question how I had happened to call that number. I reminded her that she had given me the name of the landlady. She said, 'Yes, but the landlady's name is Mrs. Mulligan and I didn't even know the name of these people.'"

Then, new names, new places and coming events may become items in experiences not trivial in the same sense as noodle soup in a bag, nor prompted by strong need. Often, items of this kind are the subject matter of realistic dreams, particularly, perhaps, of precognitive ones.

In the autumn of 1951 a woman in the state of Washington had an unusual dream, which was this:

"I was on an old-fashioned train. The conductor came through and called out a funny name—like Polygapo—and said that all Polygapoes, big and little, here you are. The train stopped in front of a white house with a fence around it. A half-dozen or so children came tumbling and running off the train into the sunny, overgrown yard. One jumped the fence, one ran next door, one chased a dog, one picked up the newspaper and ran up on the porch. The whole scene was framed by the train window. At this point I awoke.

"I rarely pay any attention to dreams and do not like to repeat them to others, nor do I bother with interpretations. This was unusually clear, though, and so delightful that I told it to my mother. I had no idea that it had any significance or that it was prophetic, so I quickly forgot it.

"On June 14, 1952, my younger sister and I took our first plane trip by flying from Seattle to Olympia, Washington. We were to return by train and inquired the location of the station. Through a misunderstanding we were directed to the wrong station and nearly put on the train for Portland. By this time we had missed our intended train home and had to take an old-fashioned one that evening. We hadn't been on it long when the conductor came through and called out precisely as he had in my dream.

"I felt a little queer the first few seconds, as though this had happened before. Then in a flash my entire dream came back. I sat there watching, saying to myself: Now that boy will jump the fence—and he did; the other boy will chase the dog—and he did; the girl will pick up the newspaper and go up on the porch and she did. So it was with everything; precisely as in my dream. The shadows, the sunlight, the wind blowing the grass, every act of the people, every word spoken all were the same.

"Being of a skeptical and doubting nature, by force of habit questions arose in my mind as to whether or not this might be imagination or some sort of self-hypnosis. But before the utter conviction I felt, this question was meaningless. I *knew* this was my exact dream come true.

"I was stunned and hardly dared to think what the significance of this might be. Was it predestined that we should be misunderstood, miss our regular train, sit precisely where we did (as no other seat on the train would give that exact view), the train would stop at that very spot, and everyone should do and say those very acts and words?"

As to her question, who would presume an answer? The present is still too early. Precognition and precognitive experiences must be studied much more extensively before their riddle is solvable. Here, such an experience counts as one on a relatively unimportant topic. As the importance of a topic decreases, one begins to inquire how slender the connection of personal involvement can be. One finds instances in which a mutual acquaintance is the only personal connection. A woman in Oregon dreamed she was visiting an old friend, a Mrs. Harker. As the dream unfolded, she says: "There was a curtain closet before us out of which emerged terrifyingly two thin arms clawing the air while the curtain shook violently. I knew an insane person was behind that curtain. I was filled with terror and screamed in my dream, 'Something terrible is the matter with Mrs. Mirelle.' I seemed to know we were in this person's home but in reality I neither knew nor had ever heard of a person of that name. I knew in the dream that she was a friend of Mrs. Harker's. I awoke, shaking with fright, and remained awake the rest of the night with the light on.

"The next day I kept remarking to my husband, 'Do you suppose there is a Mrs. Mirelle?' I felt it ridiculous to call Mrs. Harker and inquire, but a few days later she called me, and so I told her my dream. She replied soberly, 'But I do know a Mrs. Mirelle. I haven't heard from her recently.' Not long after that I met Mrs. Harker at a party. She said, 'My friend Mrs. Mirelle has lost her mind.'"

Though one might think the link in cases like the above is tenuous enough—in other instances even the intermediate third party is lacking. If any personal involvement exists, it must be an entirely unconscious one.

A young man in New York says, "One summer night I dreamed that I was skulking in the vicinity of three old untenanted houses. These houses were left in a depression by reason of a street-grading operation. When two streets which crossed each other at this corner property were raised to grade, the old houses were left about twelve feet below the street level.

"In my dream I entered the middle of the three frame houses with a basketful of wood shavings and a can of kerosene. I lit the shavings, poured the kerosene on the pile, and I remembered being very careful that the flame was subdued till I could clear the place. I remembered scrambling along the side of the street, where I waited some time until I saw flames coming through the roof where shingles were missing.

"At that point I saw a man, whom I recognized, running toward the scene and the fire engine approaching. The dream ended at this development.

"I did not attach any importance to the dream until next morning when a neighbor called at my father's shop and told him that John Henry's old shack at Fourth Avenue and Maple Street caught fire during the night. I did not say anything about my dream till my father and I were alone. Later I walked to the scene of the fire and found that the middle house had been afire and that the roof had burned just where I had seen it in my dream!"

If one were to suppose, in an instance like this one, that an unconscious urge for adventure explained that person's selection of that topic, then in the next case, doubtless some other hidden drive or interest would have to be supposed. Sometimes, for instance, it might be a humanitarian motive, as was possibly the case with a woman in Tennessee.

She had a dream one night, which she remembered next day, and which she says, "kept pressing in upon me so I could hardly go on with my work. It was about a definite person, but not anyone I knew. It bothered me until I finally went to the phone book and found there was such a person listed. As I remembered it, I thought the name was S. N. Byrd.

"So then I called the number. His wife answered. I took a few minutes explaining to her how silly I felt telling her about a dream I had just had the night before about her husband. She asked if I knew him, and I told her that I not only didn't know him but had never even heard of him. Then I told her that according to my dream he had a very bad heart.

" 'Yes,' she replied, 'but how did you know about it?' I explained that I really didn't know, but I just dreamed it.

"Then I told her about some rose bushes that he had bought and had been trying to get a fellow to come and plant for him, but the fellow kept putting him off and would not come and put the bushes in the ground for him. So before he left for work that morning he had remarked that if the fellow didn't show up by that afternoon he was going to put the bushes out himself.

"She said, 'Yes, he did say that just before he left to go to work this morning.'

"So I told her that she was to keep him from doing it because just as sure as he did and his heart in the shape it was, that he'd drop dead before he finished planting them. She had me describe her husband to her as I saw him in my dream and I did, and she said, 'Well, that's him to a tee, and you can rest assured that he will not put out those rose bushes when he comes home as he has threatened to do just before he left.' Then she thanked me very profusely for the warning."

Not even possible interest in the welfare of an unknown person, however, can account for all the "far-out" topics that occasionally are reflected in ESP experiences. Sometimes one has to say that nothing more exalted than curiosity would explain them.

A woman from Chicago dreamed, she says, that "I was going somewhere in our car with my husband and a couple we knew quite well. I cannot remember why we stopped at this farmhouse, but we did, and the lady that came to the door was old and invited us in through the kitchen and told us to wait in the next room, which was a combination dining room and living room. She said her son would be back soon, and for us to wait there in that room. As we sat there, my eyes fell on the room right next to the one we were in, but the door was shut. I got up and peeked inside to see what was in there, and saw a very old piano. Just then the woman's son came in and greeted us. He wore the clothes of a priest. I cannot remember any more of the dream than that.

"At least six months later, our friends and my husband and I were planning a vacation to Wisconsin. Having neglected to send reservations early enough, we took a chance and went anyway with the hope that possibly there might be a cancellation. Upon arriving there, they said no, that there was no place they could put us as all the cabins were gone. As an afterthought the lady said, 'Why don't you go over across the lake to the farm, they have a cottage near the lake that may be empty.'

"We did this, and as we arrived at the farm it looked very familiar to me. The lady that came to the door was old and invited us to come in, through the kitchen, and asked us to wait in the next room; as soon as her son came home he would let us know if he could rent the cottage. As we waited I told my husband that I had dreamed of such a place, and I said, 'I'll bet you a nickel that if I open the door to the next room, there will be an old piano in it.' He laughed at me, so I went over and did just that, and you guessed it, *there was the old piano*. A few minutes later the lady came in to apologize that her son wasn't coming for a while; he had been detained with his studies to be a minister. A few minutes later the son came home and was wearing the round collar of the clergy."

To go still further, however, even curiosity seems not the end of the free-ranging topics of ESP. Occasionally an experience involves a topic of so little importance or concern that it seems to reflect only a background—like surrounding landscape, say—which happens to come within range on about the lowest possible level of attention.

A woman in Dayton dreamed of sitting in a chair with the blinds covering most of the picture window before her. Suddenly she heard the whirr of a lawn mower. Glancing out the window, she saw grass flying from a lawn mower, and a pair of oversize boots walking back and forth. The shades hid the person to whom the boots belonged.

She would no doubt soon have forgotten such an insignificant dream, but the very next evening it came true. A small boy came to the door and offered to cut her grass for a dime. She gave him the dime and he went home for his mower. A few minutes later she was sitting by the window, shade lowered, and was startled by the whirr of the mower. Glancing out the bottom of the window, her dream came to life. The grass was flying from the blades of the mower, a pair of big boots worn by the small boy following it.

Thus we can follow the selection of ESP topics from those that seem to be chosen on the basis of strong need or interest, through the mid-range kind of crises, down to the unimportant. We have found selection that seemed to occur from a motive no stronger than that of curiosity (or is curiosity a strong motive force? It lies at the root of the human tendency to investigate and explore, both trivialities like someone's old piano, or the nature of man himself), and even on the level of extraneous events noticed only because they are part of the person's immediate environment.

In this glimpse of the range of personal interest covered by the topics of ESP an answer to the question we began with is suggested. We saw the topics selected on a much broader basis than strong conscious need or interest. The basis of their selection extended even to unconscious lines of motivation, and to motives too slight even to dignify with a name. But wide selection of topics, if one stops to think of it, is not unique to ESP. It represents the normal human range of interest in affairs. One's daily thinking runs the gamut from items of the greatest to the least importance. The free-ranging character of ESP, then, could be simply a mark of man's comprehensive mental activity. The difference is that here, by hidden channels, broader areas are made accessible; motives and tendencies that lie beneath the conscious level can have scope for action.

7

Men, Women and ESP

Women have the reputation for being the more "intuitive" sex. Are women, then, more psychic than men, or in modern terms, do they use ESP more than men do? The question is part of a larger one, "Who has ESP?" It is not a simple one to answer. Certainly not everyone has ESP experiences. Many people have never even known anyone who admitted having one. Yet, the cases cited herein come from persons in practically every state of the U.S.A., and from some foreign countries. Those from abroad are, as it happens, from English-speaking countries. But that certainly does not mean that ESP experiences are limited to speakers of English.

As a matter of fact, a good showing of reports from lands where other tongues are spoken can be assembled to show that ESP experiences are practically world-wide, and occur in substantially the same types and forms in every culture. Such a list would certainly show that no one group has a monopoly on the psi ability.

Who, then, are these individuals in any country who have ESP experiences? Is it true that more of them are women than men?

The common assumption that women are the more "intuitive" sex has the converse that men are more logical. Since ESP occurs in other forms than the intuitive, and since many intuitions are not the result of ESP, the feminine reputation, whatever its justification, may not necessarily be based on ESP. On the other hand, while men are rarely said to be "psychic," they do have hunches. If the hunches are correct they are likely to be put down as "just one of those things," but hunches, of course, are intuitions. Some of them could be caused by ESP. It could be that masculine ESP is thus underestimated.

However all this may be, it is true that many more women than men report ESP experiences. In the cases cited here and in the collection from which these are drawn, an estimate of ten experiences from women to one from men would not be too high. This difference might be the result of such superficial causes as women being more communicative, less inhibited on this topic than men. Men may be less quick to recognize an experience as extraordinary if one does occur. They might be inhibited in admitting it even to themselves. Almost any experience—no matter how strange—can be explained away if bias will not allow the mind to admit its unusual nature. If any of these inhibitions really do apply more to men than to women, they could well account for the difference.

At any rate, ESP is not sex-linked, for many men do have ESP experiences. Do they have the same kinds and in general on the same sorts of topics? Certainly in preceding cases no particular difference in the topics of men's experiences and those of women is noticeable. Perhaps the farthest "out" on this line would be the topic of the baby still unborn, which could be considered an exclusively feminine topic, if any is. A woman from Ohio reports: "Both my husband and I were extremely happy awaiting the longed-for event. We were in our thirties. I was in perfect health and not at all worried. I thought I preferred a girl and we jokingly referred to the baby as 'our little black-haired girl,' because we both have very dark hair.

"A few nights before my confinement, I dreamed that some person, not visualized perfectly, came to my bedside holding my baby, drew back its covering, and held it for me to see. I looked long at the face, and knew though no word was spoken, that it was a boy. The face was startlingly unlike my imaginings—very fair, hair light, the chin noticeably pointed below very fat cheeks.

"During the delivery at the hospital an unexpected complication ended in tragedy. When I became conscious, the doctors and nurses were working vainly to try to make the baby breathe. I asked, 'Is that my baby?' and a doctor (masked, of course) brought the baby to my side, folded back the cover and I saw the identical (an unusually individual) face, exactly as in my dream. Afterwards, others commented on the very features I had memorized from the dream. Therefore, the likeness must have been real, not imagined by me in semi-anaesthesia."

But the experience of a man from Missouri matches it. He explains, "After seventeen years of marriage, when our first baby was due in about two months, I dreamed I saw the child with the darkest eyes and the blackest hair, surrounded by white that confused me. The child in my dream was a baby girl. At breakfast the next morning I proceeded to tell my wife of my dream. She and her mother both thought I was wrong, that the child would be a boy and that it would be red-headed. Nothing further was said. The day the child was born, after seeing my wife for just a few moments, the doctor asked if I cared to see our child. I proceeded to the nursery and saw a number of babies, and the doctor had the nurse in charge bring ours to a side door. As soon as I saw the nurse with the child I recalled the dream. The setting was an exact duplicate of my dream some two months prior to that date and the white which confused me in my dream was the white uniform of the nurse holding the child."

The only essential difference between experiences like these is not a part of either account. It is the difference in frequency. More women than men report experiences on this topic.

Turn next to consider the forms of the experiences. The two above were dreams. What about hallucinations?

A girl who lived in Ohio was on a visit to an aunt in Florida. Washing dishes one day, she heard someone calling her, "Betty Lou." She thought it sounded like her father. She says: "I ran to the door and opened it, fully expecting to see my dad, but nobody was there. I felt very strange. Just then my aunt came in. I told her what had happened. She said, 'Go put in a long-distance call to your folks right away. It may mean your dad is really calling you.'

"Well I wasn't worried about him because I had had a letter a few days before and everyone was well. But my aunt insisted I call home, so I did.

"Mother answered and said, 'Oh, honey, it's you! Daddy's calling for you. The doctor's here now. Daddy had a heart attack!'"

In comparison, take the case of a man who traveled a lot. He was in Florida, his wife visiting her parents in Ohio, when, as he says, "One night I awoke and heard my name called twice, and since it sounded like my wife I was worried and immediately dispatched a telegram to Bucyrus to see if anything was wrong. It was verified that at the time she called me (I noted the hour) she had become ill and just before becoming unconscious had called my name. Happily she recovered."

Compare also these visual hallucinations. A young English woman was trimming her Christmas tree. She had just stepped precariously on a hassock she had placed on the dining-room table, to put the Christmas fairy on the tip top of the tree when—suddenly she knew she was not alone! Standing in the doorway she saw Jim, a friend of hers who had died nearly a year before. Smiling a trifle, he stood there with his hand on a walking stick with a white handle.

Before she thought—he looked so natural—she said she'd be down in a minute. But then she knew he could not be there! And sure enough, he wasn't. She searched the house but found no explanation.

She put on a coat and dashed down the street to the house where her friend Jean, Jim's widow lived. Tear-stained, eyes swollen with weeping, Jean told her how glad she was for company. She had been thinking of her husband and that a year ago he had still been with her. She said it had all come back so vividly because she had come upon a homemade walking stick her husband's brother had given Jim before his death, and which had been put away and forgotten. She picked it up to show it.

It had a white handle!

And the visual experience of a man: "It happened to me twelve years ago. It was about one P.M. when I walked into my furnished room in the Bronx. To the right, as you walked in, stood my dresser.

"When I saw my sister standing there, looking into the mirror and combing her hair, momentarily I was not surprised. Her presence seemed such a natural thing to me that I even called her name.

"But when she turned to look at me I suddenly realized that she could not possibly be standing there in my room—not in the flesh, anyway. My sister was in Atlanta, Georgia, with her husband at the time.

"A cold chill ran up and down my body. I was frightened. Why, I cannot say. Perhaps it was the fact that I knew I was seeing a loved one who was not actually there. I almost ran out of the room and out into the street. I returned some time later with a friend of mine. Of course, my sister was no longer there.

"The following day I received a letter from her. She seldom, if ever, wrote. She told me that she had been very ill and was having a difficult time with her husband, who turned out to be more of a tyrant than a companion. She also wrote that she had been thinking of me constantly and had been wishing that she was with me. I do not believe that she ever knew that she paid me a call."

A different kind of hallucinatory experience, the "sympathetic projection of pain," as we might call it, is one with which we are already familiar. Again, take first a woman's experience, that of a widow whose relatives all lived in Pennsylvania. She was employed in Florida during the winter.

"In January, 1956, at eleven o'clock in the morning I was standing supervising the girls in my employment. Without bending or moving in any way, a terrible pain shot through my right hip. It was almost unbearable, and I limped going to my desk to sit down. Several girls witnessed this, and I knew of no reason for the pain. Standing, sitting or lying on my bed brought no relief.

"Since I do hotel work, my hours are usually mornings and evenings with a rest period during the afternoon. In the early evening, the house physician came in to see some patients and I consulted him. He advised me if I was no better by morning to come to his office and have some X rays. As the pain was constant, I tried to divert my mind by going to the ballroom, where we have a movie once a week at nine P.M. Unrest assailed me, and the urge to go away from the ballroom was so great that I limped back to my office. Just as I entered the door I was being called by long distance. The news I received from that call was that my mother had fallen at eleven o'clock that morning and broken her hip. This fall resulted in three operations that have left her a cripple.

"By morning my pain was gone and I was perfectly well. I related my experience to the house physician without too much comment on his part. He did say this had been known of before."

Next is the experience of a young man in Indiana. He was in the midst of a poker game one evening, and, as he says: "—having wonderful good luck with the cards. Suddenly I had a very severe shock and terrible pains in my heart and felt as if I were going to burst. I jumped up, threw the cards on the table and yelled, 'I am quitting.' A man from Louisville, Kentucky, bawled me out, saying 'to quit with the luck you have you must be nuts.'

"Feeling awful, I walked to the company office, but the clerk with the Ford truck would not be back until nine. So, suffering terribly, I blindly walked half a mile to the hospital.

"Hearing two medical doctors talking, I blurted out, 'Give me something quick. I am dying. I feel like bursting. *Bleed me!*' They said, 'We don't bleed people any more,' and had me put to bed with a shot and dope.

"Next morning I awoke, feeling fine, and had breakfast in bed.

Then that afternoon, when another doctor came in who examined me and said I could go, I asked him to give my apologies to the doctors I spoke to the night before for my crazy behavior and lack of respect. As there was no truck waiting, I decided to walk back to my barracks. I had gone about halfway when the company clerk came driving the truck and yelled, 'Hi, D., where in hell have you been? I have been searching for you all over. Here is a telegram for you.'

"I opened it and read that my father died. He had a stroke the night before at eight-thirty P.M., just the same time I was taken deadly sick. He died twelve and a half hours later."

Certainly in none of these hallucinatory forms are men's experiences significantly different from women's. What then about intuitions? Even this form so generally reputed to characterize women is common, one soon finds, among the ESP experiences of men.

A woman in Missouri tells of her husband's experience thus: "On the morning of July 5, 1937, my husband came to the breakfast table not in his usual calm and cheery disposition. In his mild way he showed signs of extreme nervousness and the results of a sleepless night. Finally he simply said, 'Something is wrong with my sister, Betty. I think she is dying.'

"The day before, we had been with my husband's sister and her husband. She was apparently in excellent health, though she and her husband had not yet told the family they thought she was pregnant, so we didn't even know that.

"Knowing my husband was not a 'flighty' person, I became alarmed at his condition and said nothing when he went to the telephone to call his sister's home to see if she was all right.

"Before the operator could answer to take the number, my husband's brother-in-law opened our front door, came in hurriedly, and said, 'Herbert, come with me; your sister is in the hospital and we think she is dying.' Needless to say, he was surprised at my husband's answer, 'Yes, I know.'

"My husband's sister had been ill all night long. She had a tubular pregnancy and was at death's door many days, but somehow my husband knew of her danger before he was told of it by her husband. It goes without saying, this particular sister and my husband had been unusually close to each other from early childhood."

Intuitive experiences consisting almost entirely of emotion—which might seem likely to be restricted to women—are reported by men, too.

A young man in California tells his experience thus: "One night in July of 1951 we had just finished supper, and my brother-in-law was getting ready to go to a meeting in San Jose, which is twenty-five miles from our house. For no reason I started crying, me, crying, twenty-five years old! I *begged* him not to go. Well, there was quite a fuss and I got everyone upset. Mom kept saying, 'He will be all right.' You know, the usual soft soap you give an upset person. This went on for about fifteen minutes. Then the feeling left me, and I said, 'It's all right for Bob to go now.'

"By this time, the fellow he was to ride with had waited at their meeting place, but left before Bob got there, so Bob had to drive his own car down. He got as far as Bayshore and Charter Streets, when the traffic began to back up. A wreck, which is nothing unusual here. But when Bob got to the corner, he said he almost passed out. There spread out on the highway was the man he was to have ridden with; his head was half gone. The car was a total loss. They found later that his brakes had locked on one side, and he flipped up in the air and came down on the other side of the road to be hit head-on by another car."

Finally, fathers as well as mothers sometimes seem to know intuitively when their children are in danger. A man in New York says he is "—supposedly a sane, conservative businessman. I am president of a bank, owner of a large real estate and insurance business, a graduate economist of the University of Pennsylvania.

"It was during the invasion of France and Germany. I had a son who had just gone over from the States and I knew he was in there fighting, as I had received one brief message from him as he left England. In September I went up into Canada on a fishing trip and while I was there I became very depressed, and I couldn't help but feel Bill (my son) was the root of it. I came home, still feeling depressed, and I talked it over with my wife, as I could never conceal any mood from her. I said frankly I felt Bill was in trouble. A few nights later, we received a telegram saying Bill was critically wounded.

"We were frantic and tried every means to obtain information as to his condition, with absolutely no results. I brooded over it for days, trying to imagine what his wounds might be. One night, possibly a week later, as I sat at my desk, a feeling came over me. I could almost visualize a wound on his head, back of the right ear, and some other slight wound that had to do with his arm. The feeling was so strong that I wrote down my thoughts on a sheet of paper and placed it under the blotter on my desk. I might add, though it may sound unbelievable in light of the end of the story, that I seemed to feel the head injury somehow affected his eyesight.

"Three or four months later we received word Bill was in a receiving hospital in New York; we rushed to see him, and here is the unexplainable: Bill had two shell wounds in his head, not right back of the ear but more nearly on the back of the skull, but toward the right ear. The optic nerve had been all but severed, and he had been blind and partially paralyzed for weeks but was regaining both his eyesight and use of his limbs when I saw him. He also had a shell sliver that had entered his shoulder, passed down his right arm and came out just above the elbow.

"On our way home, I told my wife of the memo under the blotter on my desk, and when we reached home I had her get it and read it, to her amazement."

These examples show that at least some men have ESP experiences comparable in quality to those of women. The topics, the circumstances and situations are similar, and so, also, are the ways in which ESP is expressed. Men as well as women are impressed, convinced deeply, moved emotionally upon occasion by these flashes of knowledge coming in by channels for which they cannot account. The only real difference in the reported experiences is simply that of *numbers*. It is interesting to see what laboratory research shows about the comparative ESP abilities of men and women.

MEN VERSUS WOMEN IN LABORATORY TESTS

Some fairly strong hints about the relative ESP ability of men and women come from the laboratory. Large numbers of both sexes have been tested in the course of ESP research. First of all, the sex of the persons who have been outstanding as successful subjects is of interest. The British psychic researcher, Dr. S. G. Soal of London University, and his colleagues have had until recently two outstanding subjects, a man and a woman (Mr. Basil Shackleton and Mrs. Gloria Stewart). Recently, two boys have been added to this list. In the Duke Laboratory five out of the first eight outstanding subjects were men. However, over the years since the work of these subjects was recorded, probably more women than men have scored well. But the observation means little, because the total number of each sex to try and fail has not been recorded. A more revealing one could be made on the pre-adolescent boys and girls who have been tested. *Children of both sexes have scored at about the same level.*

In 1936–37, when my children were still small, I made a series of gamelike ESP tests with three of them and thirteen others from the neighborhood. The age range was between three and fifteen, but most of them were between five and ten. There were, in all, seven girls and nine boys. The average score the girls attained was 5.6; the boys' was 5.25 (when the average expected from pure chance was 5). The scores of the girls thus were slightly higher than the boys', but one of the boys had the highest average of all, 6.7, and another the lowest, 3.8. Of course, the numbers of each sex as well as the number of tests each took was too small to be conclusive. The range of the scores in this little series of tests, however, is fairly typical and gives very little indication of a difference between the sexes in childhood.

Beginning in 1953, large-scaled ESP tests in public-school classrooms have been made and reported in *The Journal of Parapsychology* from time to time. In general, in these the sexes have scored about equally well. If any difference does come in, however, usually it is the girls who have the slightly higher scores. The difference is often more noticeable in the adolescent, high-school ages. Even though the innate ESP ability of small boys and girls is approximately the same, it may be that as they get older and are exposed to the differing social influences of present-day culture, boys tend to become more objective than girls, more matter-of-fact and rational in their approach toward life. How much of this is inborn one need not decide. At any rate, as after the college years men become engrossed in business and professional life, women usually in the details of domesticity and child raising, these environmental and cultural differences alone add up and could stamp their mental habits differently; the differences foreshadowed in the adolescent years could affect the likelihood of expressing ESP.

When adult men and women—married couples, for instance—take ESP tests in the laboratory, the woman's score is likely to be higher than the man's. While this is not invariably true, it is true so often that a gambler might make money on it.

Along with the difference in scoring level—preceding it, really—one usually notices a difference in *attitude* toward the test. A young woman will easily, almost gaily, and in a gamelike spirit take the test and accept her score without much comment. To her, it's just something interesting, no matter how it comes out.

A man, particularly one older, beyond the college level, is likely to react quite differently. He may be a bit hesitant in the first place. He is uncertain that there is such a thing as ESP, and he is not quite convinced that the test makes sense. He is not certain of the mathematics, and he would be surprised if he "got anything." Whatever he gets, he accepts with reservations. It might have been this; it might have been that. He wants to think it over.

And so, if the woman's score is higher than her husband's, it may not necessarily mean that she has more psi ability than he. It could mean that because of their differing attitudes the test as she took it was different from his. ESP, as parapsychologists know now, is fleeting, spontaneous, evanescent, easily disturbed. Like humor or writing poetry or painting pictures, it functions better if not analyzed too much as it is being expressed. Thus the tests the husband and wife take, even though technically the same, may be different for each of them psychologically. The *attitude* of a subject toward ESP tests has proved to be as critical a part of them as the symbols on the testing cards.

If attitude has a critical effect in controlled laboratory tests, it would in life situations, and such a difference in attitude as observed in the laboratory is reflected in the letters in which men and women tell about their experiences. If one takes hundreds of letters from each sex, two patterns stand out: one typically feminine, the other masculine. Though there are individuals of each sex who do not fit the pattern, the comment of most women telling their experiences is likely to be limited to a hope that their accounts will be helpful in research. They may add that they would appreciate some explanation of it. Many men express similar sentiments, but a much larger proportion of them attempt an explanation or propose a theory. The difference seems to be related, in some degree at least, to cultural or to thought patterns developed by environmental influences and need not mean an inherent difference in the sensitivity of the two sexes.

It seems then that their sex itself does not explain why more women than men experience ESP. The hint is that *attitude* plays a part, and that the attitude of each could be, at least to some extent, the result of the general cultural pattern, as it discriminates between boys and girls as they grow and develop. This hint still leaves us with no reason why only a few women and still fewer men out of the entire population should register evidence of the psi ability. But are there only a few who do so? This question needs looking into, for the relative frequency or rareness of a human characteristic may tell something about it, too.

One certainly cannot expect a definite numerical answer to the question of how many people have ESP. Information about ESP itself is still too limited; and people who have ESP experiences are, as a group, still about as undefined and unrecognized as the unorthodox occurrences they report. In fact, many people may well have ESP experiences without recognizing them, either because of the unfamiliarity of the subject or because the experiences occur so unobtrusively that they go unnoticed.

I am quite certain from my own experience, for instance, that in the 1930's, if I had not been "married to ESP" I would never have considered it more than an odd coincidence that one of my small children seemed so often to voice my own unspoken thought. Only after repeated observation of a coincidence between her remarks and my own thoughts and because as a family we were then becoming ESP-conscious, did I finally begin to keep a diary recording these incidents. In time it became quite evident from this record that one of the four children had telepathic tendencies.

Beyond a doubt, hundreds of other people have had experiences which do involve ESP but which they pass off as only coincidence, as "one of those things," a "queer" occurrence. It could very likely be that the number of those who recognize ESP when it does occur will always be smaller than the number in whom it actually operates.

Another factor which makes it impossible to count those who have had ESP experiences is evidenced in many of the letters reporting them.

That factor is the attitude toward their own experiences, reflected in a letter from a woman who heard her name called when her distant husband was in an accident. She says, "I haven't talked about it much—because I was afraid people would think I was superstitious or crazy." So many other people have had this fear that it becomes a refrain.

"In case you wonder why I am submitting this," says a California woman, "it is because for years, or I should say all my life, I have felt so alone when I wanted to tell about my special dreams. No one would understand." She tells of several telepathic dreams and some intuitive waking experiences sufficiently striking not to be passed over unnoticed.

A man who is a school principal in Virginia had a striking precognitive dream. He says, "I have never told this much—for what I have told appeared to fall on deaf ears."

A young woman in Florida, who also had had unusual precognitive dreams, remarked, "I have told very few people of my experience for many would be unable to understand."

"People in this town would think I was a witch, if I discussed such things," says a girl in Tennessee who works in an office. She tells of numerous intuitive experiences.

A man in California whose wife had died recently, and who had had an unusual experience that could have been a "sign" from her, wrote, "Thank you for the opportunity to get this off my chest. I have not mentioned it to anyone before."

Reticence, of course, tends to limit the total number of people who will report their experiences. And yet, within a few years' time, the number of those who did report their experiences in spite of such inhibitions, and the still smaller number who wrote to the Parapsychology Laboratory, was large enough to contribute the thousands of cases that make up the collection on which this book is based.

This question of how many people have ESP is no new one. Formal attempts to find an answer date back into the 1880's, at least. At that time, in England, a questionnaire was sent out by some scholars of the then newly founded Society for Psychical Research to get an idea of the frequency in the population of what were then called psychic experiences. Of course, that term did not then mean the same as is meant by the ESP experiences of today. It referred at that time mainly to experiences that suggested thought transference and which we would classify as telepathic; it included various kinds of "death coincidences," hauntings, ghosts and apparitions. Nevertheless, the result of that early questionnaire is still of some interest. About 17,000 people answered, of whom a sufficient number reported "Yes" to the question whether they had ever had a psychic experience to give a rough ratio of about 1 in 10.

Two generations later, in 1925, in this country Dr. Walter Franklin Prince of the then-active Boston Society for Psychical Research, with a similar objective, sent out a questionnaire to 10,000 persons whose names were taken from *Who's Who*. He got fewer answers, but a higher proportion of yeses. Of 2290 who replied, 430 said "Yes": about 1 in 5.

Of course, estimates like these have only historical interest now, particularly because the advance of knowledge based on experimental results has necessarily changed the definitions. Psi experiences, we now know, must be defined more widely than they were in 1880 before ESP had been demonstrated to be a human ability. Since that time, a new dimension has been added to the concept of what is "psychic." Accordingly, some occurrences that would formerly have been ignored now find a place, and some that were emphasized then because they seemed so meaningful and spectacular (ghosts and apparitions in particular) now shrink in percentage of the total reported and in significance too, as their place in the orderly affairs of nature begins to be clarified. These changes in the definition of psi, then, make for unreliability in the older estimates of the percentage of those who have, as against those who have not had psi experiences.

In other ways, too, we know now that numerical estimates such as these mean very little. Research has given strong indications that the ESP process is a delicate one. Like a fragile seed it does not germinate except under just the right conditions. It is so easily interfered with that it may be here today and gone tomorrow for causes so obscure that even experts cannot always find them. Some students, for instance, do well with one experimenter and poorly with another, and all of them are almost certain not to do well just before exams —or even before a football game if they are fans and have their eyes at least half "on the ball." This shows that failure in ESP tests may result from other causes than lack of ESP ability. At one time it was estimated that about 1 student in 5 "succeeded" in ESP tests, but it is now recognized that such a ratio means very little as an indication of how many might, under other conditions, demonstrate ESP. If that is true for college students, it no doubt is just as true for others, and for spontaneous as well as experimental experiences.

The various considerations one must take into account when estimating how many people have ESP experiences show the impossibility of making reliable estimates. They indicate also that the number of such persons is by no means negligible. The suggestion is strong that the total number may be much greater than has been suspected. But the answer to "Who has ESP?" still eludes us. After all, it does not occur to everyone either as a spontaneous experience or in experimental tests, and even those who give clear evidence of it may not do so consistently.

8

ESP in Childhood and in Old Age

So many of the experiences already cited were those of adults that ESP might appear to be limited mainly to the years of maturity. If this was a complete picture of the age range, one well might suppose that the psi ability is not one "there" to begin with but that it only develops as the person grows to maturity. But as a matter of fact, many children have psi experiences, as do also many of the aged. These experiences are not only interesting in themselves, but those of children especially give hints toward understanding the psi ability and its place in the personality.

IN CHILDHOOD

Children, even very young ones, sometimes surprise their parents by some remark seeming to show knowledge of something they "couldn't have known." Most commonly, these remarks seem to indicate telepathy with the parent, usually the mother.

Although the child is the person actually showing ESP in such cases, the reports come, of course, from the parents. Because the parent's own thought is the item "read," however, the report is not really a secondhand one. And also because he was surprised and puzzled by the remark, he usually reports it while still fresh in his memory, so that these accounts are more reliable than if they depended on the long span of personal memory.

A woman in Pennsylvania noted a number of times when her small daughter seemed to catch her thought. One day she was thinking about the workman who had started a job of excavating and then had been called away without finishing it. Weeks had gone by. She was annoyed by the delay.

"At dinner one night," she says, "I was going to suggest to my husband that he phone the man. Then I thought I would not mention it as my husband had other problems and I'd only add to them by starting to worry about one more. Just then my daughter, about three, said, 'Arno Kraus,' the name of the man I was thinking of phoning. I don't remember her ever saying it again."

The reason telepathy is the most commonly reported form of ESP in children very well may be simply that only in this form does the adult himself have a role. The convincing thing to many a parent is no doubt the undeniable fact that his own thought seemed to have been repeated. But even so, many instances of telepathy are probably overlooked or dismissed by skeptical parents, indoctrinated as they are to the idea that only sensory channels can convey information.

A woman from Cincinnati explains that when her four-year-old daughter first seemed to know some thought which neither she nor her husband had expressed, they just assumed they had given some indication of it without being aware they had done so. But they began to take notice when the occasions of her doing so were repeated.

"For instance," the mother writes, "one afternoon at about four o'clock I was standing in the kitchen, leaning with chin on hands, pondering the question of dinner. I do not usually do this. Ordinarily I plan and begin preparations for dinner quite a bit later and either know all day long what I'll fix, or figure that I'll 'whip something up.' It was a quiet time however, and seemed a good opportunity to get the meal under way early. I decided spaghetti would be the choice. We don't have it often, and it is not a particular favorite of my daughter's, but immediately after the thought crossed my mind she appeared from her room and asked casually, 'Are we having spaghetti for dinner?'

"I am convinced I didn't speak the thought and she couldn't have heard me anyway. I decided she 'heard my thought.' When I asked her how she knew, she just looked blank.

"Today a similar thing happened. My husband was in the basement preparing for some painting he is going to do. He had just surveyed his equipment and regretted not having asked me to buy a brush while doing errands in our shopping center. Just then our daughter burst in the back door, returning with me from our shopping trip.

" 'Oh, Mommie should have brought you a brush.'

"We have talked it over and are left with no ordinary explanation. Painting is not a common occurrence here, and neither was my husband handling or looking at a brush when she entered. She is more familiar with a roller, if anything. My husband had thought it just seconds before she entered. He did not know we had come back.

"These are minor happenings, to be sure. We have never been people to whom such phenomena seemed acceptable, but these incidents have really stirred us."

As in this instance, if such occasions are repeated, even reluctant parents may eventually take notice. This happened in my own family, too. I have mentioned before that my husband and I at first brushed off as just coincidence the fact that one of our daughters, then about three years old, seemed repeatedly to voice my own unspoken thought and that eventually we did take notice and I began to keep a diary, recording the incidents. In time, as the entries accumulated, it was possible to notice some recurring characteristics in these little episodes. The first, as with the children in the cases above, was the ease and effortlessness of the apparent transfer. One typical example occurred when the child was playing contentedly on the floor after breakfast and I was starting to clear the table. One piece of buttered toast remained and I was tempted. Then I thought, "No, I'm gaining. I must not eat it."

Just then the little voice, in true unflattering child-fashion, piped up: "Mama, you're fatter now than you've ever been, aren't you?"

And then, back to her own pursuits again—no follow-up, just as there had been no introduction to her thought. For several reasons I was "really stirred," but she was entirely oblivious. The remark was evidently based on an impression received so easily and naturally that she was entirely unaware of its extraneous source, and also of the fact that it had no rational introduction or relation to anything that went before or after.

The episode also illustrates another characteristic of telepathy often noticeable in the experiences of both adults and children. It is the obliqueness of the remarks. For in them the other person's idea seems to have been reconstructed and adapted to the child's viewpoint, instead of being repeated exactly.

Once in a while it seems as if a child gets a telepathic impression from another child, although it is more difficult to be certain that telepathy occurred than when an adult is involved.

One day the mother of two small boys in Illinois, one-and-a-half-year-old Chris and three-and-a-half-year-old Vic, had left the younger child asleep at his grandmother's, a block and a half away. In about 45 minutes, she says, "Vic began to run to the window looking down the street and calling frantically to me that Chris was crying. I was busy and it was only two-ten; I didn't expect them till three. I told Vic he was mistaken and went on with my work. He was very persistent and burst into tears, 'Chris wants you, Mommie.'

"In about five minutes Mother arrived with a tearful Chris, saying he had awakened crying at two-ten and then ran all over the house sobbing, 'Mommie, Mommie.' "

All of the telepathy experiences above occurred in preschool children. It is notable that in most instances episodes like these may first be noticed when the child is very young, become frequent about the ages of three to four, then decrease again, and cease entirely when the child enters school. It was true of the little girl who said, "Arno Kraus," and also of my own child, with whom no more instances were noted after she went to school. In later years when tested for ESP she scored no higher than her brother and sisters. As an adult she has had no recognized ESP experience.

Starting to school, of course, brings a great change in any child's life, but possibly telepathy with parents would decrease in any event, as the child's intimate family horizons widen. At least one is safe in saying that close dependence on the mother and the number of telepathic experiences decrease at about the same time. This fact suggests the kind of psychological situation most conducive to telepathy—in adults perhaps, as well as children.

One of the most significant points to notice in telepathy experiences involving young children is that they occur without the least intention on anyone's part. The child is quite oblivious of the source of his idea; and the parent not even aware of the child in connection with the thought, much less of "sending" it to him. That observation is important in understanding telepathy on any age level.

Other types of ESP besides telepathy sometimes are noticed in children, although, just as with adults, one cannot always tell whether an experience involves telepathy or clairvoyance. Children sometimes seem to be affected by coming events as well as those of the present, although if the episodes are dreams, it may be especially difficult to tell whether anything more than a nightmare is involved.

At four and a half, a little boy in Michigan dreamed on several different nights that a snake "got" him, and then one day to his terror he actually did come upon a snake in the yard. His parents thought it only coincidence, although no more snake dreams wakened them after the snake had been disposed of.

But again at six he began to have nightmarish dreams: this time he thought he "fell in a hole." For three weeks he wakened nearly every night, sweating and screaming in fright.

Then, his mother says, "One day he was playing in our neighbor's yard where there was still snow on the ground. I heard terrible screams coming from what sounded like a long way off. I hurried in the direction of my neighbor's basement. The screams sounded almost as if coming from underground. Then I saw the hole of an old septic tank with rotted cover, and Steve up to his waist in the water and sinking rapidly. But my neighbor and I got him out, though the water was up to his shoulders before we finally rescued him. I thought dreams coming true were all a bunch of nonsense until this happened."

Occasionally a child's description of his dream may be more detailed, less like a nightmare, and, particularly if the event is one concerning someone other than himself, may rather definitely be precognitive. In a New Jersey home on November 18, 1950, a little boy named Craig, four years old, woke up screaming. His father went to him and with difficulty succeeded in soothing and quieting him. Then the boy told his dream.

"I dreamed you were in the water, Daddy. There was tall grass all around, and you were in the water. I called and called to you and you kept trying to come out of the water to me."

Of course, the parents promptly forgot the episode. The father and his brother had a duck-hunting trip planned, and two days after Craig's dream they set out.

The two men sat in the duck blinds in the tall weeds for most of the day. Before they were ready to come home they shot two ducks that fell out in the water. They got into the boat to retrieve the ducks. Before long, a terrific wind came up and they were forced a long way out. The water was very rough and the boat capsized. The brother was drowned and Craig's father thought he would never make the shore. He said the thought of Craig's dream was before him constantly.

Occasionally an adult watching a small child gets the idea that the child "sees things." Considering the ease of imagination and the uncertain distinction between the real and the unreal so often observed in little children, it is difficult to tell just what their experiences of this kind may actually be. However, they seem to be having hallucinatory experiences.

A California woman says that her little boy when about two began to act as if he "saw" things. For instance, she recalls, "One time, sitting in his sandbox, he got very still and with a faraway look in his eyes seemed to be staring at something. He said, 'Daddy stand up —long time.' My husband had gone to get our car license. It was the deadline and he had to wait in line several hours."

Of course, when a small child says he "saw" a distant event, one cannot tell if his use of the word is exact enough to mean that he had a hallucinatory experience or a bit of realistic imagination although it could mean the former. A Wisconsin family was returning home from a trip when the four-year-old in the back seat stood up unexpectedly and asked, "Did Aunt Myrtle and Uncle Charles have a wreck with a train?"

The father in a disgusted tone, he says, asked, "What are you talking about?" The answer, "I see'd they did."

The next day word was received that the aunt and uncle had stalled their car on a railroad crossing. They had gotten out of it before a train hit and demolished the car. As far as could be estimated, it was at the time of the child's remark.

Whether or not, in a case like that, the child actually thought he *saw,* is seldom considered a point of interest, but on the other hand, if the person he said he saw was someone dead, the effect on the parent is likely to be quite different. In the latter kind of case, the "seeing" is likely to be taken as significant.

In New York City a bright three-year-old girl had a playmate, Anne, who was seven. Anne, a diabetic, died. The little three-year-old was told that Anne had gone away on a trip. She did not see her or go to the funeral.

Several days after the funeral, the mother says, "I sent my daughter to get a broom for me from the hall closet and she returned without it. I asked her why. She said Anne would not let her. I asked what she meant, and she said Anne was standing in the hall closet and would not let her by. When I was convinced she was not joking or telling a story, I asked what Anne had on. She said a pretty white dress and veil, and that they could not go out because Anne had no coat.

"Anne had been buried in her communion dress. I tried not to become upset, but the following day while I was sitting in the living room I heard my daughter talking to someone in the hall and called to her. She again told me the same story, that she had seen Anne. I went to the hall and asked where. She pointed but said Anne was going out the door. I took her to play at the neighbor's and I told the neighbor of the incident. Together we prayed and sprinkled Holy Water in the apartment, but I had a very uneasy, sorrowing feeling. Two days later my daughter became ill and two weeks from the day Anne died, my daughter died of pneumonia."

Was the mental process any different in the two cases above? Or was it the subject matter only that impressed the parent in the second case? Such occurrences at least give a degree of evidence that children experience the hallucinatory form of ESP. However, they are rarely reported to have had unrealistic ESP dreams. Perhaps it is too much to expect that that form, if it did occur, would be recognized by an adult.

Just as one would expect, the childhood experiences remembered and recounted later by the individual himself, rather than by an adult at the time, do not go back to occurrences in the tender preschool years. Another conspicuous difference to be expected is that telepathy with parents is not reported. After all, the child himself is quite oblivious of such occurrences, and even if he were not, at that age knowing someone's thought or having someone know his would be taken as a matter of course like the sunshine and the shadow.

Frequently recalled from childhood, however, are precognitive experiences. They seem to make an indelible impression, possibly sometimes because the occurrence itself was unusual, but more than that the fact that an earlier impression *came true* is arresting, even to a child. A woman in Maine recalls an experience when she was only ten years old. She says, "I awakened that morning terribly frightened from a dream in which I had seen a man standing before me in our front hall. He was of dark complexion, and his clothes were covered with mud. The thing that frightened me most, I believe, was the fact that he had the most evil-looking eyes I had ever seen. I told my mother about this and she comforted me by saying it was only a dream and to go to school and forget it.

"That evening, while we were at supper, there was a rap on the front door, which my father answered. We could hear Father talking, and after a few minutes he came up to the dining room and asked Mother if it would be possible for a stranger who was stuck in the mud to have shelter for the night. This was not the custom, but knowing the roads were almost impassable it was agreed that the man might stay for the night. Father went to the stable to make the badly spent horse comfortable for the night, then returned to the house with the man. When he brought him into the dining room for supper, I nearly fainted. It was the same man that I had seen that morning in my dream—evil eyes and mud-stained clothing. We never knew who he was; he left early the next morning after his light carriage had been freed from a frost hole."

As perhaps might be expected, visual hallucinations, particularly those that involve the dying or the dead, are likely to be remembered. Memories of childhood may, of course, be quite unreliable, but when the kind of occurrence remembered is similar to that reported by other adults as a recent happening, such memories gain considerable support. Another woman in Maine recalls an experience when she was ten that, if not a dream, was hallucinatory. She knew her father had had an operation and was in the hospital, but as she says, "I did not know about death as I had never had anyone die that was close to me. I was sent next door to stay overnight with my girlfriend. I woke up and at the foot of the bed was the most beautiful light I had ever seen. There was my father with his arms open to me and as I watched he was rising up. I called to my girlfriend, telling her my father was dead. We got up and lit the light. It was just ten after four in the morning; soon my uncle came from the hospital to tell us my father had passed away, and that he called to me as he was dying. He passed away at exactly ten after four. I was a child that knew nothing of death; yet I knew he was gone."

The early age at which an idea from the religious or cultural background may be inculcated is illustrated in that instance, as well as the probable occurrence of hallucination in childhood. It is easy to see that this form of experience would make a particularly indelible impression on the person. As it happens, the number of childhood memories of experiences that appear to be hallucinatory seems larger in proportion to other forms of ESP than the number reported by adults.

In families of several children, if any show tendencies toward ESP, usually only one does so. In a California household some ten years ago, Joan, the youngest of several children, when about three began to stand out from the others, because she seemed to know things in a way her mother could not explain. For instance she "knew" what Christmas gifts had been bought for her ("my little blue purse," etc.). Her mother was sure the secret had not been "given away," and the gifts not the expected ones. She also began to tell her mother (correctly) when certain relatives were coming to call, even though her mother thought their coming impossible.

Then, her parents being separated (her father had deserted the family and her mother later obtained a divorce), Joan began to tell things about her father, even though in reality she scarcely knew him. In fact, one of the unexpected visitors she had predicted had been her father. Later her father was very ill. He was taken unconscious to the hospital and put on the critical list, the doctors thinking he could not get well. At home, Joan kept insisting her father would get well, and in spite of the opinion of the experts, he did so. She told her mother correctly when her father's blood transfusions stopped, and when he was first given food, when he first walked to the window.

By this time Joan was nearly five, and her mother wrote for advice to the Parapsychology Laboratory. To help to decide how outstanding Joan's ability was some ESP tests were suggested.

Under the informal conditions of the home and with tests as much like a game as possible, Joan's mother succeeded in having her "guess" some cards. Using the ordinary ESP deck, in which five is the expected chance number, she got first fifteen, then eleven, then twelve, and finally only four correct out of the twenty-five-card pack.

As ESP scores, of course, these were high, except for the last. They could scarcely be explained as only "chance." When she got the twelve her mother noted that she was "nonchalantly sucking a lolli-pop." When she got the eleven, she was drawing with a stick in the dirt. When she got the final four, *she had not wanted to do it.*

Understandably, with a five-year-old, the novelty of calling cards soon wears off. And novelty, enthusiasm, interest—from childhood to old age—appears to be a necessary psychological condition for positive scoring in ESP tests. But Joan had shown by this more for-mal method too that she "had ESP."

The fact that this one child could guess correctly so many more cards than could the others began to create a problem in the fam-ily, just as any unique characteristic of a single child often does, and the mother decided not to make any more tests. For one thing, she did not want the little girl to be thought "different," or to start considering herself different.

Joan's mother had another worry, too. Her older child had had rheumatic fever, but was recovering. Joan said that her sister would go to sleep and not wake up. Must this come true like Joan's other predictions? It could be pointed out, however, that not all of the earlier ones had been correct. Obviously, not everything she hap-pened to say was on the same level, and even those remarks that seemed to involve ESP had not all come true exactly.

For instance, one night before the family was to start on a "gypsy" (unplanned) trip, Joan wakened her mother by crying, "Don't take me to the water. I will drown." Her older brother and mother both tried to assure her they were not going to the water and she was not going to drown. They thought of it only as a dream. However, the next day they came to a beautiful camping ground and decided to stay for a few days. Only hours later did the mother realize they had camped on a river bank. She said nothing but watched the children closely while swimming. They spent three lovely weeks by the river and no one drowned. Joan also predicted that her father would "come home and hang his clothes in our closet again," but that did not come true.

By emphasizing these misses Joan's remark about her sister took on a different cast, and no longer seemed to her mother anything to worry about especially.

The case of Joan is unusual in that it was one of the first instances in which a child with so much spontaneous ESP to her credit was also tested by the card-calling methods (informally at home) and shown to be able to demonstrate ESP that way, too. But the sequel to it is the familiar one already mentioned. Her ESP—at least as a noticeable element—was apparently evanescent. In her fifth year, evidence of it decreased. For the last summer before she started school, and after that, as far as the record goes, she neither made predictions nor gave any other evidence of ESP.

The interesting general fact that emerges from studying ESP in children is that their experiences, though simpler, still are similar both in form and type to those of adults. It seems that ESP may be "there" even in childhood.

IN OLD AGE

Though changes come with the years, most human capacities persist into later life, their expression over the years being adapted accordingly. ESP, too, can be traced from very early years on through adulthood and into the advanced years without any clear lines of demarcation.

It may be, however, that the number of experiences reported by those over seventy is smaller in proportion than is that of younger people. Many individuals in the older decades write to tell of their experiences—they feel the underlying significance of the material they have to contribute and often go to great inconvenience to record it—but more often than not, the experiences they report are not those of the present, but of the past, often the distant past. To reminisce may be characteristic of age, but it also seems that mature reflection on the significance of these experiences has helped to preserve them in memory over long intervals.

An elderly minister now living in Florida writes, "Being now 85 years of age, I still remember an experience at sixteen years. I was a poor boy, on my own, in September, 1886, working for Sam H. on his farm, three miles from an Iowa town. Sam bought cattle and hogs for the Chicago market, and used two ponies, a bay and a roan.

"It was Sunday morning. I was in my room dressing, after doing the chores. I was given to day dreaming. As I dressed I saw Sam's pony throw him, roll on him, and crush one of his legs. I heard Big Sam's wife call me: 'Come quick, Vic. Sam's hurt.'

"I saw myself get on the pony and gallop the three miles to town for the doctor. I saw myself near the corner of the barn talking to the son, a boy my own age, telling him how we must carry on. I saw Sam on the bed and the doctor at work.

"Then, it was the same time the next Sunday morning and as usual I was dressing in my room. Then came the call: 'Vic, come quick. Sam's hurt!'

"I remember saying to myself, 'There it is and I know what to do.' Soon I was on the pony racing for the doctor. At the very spot where the previous Sunday I had talked to the son, I talked to him again.

"The one difference between the waking day dream and its realization was that I thought Sam had been thrown by the roan. Instead it was the bay which threw him and on which I raced to town."

Older people, however, do sometimes report experiences of recent occurrence—often just the latest of a long series. In 1949 a man from Florida, then 75 years old, who told of several precognitive dreams in times past which served him as warnings against such dangers as drownings, fire or other accidents, wrote of his most recent one. "In August of 1945, my wife and I drove to New Jersey where some of our children were then living.

"About daylight on the sixth, I was sitting up in bed spelling, 'Bay —Bayone—Bayonne,' aloud. My wife said, 'What are you trying to spell?'

"I said, 'There is going to be an explosion of two or three millions of gallons of oil or gasoline in Bayonne in three weeks or three months—I can't quite get it. Many lives will be in danger, but if precautions are taken the explosion will not take place.'

"I repeated the name to my wife, lest I might forget it. I asked my son if he had ever heard of a place called Bayonne. He said, 'It's on the Jersey side of the river and the Standard Oil Company has a refinery there. Why do you want to know?'

"I told him, and he, knowing of my many earlier premonitions, took it seriously and later . . . (he arranged) . . . that the commander of the base had me tell him of my premonition.

"He thanked me and said he would have warnings posted.

"The accident happened, as you know. You might get copies of the papers in that vicinity for November eighth and seventh, and see what they say. As my daughter said when she wrote me about it, 'Well, Dad, you hit the nail on the head again, and right to the day.'

"So far as I can remember I had never heard of the name, Bayonne, before the morning of August 6, 1945. Did the commander warn the Standard Oil Company?"

Precognitive experiences are the most frequent in this age group, as in each of the others, but other types are occasionally reported. One can see that ESP may still occur as the years pile up, although the topics may not range as widely as in earlier years. A few may concern events of relative unimportance, but most are heavy with the crises and tragedies of life. Since the big event that looms for many in this age bracket is death itself, that is the topic one might expect to meet most in experiences of the aged.

On Sunday, August 24, 1941, a 78-year-old man in North Carolina told his wife a dream he had the night before. He dreamed he was standing at Butler's Crossing about three miles from his home when he saw a vehicle coming toward him at great speed. The light was so bright it blinded him. He screamed to his son, "Oh, David! It's Judgment Day." At that moment the vehicle struck him, as he said, "hurling him into everlasting darkness."

His wife said it was a terrible dream, but she did not know then that it was also precognitive. Her husband at the time was suffering from an allergy, for which twice a week he was taking treatments from a doctor in a nearby town. Three days later, he went to town for his shots. On the way back he caught a ride to Butler's Crossing, where he got out of the car, stood a few minutes by the road lighting his pipe, and then started across the highway. He was at the center white line when a speeding car came around the curve. He stepped back, the car swerved to the left, hit him and threw him sixty feet. Fifteen minutes later he was dead.

We have already seen that occasionally the subject matter of a precognitive ESP experience may be an event to come after the end of a person's lifetime. Instances in which this proved to be the case naturally would be likely to come in this age group to which death itself is so much nearer.

In the summer of 1953 a woman in South Dakota had received

an urgent call from her sister to come to her mother's bedside in Independence, Kansas. Her mother had suffered a coronary occlusion several months before, and this was her daughter's third trip home. When she arrived she found her mother very weak. She recognized the daughter, but asked no questions about the family. After several days she lapsed into a coma, and they knew the end was near. One evening (July 5), as the daughter came into the hospital room, her mother was talking to her nurse—actually carrying on a conversation, though she seemed confused. She was saying, "I have two girls, and there's a boy, too. The boy is Franklin." She had no son; her daughter's twelve-year-old son was the only Franklin in the family. Then the mother looked at the daughter, seemed to know her, and asked, "Where is my boy? Where is Franklin?" The daughter took her hand and said Franklin was at home with his Daddy. "Is he all right?" the mother asked.

Sometime before, the mother had visited her daughter's church camp and loved its rustic beauty. Since then she had always been happy to know when any of the family were to spend some time there, and it was natural for the daughter to tell her now that Franklin was getting ready to go to camp. "Oh, *no*," the ill woman moaned, "I don't want Frankie to go to that camp. He must not go there." And she began to cry. They talked to her soothingly, and soon she either slept or drifted into unconsciousness, still clinging to her daughter's hand. Perhaps a half-hour later as the daughter still stood beside her, she opened her eyes and looked at her with an expression of great fear. "Helen," she said, "did Franklin die too?" The daughter assured her that Franklin was all right and asked her mother if she had had a bad dream. "Yes, and something terrible, just terrible happened to Franklin," and then with the tears running from under her lids, she closed her eyes and did not speak again. The next day, July 6, she died without awakening.

On July 21, the second day Franklin was at camp, he dived into the creek and struck a submerged log, dislocating his neck in such a way as to sever the spinal cord. The doctors gave little hope that he would live and for weeks it was a hard fight, but he survived, a quadriplegic, but as his mother says, "The same boy, full of fun, courageous, and hopeful for the future."

We have just seen that ESP occurs at all ages—in certain persons. The picture is complicated, however, by the fact that some persons who as adults "have ESP" do not show it in childhood, though some do report it as a life-long tendency. On the other hand, some of the children who give evidence of it while very young, no longer do so as they grow older. The fact that this change comes about the time their family relationships, particularly parental, widen may be significant. Yet it does not appear that the mere closeness of mother and small child could be more than a partial explanation, for the children that show ESP are too rare for that. Also, in families of several children, the fact that only one shows it would indicate at least that it is not the result of an intangible something which one could perhaps call "family atmosphere." More than that, none of the mothers who have reported the ESP tendencies of one of several children has indicated that she felt closer emotionally to this child than to the others. If such were the case, presumably it would be mentioned, at least by some.

If fact, nothing in the expression of ESP in the various age groups gives any indication why some individuals and not others should experience ESP. Obviously, the reason why some adults do, and some do not, must be one that applies in childhood too—an observation that may have a bearing on the question still with us, "Who has ESP?"

ESP and Peace of Mind

9

Is it healthy to have an ESP experience or does it mean that the person is somehow peculiar, if not actually ill mentally? Occasionally a person is very much disturbed, asking himself, "How could I have known that? Are my mental processes abnormal?" Knowing no place to turn for information, and with friends and relatives who look askance at any unusual mental tendencies, his worry is likely to be suppressed and secret and perhaps all the greater on that account.

The worry may go back to childhood, if his parents took a strong stand against anything unusual of this kind. A girl in New York, now a young lady of twenty-five, had a series of unusual experiences as a child. One of them, at least, had the earmarks of ESP. When she was eleven she had been sent off to camp for the summer, knowing that her mother was very ill and would have an operation. One night she had won the swimming contest, and had gone to bed very happy in consequence. When falling asleep, she thought she saw her mother lying unconscious in the street with her aunt standing beside her and calling her.

The impression was so real that she cried until she finally fell asleep on the counselor's shoulder. When the message came next day that she must go home, she took it calmly. She already *knew* her mother was dead, before the circumstances had been confirmed just as she had seen.

Perhaps if this had been this girl's only unusual experience it would have been easier for her. But others, some evidently mixed with and confused by a vivid imagination, kept occurring. Finally, at thirteen, she told her father about it. He gave her a spanking—a doubtful cure either for imaginative fantasy or ESP. It convinced her, at least, that experiences like hers were not normal, and raised questions all the more worrisome because she dared not discuss these; questions only answered when as an adult she learned about ESP.

Probably today few parents would use such extreme measures. But even without being expressed by outright punishment, the attitude of parents can make the youngster feel odd or different. Some children, too, may be so sensitive that without knowing specifically their parents' attitude, they may feel intuitively that it would not do to tell their experiences.

In Nova Scotia some years ago, a nine-year-old girl had a dream which as an adult she recalls in these words: "A coffin stood in a corner of our living room. As I approached I saw that the face therein was that of my beloved grandmother. I awoke stricken with grief. I slept no more that night. I could not bring myself to tell anyone of the dream that haunted me so—not even my grandmother. After several days my spirits rose again and the dream was almost forgotten.

"Within a fortnight my grandfather died suddenly of a heart attack. On the day of the funeral I was taken into the room of my dream. There was the coffin as I had seen it. The only difference lay in the cold still face—the face of my grandfather and not, as in my dream, of my grandmother.

"My grief was now mingled with a strange, gripping alarm, almost terror. Still I spoke of the dream to no one. In my child's mind, I feared mentioning the dream would in some way add to the sorrow of an already stricken family.

"Years afterward my mother told me that on the day my grandfather died he had said to her in the morning, "Last night I dreamed that everybody in town was dead—I was the only person alive." She told me that he looked at her keenly as if to ask whether she understood what he was thinking. Then he went out, waving his hand in his usual lighthearted manner. Within an hour he was dead.

"It was then I told my mother of the dream I had had almost twenty years before. For years it had the grip of an icy hand, and as I write, the retelling of it opens old griefs as if they were yesterday's wounds."

In twenty years a perfectly healthy "wound" should have so healed that retelling would no longer raise the old emotions so vividly. No doubt the reason it still did so was because the question raised had gone unanswered all those years. If the girl had been able to discuss her dream normally with her parents, much of the disturbing mystery of it would have disappeared, the strain would have been relieved and the episode taken for what it was: a perfectly healthy precognitive experience remarkable mainly for having occurred to a young child.

Parents, however, are not always to blame for worries in later life that result from the realization that one has experienced ESP. Occasional individuals acquire such firm ideas of the limits of normal mental action that an ESP experience, going beyond these limits, confronts them with an insoluble dilemma. As a California woman puts it, such occurrences seem so fantastic that one cannot expect others to believe they could happen except to someone who was going "haywire!"

One of her experiences, for instance, came to her one day when baking a cake. Suddenly she had a mental picture (one of the rare "waking" realistic dreams, evidently) of her husband in an auto accident. She saw him badly injured, his head bleeding and his body from the waist down twisted so that it lay on the right side, while from the waist up he lay flat with his arms arched over his head. She knew he was unconscious. She saw no car, yet she knew it was a car accident. The impression came with such force and vividness that she burst out crying. Then, realizing she was crying about something imaginary, she felt frightened and ashamed, thinking perhaps the kitchen heat was affecting her.

Seven days later the accident happened. Her husband was standing by a parked car which was side-swiped by a speeding one. The position of his body as he lay unconscious in the road was precisely as she had seen it. But how could she expect anyone to believe she had foreseen this, when even to herself such foresight seemed impossible?

If intuitions can disturb a person's peace of mind because they come true, hallucinatory experiences are even more likely to do so. In North Dakota one night, a woman whose son was in a boys' school two-hundred miles away, was walking into her living room when she suddenly heard the son call, "Mom," so clearly she turned around in surprise to see if he were behind her. A letter a few days later told how he had broken his arm in basketball that evening. She learned that at the time she heard him call, his pain was so intense he thought he could not bear it. The form of her experience, an auditory hallucination, was so unfamiliar to her that she says, "I feel awed by such an experience, and I don't like to relate it to relatives or friends. In fact, I did not even tell my husband till long afterward."

Embarrassment or worry over having had a *hallucinatory* psi experience is understandable, for in ordinary mental life hallucinations are very rare. In the public mind, they are associated directly with mental illness or drug addiction. The fact that psi can occur in the hallucinatory form in perfectly sane and healthy persons is still an almost entirely unrecognized fact. The individual himself, his parents, his friends, his doctor, even his psychiatrist, may be entirely baffled by it, and have no idea that it is simply one of the less common forms of ESP experiences, no more abnormal than a dream.

The emphasis in all the experiences above has been on unhappy effects on individuals and their peace of mind, resulting from their experiencing ESP. Fortunately, only a minority of persons seem to be thus adversely affected; an opposite attitude is very often expressed.

Apparently, a person's reaction to an ESP experience when it is entirely inexplicable to him is to a large degree a measure of his inner confidence. Some, like those above, seem easily to come to doubt themselves. Others can stand on their own conviction and say, simply, as does a woman from Indiana, "How can you explain the impossible? I only know it happened." She awakened suddenly one night when her army husband was stationed a thousand miles from home and had no expectation of a furlough for some time to come. Something had happened. She did not know what. It was ten minutes after four. She continues:

"I began to prowl around the house to see if everything was as it should be. I searched the house. It wasn't on fire. I went to the front door. There was no auto accident that night to have awakened me. Finally I looked in on my mother to see if she was all right. She awakened and wanted to know what was wrong. I didn't know. Something had wakened me. But nothing was out of order, so I gave up and went back to bed. As soon as I was settled, the doorbell rang.

"There stood my husband! He had been given emergency leave, had driven all day and all night to get home and had reached the city limits at exactly ten after four. He had not sent word because he wanted to surprise me."

With similar self-confidence, a person may staunchly consider a baffling experience as nonetheless meaningful, to be taken seriously and to be explained, if possible. Feeling no insecurity about it, he can say, as does another Indiana woman, "I hope my little story can help you in some way to come a little closer to the reason and truth about such strange occurrences. I do not mind having my experience used in this way. It is certainly nothing to be ashamed of!

"My first experience was a dream when I was seventeen. My sister, Frances, nineteen, was married to a wonderful, talented musician. They were very much in love and happy together. One night I had a dream that was so real I remembered every single detail of it. I dreamed that my brother-in-law, Eddy, was out hunting with a young boy who was faceless in my dream. All of a sudden Eddy dropped from a discharge from the boy's shotgun. He had climbed through a fence and didn't have the safety on. The pellets hit Eddy in the hip and he bled to death before they could get him to a doctor.

"Then in my dream I thought I was asleep and that my mother's screaming awakened me. I ran down the hall to the kitchen and my mother came through the living room and dining room and we met in the doorway. At the same time another woman, also faceless in my dream, got there. Mother had a telegram in her hand, telling of the tragedy.

"The whole thing bothered me so I wrote to my sister and told her about it. They got my letter on Saturday and laughed about it. But Monday morning Eddy was killed just as in my dream. The telegram arrived just as I had seen it, and my mother had a friend visiting, and she was in the kitchen. We all met in the two doorways leading to the kitchen."

Some of the more religious individuals explain their experiences in terms of their faith. They may wonder about the occurrences but feel no personal responsibility for their explanation. As one woman says, "The Good Lord prepares me for certain shocks that lie ahead."

Many, perhaps the majority, of those who report ESP experiences make no comment expressing a reaction. They apparently feel no strong self-consciousness about it. From comments like these above it appears that the attitude the person takes depends on the individual himself; on factors in the specific individual, such as the strength of his self-confidence.

A person whose peace of mind had been disturbed by having an ESP experience is usually reassured merely by the information that many other people have such experiences. A Chicago woman who had had several precognitive dreams, when informed that this was a kind of dream quite frequently reported, expressed the relief shown by many at similar information: "I am so glad to find out that other people have this kind of dream, too." She did not ask for an explanation of precognition or of ESP, but wanted only to know she was not alone in her experience and therefore not odd, different or abnormal.

It is not surprising really that these worries about whether the ESP process is normal and healthy should be easily resolved, for after all the reason for them in the first place is mainly that ESP is entirely unfamiliar to the person. Psi experiences are relatively rare, and since many people refrain from telling about those that do occur, they seem even more unusual than they are. And after all, it's not the inexplicable but the unfamiliar to which mystery clings the closest. On that account, the worry disappears once the person learns that he is not alone in having this kind of experience.

Sometimes a physician, especially a psychiatrist, is in a less easily solved quandary. He may need to know not only the fact that ESP does sometimes occur, but how to diagnose it when it does. During the war a woman who had occasionally been under the care of a physician because of a tendency to be anxious and over-nervous awoke one night crying hysterically, "Jack is dead. Jack is dead." She said she saw him go down in a burning plane. Jack, her son, was in the U. S. Army in the Pacific. When her husband could not calm her, the doctor was called. He finally gave her sedatives and had her hospitalized. Neither he nor her husband took seriously her idea that Jack *was* in a plane crash, for he was not even in the Air Force.

But word came later that her son had been on a plane, and had indeed gone down in flames. He had been killed at approximately the time of his mother's experience.

Because her husband and doctor knew of her previous tendency to over-anxiety, they considered her conviction that her son was dead as a pure delusion and therefore pathological. But in reality, her behavior was the perfectly natural reaction of a mother who had just been acquainted with and convinced of terrible and heartbreaking news. As the physician himself later realized, her inability to convince them of the truth only increased her distress and lessened the possibility of self-control. He was, in fact, not a little disturbed by the case, realizing the difficulty of avoiding an erroneous diagnosis in future cases. As we know, the immediate and certain recognition of the element of ESP in any episode is often impossible, even for experts. Fortunately, the combination of emotional instability and ESP, as in this instance, is rare, and the doctor in such a case can only consider the possibility of ESP and suspend his judgment until a check-up can be made.

Presumably, if ESP were an unhealthy symptom, it would long ago have been recognized as such by the profession of psychiatry. The fact that psychiatrists have never taken it as a symptom, then, can be considered an indication that the two are not necessarily related. Psychiatrists, however, have to date given more attention to the subject of ESP than have individuals from any other branch of medicine, or the psychological sciences. Psychiatrists are concerned with those hidden aspects of mind that become unhealthy. They deal with the unconscious processes of mental life, and as "depth psychologists" probe into them. The forms of expression of ESP—dreams, hallucinations, compulsions and automatisms—perfectly healthy and normal forms of expressions as they are, may also be used by the mind in morbid states.

In the psychoanalytic branch of psychiatry, particularly when patients' dreams are recorded and studied, occasional instances of telepathy have been noted. Usually the patient's dream was found to play around the thoughts or actions of the analyst in such a way that telepathy was suggested. But analysts have interpreted such occurrences as the result of the close rapport established by the treatment and not as a symptom of the patient's illness.

The method of dream analysis and the close interpersonal relation of patient and doctor would encourage telepathic exchange, but the number and frequency of such telepathic experiences is not so great as to raise a special issue. Such occurrences, however, have had the effect of arousing the interest of a number of psychiatrists in ESP ability.

The lack of a connection between ESP and unhealthy mental states can also be noticed in the reports of the persons whose experiences are given in this book. As far as their letters show, these people are a sane, well-balanced lot. Nothing about their experiences and nothing in the manner of reporting them suggests the pathological in the least. A few of them, as mentioned above, do wonder, on account of the strangeness of the experiences, if such a connection might exist. But that strangeness is one of unfamiliarity, as we have seen;

it comes from lack of information about ESP, and perhaps also from lack of knowledge about the symptoms of mental illness.

It does, of course, occasionally happen that an individual who has already had, or who subsequently has a mental breakdown may also have ESP experiences. A man from Georgia, who later was diagnosed as a schizophrenic, was going to California by train in 1944 to look for a new job. Acquaintances of his, a Mr. and Mrs. B., occupied the seat opposite him, but the halfseat beside him was vacant, except for a time when, as he thought, a well-dressed young lady occupied it.

He thought he fell into conversation with her, got her name and discussed his future prospects in California with her. "You will be all right," she said. "You will meet a man, named John E. His wife will be with him. He will be your friend and will be instrumental in your finding a position."

Later he mentioned the young lady to his friends across the aisle. They, however, said no one had been in the seat, and he did not tell them of the conversation. When at the city of his destination he applied for a job at an employment agency, the receptionist was a Mrs. E., and her husband, John E., did help him find a position.

The experience, as reported by the man himself some years before his later breakdown, depends only on his word. One can take it or leave it; but if one takes it, it could tentatively be classed as a regular precognitive unrealistic experience, whether it occurred as a dream or as a day dream. It does not appear to be significantly different from unrealistic precognitive experiences or visual hallucinations reported by people with no known tendencies to mental illness.

A few persons who think they are reporting instances of ESP are actually too seriously ill to realize that they are suffering from delusions or mistaken beliefs. (Their experiences would not be included in an ESP collection because of lack of evidence that true information was received.) The kind of experience reported by mentally disturbed persons is, like the following, obviously quite delusory.

"In August, 1955, I had a nervous breakdown. Something happened by which every single thought in my mind could be read. I have been under this force for a year. Every thought asleep or awake could be heard by most anyone for miles around. . . ."

One could say that illness was shown in that case, if only by the defective judgment which allowed the person to be convinced of something without any objective evidence of it. The delusion was built on a fantastic idea of the way telepathy works and a complete disregard of the fact that the person had no evidence that his "mind was read."

The idea that unlimited telepathy can occur often fits the needs of one suffering from a delusion that he is being persecuted. "About December 15, 1955, I began hearing a voice in my mind. It was the voice of Henry W., a man living in the room next to mine. He admits mentally that it is he, but orally denies it. Although I am now in an institution, this man continues to plague me and they will not believe it."

Individuals with delusions like this man's, when given telepathy tests, have never demonstrated exceptional ESP ability. In fact, delusions about telepathy have no more to do with telepathy than those about Napoleon have to do with the famous general.

The final and most definite evidence that no relation exists between psi and mental illness comes from tests for ESP made upon patients in mental hospitals. Not only did those with the "pseudo-telepathy syndrome," as the delusion above could be called, fail to show special ESP ability, but groups suffering from other forms of mental illness also failed to demonstrate unusual ESP.

This is not to say that no ESP was found among mental patients. They gave some evidence of it, but this evidence did not characterize any particular group on the basis of kind of illness involved. In certain investigations, patients suffering from mood disorders made higher ESP scores than others. But in one research, at least, the most meaningful fact was disclosed when the ESP results were compared with the hospital records of the patient's degree of *co-operativeness*: the patients who were more co-operative gave higher scores in their tests for ESP than did the less co-operative groups.

These results seem to point the same way as those of certain tests of normal college students. In the latter, measurements were made touching on the students' "adjustment," and the well-adjusted students scored slightly higher than their opposites.

Again, as in the differences found between men and women in ESP tests, results on this point seem related to the *attitude* of the person toward his test. In mental hospital studies, in classes, and in the laboratory, test results seem to be affected by differences in attitude, rather than by differences in *amount* of ESP. The differences are analogous, perhaps, to the contrast between the work an artist might produce when he is at ease and when he is under strain. In the latter situation, his product would not measure his natural ability, so much as it would the way he felt about his surroundings. If one so interprets the tests made in the hospital, the ESP displayed in them seems to be a measure of the remaining *normal* tendencies of the patients, rather than an indication of their illness. And so, the final conclusion given by all the lines of evidence is that the ESP process is a normal healthy one, and its operation need not worry anyone. Whatever may be the factors that mark off those who do from those who do not have ESP, mental illness is not one of them.

10

The Stamp of the Personality

Who has ESP? Are the persons who experience it of a distinct personality type? Do they have definite and distinguishing characteristics? If the answers to these questions were easy, they should already be evident.

The answers are *not* easy. The difference between those who do and those who do not give evidence of ESP is still obscure, even to those who know the most about psi and how it operates. If one could study carefully a large number of persons who have ESP experiences and contrast them to a similar number who do not, it might be possible to make generalizations about the two groups. Such a study, however, has never been practicable, and so one must draw whatever inference he can from the experiences themselves. By observing special aspects of them, it turns out to be possible to arrive at a first-stage answer, or at least a hint of an answer to the question of who has ESP.

In considering a large group of people like those who have reported the experiences in the preceding pages, the most obvious observation is that they do not, rather than do, show similar characteristics. They do not even seem to "have" ESP to the same degree: a few report having had many experiences; many report a few; and occasionally a person says he has had only a single one in a lifetime. The experiences reported, however, and the circumstances under which they occur are so variable and complex that clear and definite impressions are not easy to get. But, by studying the different kinds and numbers reported by different people, one can begin to see some broader outlines and the direction they point.

When a person says, as does a woman in New York, "Never before or since have I had any such premonition," one wonders at once if it involved some great personal crisis, and what form the experience took. This woman goes on to say, "It occurred on the night of October 27, 1948. I was in bed resting, reading a little. My husband was lecturing at a school some miles away. Finally I turned off the light and was falling asleep when I was brought back to full consciousness by my heart suddenly beginning to beat like a sledge hammer. I turned on the light. It was a few moments after eleven. I lay down again, only to have the furious beating get worse still. It felt as if my heart was leaping out of my body. I couldn't imagine what was happening, and got very frightened. But after a little time the wild beating ceased and I dozed off.

"At twelve-thirty the doorbell rang. Two policemen were there to tell me my husband had died of a cerebral hemorrhage at a little after eleven."

The event was indeed highly critical and important, the form of the experience far from common. It seems probable that it was a telepathically induced hallucinatory experience, the pain or general bodily symptoms modeled to some extent on those of the dying person. Since no *idea*, no rational accompaniment of any kind got into consciousness, the difficult, almost inhibited expression of an item secured by ESP is suggested.

We may presume that each individual expresses his ESP in the form that is easiest or most appropriate for him; then, when an unusual effect like the one above occurs, one supposes that it was the only or the easiest method of ESP expression available for this person, one which possibly only an extreme crisis could induce.

Many "solitary" experiences, however, come in more familiar forms, and sometimes an "only" experience may have no personal bearing whatever. The wife of an Air Force lieutenant, a person who says she rarely dreams, or at least rarely remembers having done so, had a vivid and terrifying dream one night. It was in 1927 and she and her husband were in Japan, a post to which her husband had recently been assigned. They arrived a few weeks before at Nagasaki and had taken a train to Tokyo, where they were living at the time of the dream. The dream was that she was standing high on a hillside overlooking a bay shaped like a half-moon. A railway track ran along the rocky shore rather close to the water. As she watched, a long heavy freight train came into view from the south, traveled around the bay and disappeared in the north. Presently along came a passenger train from the south traveling in the same direction.

She seemed to know what was going to happen. The heavy freight had weakened the track and it was ready to break. When the passenger train was directly beneath her position, the track gave way and many cars turned over and fell into the bay. It seemed shallow and she could see people far below crawling like ants out of the car windows and the waves breaking on the wreckage. She woke up horrified.

At a luncheon at the hotel to which she and her husband had been invited that day, she sat on the left of Mr. S., one of the undersecretaries of the United States Embassy. She heard the woman on his right ask him if any Americans were on the wrecked train. At mention of a train wreck, she asked where it took place. It was on the line she and her husband had traveled to get to Tokyo.

Before he gave details, she told her dream; and the dream wreck coincided exactly with the actual wreck. When pictures were published, they agreed in every aspect with the dream. The weird part to her was that it was as if she had actually been there and seen it happen! She had not known anyone on that train. And it was the first and, to date, the last experience of that kind she had ever had.

One certainly can make no generalization from cases as different as those two. This one, even though it concerned a great calamity, had almost no personal significance for the individual; far from being in a rare or difficult form, it was a realistic dream, the commonest and therefore presumably the easiest form of all. However, the event was a great crisis for many people, even if not for the dreamer.

Sometimes even this does not hold. The event may not be a crisis for anyone, and may not even have any particular significance. In 1943 a woman now in California, but then in Oregon, dreamed, as she says, "I was helping my aunt and uncle move in the same building from downstairs to upstairs. The dream had no sound effects—just struggle. We (my uncle and I) seemed to be on a narrow stairway and we were having an awful time with two big pieces of furniture getting them up—first one and then the other. It seemed a difficult, almost impossible task and there were two flashes or episodes of different pieces of furniture, but with the same problem.

"The dream was so vivid and ludicrous that I told my landlady about it. And I wrote my aunt in San Diego. My aunt and uncle lived in their own one-story house in San Diego and had no thought of leaving. As you do with such dreams, I 'forgot' about the dream and the war went on. When my husband went overseas, I moved to San Diego. My aunt and uncle had sold their home, and were living in a downstairs apartment. My aunt assured me that they were only living in the downstairs apartment until they could move upstairs, for she disliked being 'underneath' anyone in an apartment house. It was not until one day I was helping move the chesterfield up a back stairway—narrow with a wood railing—that suddenly I remembered. I set my end down and almost fainted. My uncle asked what was the matter. Still I didn't trust myself until I asked my aunt first, 'What was the dream I wrote you about from Oregon?'

"I think it was the most profound—although seemingly completely meaningless experience I could have had—to have that dream come true."

Nothing in an experience like the above nor in the one about the train wreck suggests any reason why these events should have been picked out and made the subject of the only ESP experience the person ever had. Presumably some nameless and shifting subconscious current was responsible, but just what or why, one can have no idea.

One fact that stands out when one considers all these "solitary" experiences together is that they show little regularity. Each one is different. The events dealt with run the gamut from strong personal involvement to triviality and the forms in which they come vary just as widely.

We do know, however, that the persons, too, were different. Each was a unique individual, with his own special set of personal characteristics. It could be that the circumstances necessary to permit an ESP experience are different in different people, just as the form available may vary from person to person. Since the individual, the events, and the preferred form all vary, should one not expect the end products to be equally varied?

What about the successive experiences of those people who have more than one? Is a personality stamp visible at least in the *form* of the experience? Is the second experience noticeably like the first, even if the occasions and events are very different?

Among the people who report two experiences, a woman from Minnesota is typical of many, because her second experience was recognizably like her first. In the first, she was about to take an elevator in a downtown office building, to keep an appointment which was in actuality set for the following day. She had been in the office building before, so dreaming the actual layout as she did was explainable enough. But in the dream she noticed especially the two elevators in the lobby: one hydraulic, the other the conventional cable type. She dreamed the cable elevator came down and its operator was dressed in funereal black. He opened the door, took some people in, and in a sepulchral voice that "gave me the chills said, 'Are you ready?'" And there the dream ended.

At breakfast that morning she told the dream. The children wanted to know what an hydraulic elevator was. In the ensuing conversation the dream was all but forgotten, though her husband said as he was driving away, "Be sure to take the hydraulic elevator."

When she got to the lobby the cable elevator came down. The operator was wearing a regular uniform, not the funereal black of the dream. Several people got on and she started to do so when, she says, "I remembered that silly dream so I stopped and the elevator man said, not in a sepulchral but a perfectly natural, pleasant voice, 'Are you ready?'

"I said, 'No,' and walked toward the directory on the wall. When the hydraulic elevator came down, I got on. As we went up we passed the other stalled between floors. It took some time to clear up that difficulty. No one was hurt, but I was glad I was not on it."

The funereal clothes and sepulchral tones of the operator show, it would seem, a mind quite ready to make something interesting, perhaps a bit morbid, out of any available material. The incident was rather on the trivial side, one that was to happen as she went about her next day's activities.

In the second experience, she recalls, "I dreamed I was driving along a country road when I saw a man lying in the ditch on the right side. He was dressed in shabby trousers and nothing else. In my dream I thought he must be dead or why would he lie in that very long wet grass. But just then he raised up and turned and looked at me. Then I awoke.

"Later I did drive out and beyond a bridge, in the ditch, a damp, almost wet place, a man was lying dressed exactly as in the dream. He raised up, turned and looked at me.

"There were workers in the field a little way off and he may have been one of them taking a rest. It was very warm, so maybe the damp ditch was cool, inviting. The whole thing was completely unimportant, except for the fact that I had dreamed the scene just before I woke up."

Again, a realistic and precognitive dream, although it lacks the touch of fantasy in the first one. Yet the dreamer "thought he must be dead"—certainly a more exciting idea than the actual fact that he was just a farm worker taking a nap. And, as she says, the whole thing was unimportant. Like the other instance, this too was a slight occurrence picked out of the next day's activities ahead of time. The two dreams are sufficiently alike to suggest a "personalized" aspect.

Just as some individuals consistently have their experiences as dreams, others have theirs *only* when awake. In the summer of 1934, a woman in St. Louis had a sudden irrational, intuitive impression. She was riding through the park on a bus, when she suddenly felt she must leave it. She jumped up and got off at the next stop, and found herself standing there feeling very foolish, as she had to wait some time for the next one. When it came she entered, still feeling uneasy. When this bus came out of the park, a group of people were standing on the street. The fire department was there, and the bus she had left was burning.

This woman's second experience was also intuitive and equally sudden, though the event it concerned was very different and the circumstances such that compulsive action, as in the first case, was not possible. It occurred Thanksgiving Day, 1941. She was a guest that day at a lovely country place and surrounded by happy people. Nevertheless, around 11:30 in the morning, when conversation consisted of nothing more serious than chitchat about the Thanksgiving dinner, she suddenly knew that her mother, who lived in California, was in great distress. She tried not to disturb this party of fourteen people, and managed to finish dinner. By then her thoughts were perfectly clear. She knew her mother had passed away. She excused herself and went home.

Hanging on the door was the notice of a death message. Her mother had died about 9:30 in the morning, making the time of the daughter's reaction and the mother's death about the same. The mother was aged, but she had not been ill, and the daughter had had no reason to expect her death.

Visual hallucinations may also, though rarely, prove to be a characteristic form. A woman who now lives in Florida but who was working and rooming in Washington, D.C. in early December,

1944, came home from work one evening, very tired and quite late, and went at once to bed.

"As I lay there," she recalls, "my mother stood at the foot of my bed, her hair down to her waist as she used to wear it sometimes when I was very small. She stood there with tears running down her cheeks. How long she stayed I have no idea, but I finally went to sleep. The next morning I put it down as a dream, though I remembered it clearly."

The second experience followed immediately after and was almost identical to the first. The woman continues, "That afternoon about six P.M. I arrived home, went to my room and took a change of clothes to the bathroom, which was down the hall. I took my bath, got dressed and started to return to my room for my coat and purse.

"My mother was standing at my door. I could see her plainly. She looked the same as she had the night before, even the same clothes. Needless to say, I called my mother in Miami. She had received a telegram from the War Department that my brother in the Army overseas was missing in action. I asked her if she had been thinking of me and she said, 'No more than usual.'

"I have never had any similar experience before or since."

Two similar experiences, such as these paired ones, in each instance suggest a personality pattern. The form of the second is much the same as that of the first, and often the second resembles the first in other ways beside form. But not all persons fall into patterns like these. If they did, the fact that a personality stamps the experience in its own characteristic way would be more obvious than it is. In certain persons, the form of the later experience may be quite *unlike* the first. A woman in Michigan in March, 1944, was applying for a job, her mind quite absorbed in the process of filling out a questionnaire, when in a sudden intuition she knew, she says, "Something terrible had happened to someone in my family."

She suddenly just knew it and she could not shake the horrible feeling that overwhelmed her. Later in the day, she received a wire from Detroit saying that her younger sister had been struck by a car earlier in the day and was in critical condition in the hospital. She later learned that the accident occurred approximately at the time of her strange intuition, an intuition of which she says: "It was not a flash of light, but more like a message from somewhere." (Incidentally, her sister lived but was unable to walk again for months.)

That experience, a waking intuition occurring just at the time of a distant accident, was the only one this woman had for ten years. Then on March 4, 1954, she *dreamed* that her father was dead and lying in a coffin. She noticed how young he looked in spite of his 73 years and woke up in fright because the dream was so realistic. She was so bothered by it that she wrote her mother asking about him. But on March 7, before she could get a reply, she got a telegram saying that her father had slipped on the ice and was critically injured. He died a week later, and in his coffin looked exactly as he had in her dream.

With two experiences so different in every way, it might seem that this personality shows no pattern. However the observation that personalities leave a characteristic stamp will still hold if one supposes that here the personality, instead of imposing a rigid pattern, is *unrestrictive* and able to express ESP in different forms.

The idea that a personality pattern stamps an individual's experiences is strengthened when one examines the successive ones of those occasional individuals who report many. In instances like that of a woman from New York, the rather rigid channeling suggested in the first and second experience seems to be a feature of later ones, too. The first occurred just after she had graduated from high school and before she had secured her first job. She *dreamed* she was in a strange room among strangers where people were working with strange equipment. She saw the layout of the room so vividly that a few months later, when she walked into the laboratory at the Du Pont plant where she had gotten employment, she felt she had been there before, and then her dream came to mind. "It was the dream exactly, even though I had not known anyone who worked there, nor had I any description of the lab before I entered the room."

In her second:

"About three years later I *dreamed* of being in a large building, standing on the staircase talking with three other people, three men: my husband, my father-in-law and one other who was hazy. We were having a conversation and quite concerned over something. I awoke crying and told my husband his sister needed blood and he must give a transfusion. But I said it before I was fully awake.

"About a year afterward I was in a hospital standing on the staircase talking with my husband, father-in-law and brother-in-law about the very serious illness of my sister-in-law. We were standing in the positions I had 'seen.' My husband had been called to the hospital to give his sister a transfusion. She died a few days later."

And now the third:

"Thirteen months ago I *dreamed* of the death of our good neighbor and close friend, a young man thirty-four years old and father of four youngsters. In the dream I saw him lying in the coffin in the living room of his home. His children were running in and out and I asked his wife if I couldn't take them home with me.

"When I awoke I told my husband, because he knew of my other dreams and this one frightened me. He told me to try to forget it and not talk about it.

"Three weeks later the man was fatally stricken with a heart attack. I brought his four children over to stay with me.

"I have had other small unimportant dreams that later happened, sometimes a week later, sometimes months."

The rest of the experiences of this person follow closely this same pattern, each being likewise a precognitive and realistic dream.

Among the people who have many experiences, those of certain ones show a degree of variation. In these, although the personality stamp is harder to see, similarities can still be noted.

Another woman, from New Jersey, reports a long series of experiences. They were all alike in two aspects. All occurred when she was awake and all were precognitive. But strict similarity ends there. Some of her experiences, which began in childhood, were intuitions. In the first instance, she "just knew" she would get hurt on a coasting expedition. It ended with a broken leg. Some of her later experiences seem farther removed from the to-be-expected.

One time she saw a woman walking safely on the sidewalk. "She will be hit by a car," she says, "an inner feeling told me." A few blocks later the woman lay near the road, writhing in pain from a broken leg. She had been grazed by a passing car after she stepped off the sidewalk.

Some years later came a somewhat different form of experience. She says, "I was walking to work one morning when, to my utmost horror, I was stepping right into a room in a hospital. A figure lay on the bed, his head bandaged. I gazed at the face of my boyfriend. Then, as suddenly as it happened, I was again back on the sidewalk.

"A few blocks farther and I saw him alive and well and I laughed to myself about my ridiculous vision. The next day he was severely injured at his work and died soon after of multiple skull fractures."

The "picture vision" type of waking experience, however, did not become an exclusive pattern, for a few years later another of intuitive type occurred, of which she says: "One day my aunt called to me as I walked up the street. We chatted a moment and then the same inner voice told me I would never see her again alive. The next day she died of a heart attack."

The last experience to date is again one of the "picture" type which she describes by saying:

"A year ago in September" (written in 1955), "as I drove home one balmy evening I suddenly envisaged my car a wreck, an ambulance along the side of the road and myself being put on a stretcher which stood at an angle in the roadway.

"About four minutes later a car traveling at high speed and out of control struck mine head on. I was very severely injured. My car was demolished and the stretcher stood in exactly the angle in the road that I had envisaged it."

The successive experiences of a number of persons are like this woman's in that both similarities and dissimilarities appear. The personality stamp is there, but the personality appears to be, shall we say, somewhat flexible.

Then we come to a final group, small but definite, of persons whose many experiences do not fall into a recognizable pattern of similarity at all. They seem upon occasion to have utilized every form on the list. A typical example is a certain woman from Illinois who has reported so many cases over the years that there is space here for only a few examples, selected to show the more widely differing forms. We can begin with an apparently telepathic episode which came in hallucinatory form.

One night the woman's teen-age son went with some neighbor boys, as she says, "in their jalopy to look for Christmas fireworks at the country stores around about. I had retired and fallen asleep when I awakened by a loud report and a cry, 'Mother!'

"I arose and went through the house. My daughter was doing her school work and said there had been no sound. Then I knew the boys had met with an accident. After the first shock I felt they were all right and decided not to go looking for them. They returned shortly. They had had a blow-out and been thrown in the ditch but were unhurt. My son had been very frightened and thought, 'Mother,' as they went over."

This person's clairvoyant experiences come as waking impressions not spontaneously but by effort. For example, she says: "I felt so badly about my son's loss of a new fur-lined helmet that I gave it deep thought. I 'saw' it hanging on a *hook*. I saw a row of hooks rather high up. I thought, a school? The hooks are too high. I saw a vestibule and thought, a church? But we had asked at the church and no helmet had been found. But I sent my son back to look for a row of hooks high up in a vestibule where adults hang their wraps. The helmet was there."

She has other waking experiences, on the other hand, which are entirely spontaneous and intuitive. Of one of these she writes: "Shortly after February 17, 1944, my neighbor had been notified that a son, James, a soldier, was missing in action. She received no further word whatsoever but she knew he was missing in Italy. She wrote several places for information with no success.

"A few days after Memorial Day, 1945, I picked up a paper containing a news picture of services held in a cemetery near the Anzio Beachhead battleground, Fifth Army. I gazed intently at the picture of the hundreds of rows of crosses and began to cry. The certain sure feeling came to me: 'Jimmy is buried here.'

"Against my husband's wishes (because it was so preposterous) I wrote the Lt. Commander at the location mentioned, asking if he would try to find out if Jimmy could have been buried there.

"On July 10, 1945, I received a reply, a letter which I gave to the dead boy's mother—that he had made a search and James A. C. *was buried in this place,* and that snapshots of the cross bearing his name would follow." Further inquiry revealed the clerical errors through which the fact and place of this soldier's burial had never reached his relatives.

His grave had been discovered actually by a clairvoyant intuition.

And then come this woman's precognitive experiences. One of the simpler examples of these was a repeated dream which she called her "lovely dream." "I used to tell the children I'd had my lovely dream again. My heart's desire was a new piano, as hopeless as owning a yacht. The dream: a huge space in the air divided into rooms, each holding a wonderful piano. I ran from one to another, playing on each, so thrilled to play again after seventeen years. Then at last I saw a special one. This one must be mine. No other would do!"

(Those dreams were before 1948 and before the family moved to Illinois.)

"In Illinois, on October 15, 1948, my daughter was sent on a high-school project working on Saturdays at the Conservatory of Music. I went there to meet her after work. Here, seven hundred miles from where I had the dreams, is the huge space in the air, an entire second floor. There are nine studios for piano, voice, dancing—each with a piano. I tried them all. One I wanted *so* much. A spinet-type Wurlitzer. The owner of the school is buying one wholesale for me as a special favor."

This woman's list of experiences, as these examples illustrate, covers practically the entire range of forms and types of ESP. They show a personality pattern represented, not by any preferred form of experience, but one to which various forms apparently are equally easy or characteristic.

From all these observations one may gather that personalities vary —some are limited in their ways of expressing ESP, restricted by fixed and rigid bounds so that only one form is possible; others, more versatile and adaptable in this respect, use practically any kind. After all, each individual has his own unique physical characteristics, his own type of mind, his own special combination of general abilities and proclivities. Why should his ESP too, not be "personalized"?

But one must remember that ESP experiences are combination affairs. Besides the personality which expresses them, the nature of the event involved and the circumstances under which it occurs also have something to do with the result. A certain combination of his personality type with the event may be necessary for some persons. It well may be that for those persons who have but a single experience the required combination has happened only once. As for those at the opposite extreme who have many experiences, one may suppose that their life situations more easily supply the necessary combination of factors.

If these surmises are sound, then by carrying them still a little further, a tentative answer arises for the question, "What about those people who never have an ESP experience?" Perhaps the difference between them and those with only one experience is not a sharp and definite one. Perhaps for the former the combination of personality plus circumstance necessary for the expression of ESP is so rare that it never happens to be fulfilled. After all, an ability that is clearly present in certain members of the human race can hardly be entirely lacking in the rest. Each human being has certain innate abilities and potentialities. But which of these will be developed, which will not, varies with each life situation, as well as with the strength of the innate ability.

What is it in people that determines the kind of ESP experience they can have or whether they will have few, many, or none? This question has concerned experimenters ever since research on ESP began to be convincing. It is still unanswered, but not for lack of experimental attempts to answer it, to pin down a specific personality type and link it with the ability to use ESP. At first it looked like a fairly simple problem and a research plan to solve it could have been stated simply: separate those who do from those who do not give evidence of ESP and then give personality tests to each and find out what their differences are. The simplicity of this idea, unfortunately, was deceptive. In the experiments which have been carried out, most of the major ready-made psychological measures have been used repeatedly to see whether they would separate those with high ESP test scores from those who fail to score above chance expectation. The result has not been a neat separation, although some differences have been found.

One of the most pronounced of these differences, small though it is, is connected with the familiar psychological distinction of introversion and extroversion. In a very general way, and subject to too many qualifications to go into here, the more sociable extroverts scored somewhat higher than their more reserved and less expressive brothers, the introverts. The margin of difference, however, was small and was far from being so definite that one could safely predict the results if he gave an ESP test to two friends, one more extroverted than the other.

One criterion that distinguished somewhat between high- and low-scoring ESP subjects has been found, although it is not exactly a measure of personality. It is that of whether or not the subject "believes in ESP." In a series of experiments made by Dr. Gertrude Schmeidler of the City College of New York, those who believed in it got higher scores, on the average, than those who did not. The difference, however, was not great enough to make it safe to bet that this "believer" will make higher scores than that "disbeliever." And so the tests to date have not shown a specific type of personality which has ESP.

ESP tests given in conjunction with personality questionnaires, however, quite unexpectedly opened a new avenue of insight, even as they also made the problem more complicated. The unexpected complication was this: in all previous ESP research, individual subjects had occasionally been found who not only failed to give positive evidence of ESP, but who got *less than chance*. In other words, their scores were *negative*. If five correct was the chance expectancy, these, instead of averaging five or higher, averaged less than five. When something like this occurs consistently, it becomes meaningful, as any statistician knows. In this instance, it meant that ESP was at work to *avoid* making hits. The laws of chance produce *chance* results, neither more nor less.

When the subjects were separated on the basis of extroversion versus introversion, it turned out that many of the introvert subjects had not even scored at the chance level, but consistently below it. In other words, as a group they "went negative," missing the target so often that they could only have done so by ESP. It was realized then that ESP differences between groups that score like these do not mean that the positively scoring group does, the negatively scoring one does not, have ESP. Instead, it seems that the two kinds of personalities tend to have different ways of directing their ESP. Those of one group are to some small extent able to direct it as they wish and hit the targets and produce positive scores; the others, in reverse, tend unconsciously to direct it to miss the targets, and negative scores result.

The research on the topic is still at this stage. The separation of subjects on the basis of personality differences may give some indication of whether the individual will hit or miss, but it does not necessarily show *how much* ESP he may have or that one does, one does not have psi ability. If psi is something that everyone has, however, this is just the result that should be expected. Certain personality traits should tend to favor its expression, while others should discourage it, or throw it into reverse. It could be that other measures of personality than those used so far might show other relations, as for instance why the forms of expression differ, some people having intuitions, others dreams, etc. After all, the measures of personality used so far were devised by psychologists for quite other purposes than for making discriminations in connection with ESP. They were shoes made for other feet, not for the still unmeasured ones of ESP. That job of measuring is still ahead.

Until the measuring has proceeded beyond its present stage, it appears that the answer to the question we have been asking so long—"Who has ESP?"—can only be a tentative one. It could be—"Potentially everybody." But that answer is still unproven, naturally. It can only await the confirmation or rejection the future may bring, the future when the tangled skein of factors that operate in each personality has been unravelled, and especially when those in the unconscious have been further disentangled.

11

Can a Precognized Danger be Avoided?

Once one recognizes that under certain conditions the future can be known beforehand, a question comes immediately to mind. Can foreseen danger be avoided? The answer is especially important to anyone who has an experience that could be a preview of a coming catastrophe. If the impression is a genuine instance of precognition, must the calamity occur no matter what he does? People and circumstances differ and it is only by considering a large number of cases that one can get any idea of what really happens.

Some people may not do anything to prevent the catastrophe. They may forget the warning, as did a man in Maine. He had a fourteen-year-old son, Walter, who was spending the summer with a friend living about a mile from the father's store. Walter was a good swimmer and often went swimming in the stream with other neighborhood boys.

One night the father had a dream. He thought Walter had gone in swimming below a certain big tree above the dam and had been drowned. He dreamed that when he got there the body had not been found but that John McC——was diving for it.

He awoke in great fright, crying and scarcely able to control himself. His wife tried to calm him, saying that dreams do not come true but that just to be safe, he should tell Walter, when he came in next day, not to go swimming.

The next morning the father went to his store and was busy and preoccupied there when Walter hurried in and said he was going swimming. At the moment the father did not think of the dream.

Soon after someone came running and called, "Come quickly! Walter was diving and hasn't come up."

Then the dream came back with full force. He hastened to the swimming hole; the body had not been found but John McC— was diving for it. It was at exactly the same place as the dream, with exactly the same circumstances. The father's torturing afterthought was, "If I had heeded the dream, Walter would be alive today."

In other cases, efforts to avoid the danger are inadequate, as in the case of a woman in New Jersey. On a July evening in 1952, she was relaxing in a darkened room, while waiting for her husband, who worked the early night shift, to come home. As she sat there, almost asleep, not quite awake, she had a "vision." She thought there had been an awful accident. A child had been killed and was lying covered on the ground. She could not tell if it was girl or boy, but by the size of the body she thought it was a child about five or six years old. Entirely covered as it was, she could have no idea who it was.

She could not forget the experience. In the morning she told it to her next-door neighbor and urged her to keep an eye on her five-year-old child.

Then she called a son who lived in the heart of town. She told him to watch his two small children. She had another son, who lived in the country, but she did not call him because his yard was fenced in. His little girl, Kathy, seemed safe. But that day Kathy was playing in the driveway when a township truck backed into it and killed her.

If one judged only by experiences like those two, he would no doubt decide that it does no good to try to avoid a foreseen catastrophe. "What will be, will be," and no attempt to avert the coming event can succeed: a truly fatalistic attitude. Fatalism is defined in the dictionary as the view that all events are "necessitated by the nature of things, or by the fixed and inevitable decree of the arbiters of destiny." The fatalistic view is one that has been widely held in certain times and places. The idea that "it was meant to be that way" has seemed to some religious groups the answer to the question of avoiding "destiny."

This view would be justified if all the experiences on record turned out as did the ones above. Fortunately, not all do. When one surveys the wider scene, it is not nearly so austere and forbidding. Religious and philosophical theories are concerned with the question of whether the universe is fixed and immutable. The answer we seek here, however, has to do only with what actually occurs: with whether or not foreseen dangers are ever avoided. Since they sometimes are, let us turn first to such cases.

FORESEEN CALAMITIES PREVENTED

The idea that an event could be foreseen, and then not occur, seems like a contradiction in terms. Life situations are no simple one-item events but are made up of a combination of items. What really happens is that part of a complex foreseen event does not occur. Some kind of action prevents it. There may be various reasons for the action. Sometimes the action is almost intuitive and made without deliberation or recognition that the impression that led to it was a true one.

In Washington State a young woman was so upset by a terrifying dream one night that she had to wake her husband and tell him about it. She had dreamed that a large ornamental chandelier which hung over their baby's bed in the next room had fallen into the crib and crushed the baby to death. In the dream she could see herself and her husband standing amid the wreckage. The clock on the baby's dresser said 4:35. In the distance she could hear the rain on the windowpane and the wind blowing outside.

But her husband just laughed at her. He said it was a silly dream, to forget it and go back to sleep; and in a matter of moments he did just that himself. But she could not sleep.

Finally, still frightened, she got out of bed and went to the baby's room, got her and brought her back. On the way she stopped to look out the window, and saw a full moon, the weather calm and quite unlike the dream. Then, though feeling a little foolish, she got back into bed with the baby.

About two hours later they were wakened by a resounding crash.

She jumped up, followed by her husband, and ran to the nursery. There, where the baby would have been lying, was the chandelier in the crib. They looked at each other and then at the clock. It stood at 4:35. Still a little skeptical they listened—to the sound of rain on the windowpane and wind howling outside.

In other situations, the possible truth of the impression is recognized, and the action taken consequently is quite deliberate. A woman in Maryland dreamed that her little son, just a toddler, followed two small Boy Scouts, whose faces she saw clearly in her dream, to the creek bank nearby. In the dream her child fell into the creek and was drowned. The next morning the very Scouts about whom she had dreamed, and whom she did not know and never had seen before, were seated on the curb of her front lawn. What did she do? Her solution was very simple. She says, "My son did not get out of the house that day."

Occasionally a person who has had the impression of danger ahead believes it with such conviction that he takes preventive action almost compulsively.

During World War I the husband of a woman in California was chief engineer for a steamship company. He had been out to sea for about three months one time, when she was notified to go to Philadelphia to meet him. She left, and as she recalls, "—on my arrival at Philadelphia I called the company. They notified me he would be at Pier 101 the next morning at four o'clock. I had a bath and shampooed my hair and went to bed at about nine-thirty P.M. I dreamed that the ship came in, unloaded, and reloaded without my knowing and sailed for parts in India; and about thirty hours from India what they called a 'tin fish' hit the ship and sank her, and my husband was the only casualty aboard. When I awoke it was three-forty A.M. I tied my head up and had my clothes on in five minutes. In the meantime, I had called the desk clerk to get me a taxi. He took me to Pier 101 and they were finishing tying up. I handed the taxi a ten-dollar bill, ordered him to wait, ran by the guard at the gate and up on the ship, hysterical and crying, and the guard chasing me. My husband was on deck and I ran into his arms saying, 'Don't go, don't go, the ship is going down.'

"When I was so very determined that he was to get off, he asked permission to be off. The company granted it. The ship sailed and her destination was India. She was torpedoed and sank. All the men aboard were on a raft for sixteen days, floating around before they were picked up.

"When my husband went into the office here three weeks later they told him about the incident."

In these various cases, different kinds of countermeasures were successful in avoiding a foreseen calamity, despite the ever-present difficulty of rcognizing the ESP impression. In each instance, the action taken was *appropriate to the situation,* and thereby the danger was avoided, even though the rest of the event occurred just as precognized.

Attempts to stave off calamity, however, are often futile. The reasons for failure can be as revealing as the reasons for success.

FORESEEN DANGERS, NOT AVOIDED

It would be saying the obvious to observe that efforts to avert a foreseen event fail because the measures taken are not adequate. One must find the reason why they are inadequate.

The most frequent reason of all is simply that the ESP impression was incomplete; the information received was insufficient to guide the person to the proper action. The grandmother who could not save her grandchild from being struck down by a truck failed because she did not know which child was involved, or where the accident would occur. The lack of knowledge *where* often makes all the difference between a successful and an unsuccessful interventionary act.

One morning the ten-year-old son of a woman in Utah said, as she was getting him and her two other children ready for school, "Oh, Mom, I had a terrible dream last night. A car ran me down. It was so awful."

As she says, "My first thought was to keep him home. I realized I had to be calm, although my heart was racing with fear. I said that we could not live by dreams or we live a life of horror.

"When they left I uttered a silent prayer and said to stay on the sidewalk, which they did, as they were very obedient children. Some three minutes later someone came running to me. A truck had run up on the sidewalk and struck him down. He died seventy minutes later, never regaining consciousness."

Occasionally the *time* element is the missing item.

A woman in New York State dreamed she saw her four-and-a-half-year-old son bloody, having been bitten by a dog which she also visualized.

Worried by the dream, for the next three days she kept the child indoors. On the fourth he ran out to the store next door. As she says, "Before I could get to the store I heard piercing screams.

"I found he had run into the store, bumped into a dog with a sore tail. The dog whirled and bit my son in the eye. The injury was a slit just under the eye. I thought he was blinded and fainted.

"It was the same dog I dreamed bit him."

Some of the attempts to avert a situation fail because of carelessness or forgetfulness. In a western state after a cyclone had destroyed some buildings belonging to a certain company, all hands were called to help rebuild. One of the men, not a carpenter, was nevertheless helping with the carpentry. He recalls: "Early one morning about two weeks after I started, I went up the ladder to the third elevation of staging and as I stepped onto the staging boards there came into my mind a clear picture which puzzled me several minutes. Every detail was so clear that I was completely dumbfounded. It seemed as if I had stood at that exact spot before. Even the design of the wall and the pattern of the paneling was an exact duplication. I was puzzled for several minutes, for I had never been up there before nor had I ever done that kind of work before. Finally, it made sense. Some months before I had dreamed it. Naturally I remembered the dream in detail from there on and in the dream I fell, was hurt and taken to the hospital in an ambulance. I immediately went back down the ladder to the floor below, found the foreman and told him I didn't feel like working up there so he gave me a job trimming around a large sliding door in one end of the building.

"From here on I will relate what happened, for it was like following a written script. About eleven o'clock, having forgotten about my dream, I went up to the first-floor staging to nail in some blocks. As I crossed the staging, a plank suddenly snapped into three pieces and I fell about seven feet, landing backwards over the concrete sill just below. The blow on the small of the back temporarily paralyzed me from the hips down. I was placed on a sheet of Celotex until the ambulance arrived. I was in the hospital fifteen days—"

The most common reason for failure, next to insufficient information or forgetting, is that the person does not have complete control of the situation and therefore, in spite of his efforts, the proper action is not taken. One reason for lack of control arises when a second person's cooperation would be necessary, and that person does not give it.

A Reverend D—— from Australia writes,

"My father had a friend named T—— with whom he often went shooting. One year they planned to go hunting on Good Friday. Both my mother and Mrs. T disliked the arrangement, feeling that it was quite out of keeping with that sacred day. However, both men were adamant and refused to change the day.

"At seven-thirty A.M., when Mr. T should have arrived at our home, he did not appear, so my brother was sent to make inquiries. On arriving at the T home he found Mrs. T pleading with her husband not to go. On the previous night she had had a dream in which she saw, as she stood at her front door, a cart being drawn by a white horse passing on its way to the hospital. In that cart was her husband.

"Mr. T, on seeing my brother, ignored her pleading and they left on the excursion. At noon they stopped near a stream of water. When Mr. T had eaten his sandwiches, he leaned forward to dip his lips in the water. As he did so, he pushed his gun and the trigger struck a stone and the gun exploded. He jumped back exclaiming, 'Oh, I'm shot!' My father laid him gently on his back, and went at once to get help. He found a man nearby with a horse, a white horse and cart. They lifted the injured man into the cart, and drove toward town. Nearing the outskirts, my father advised the driver to be careful and not to go up the street that passed the T house. He, however, missed the way and instead drove up that very street. As he neared the T home, Mrs. T was standing at the door. Seeing the cart, she collapsed. Mr. T died in the hospital that night."

Many precognitive experiences concern complicated situations involving people and events which the subject could scarcely expect to control. This is particularly true when the event is of public, rather than purely personal, concern.

A woman in New York awoke one morning very depressed because of a bad dream. "I had clearly seen a plane crash at the shore of a lake and the roof of the third cottage on that dirt track in flames as a result. There was only one man and he burned up. I tried to write two overdue letters that morning, but I found myself telling my correspondents about it and also the fact that the fire engine would go in by the canal and be unable to get to the plane until it was too late. It was so clear that I was conscious of every plane that went over that day. Late in the afternoon I was at the electric range stirring something for dinner when I said, 'That's the plane—the one that's going to crash! Robert, stop the firemen before they try the canal; they have to take the Basin road and they don't know it.'

"My husband went outdoors to listen, put his head in to say, 'That plane's all right,' only to have me shriek, 'It is *not!*' Within seconds the plane crashed, the firemen took the canal instead of the Basin road, the pilot was burned to a crisp, the cottage was only slightly damaged . . . and I was a wreck for weeks wondering how I could have prevented it."

Still farther beyond the power of human intervention, of course, are the elements. But although a natural cataclysm may happen regardless of the wishes of the human beings concerned, a person still can act to protect himself—to some extent—from its effect.

A man in Georgia had bought a building for an automobile showroom, putting in a large plate-glass window and hanging a large electric sign in front. One night his wife dreamed a tornado came and blew the sign down, swinging it into the window, shattering that. She also dreamed, she says, "an older woman was hurt and I was giving her ammonia. The next morning I told my husband of the dream.

"He said, 'I don't have any tornado insurance or any insurance on that plate glass. I will get some,' and he did that very day." Then, she says, "Not long after a tornado came and blew the sign into the window just as I dreamed. A lady who ran a little candy and popcorn business next to us was knocked unconscious by the flying glass. I hastily got some ammonia and gave her some."

All these people failed to prevent the foreseen event from occurring. But in some of the situations preventive action was less possible than in others: the woman had less chance of averting the plane crash than the man of avoiding his own injury on the scaffolding; the cyclone could not be prevented; all the man in Georgia could do was take out insurance. Though some dangers can be avoided, one glimpses a limit of preventability in the background.

The old question of free will, however, never involved the will to affect such rock-ribbed elements of the universe as death or the weather, the climate, earthquakes, floods or the celestial bodies. Man has not aspired to change the stars in their courses. But he has wanted to feel that he was free to say yes or no about his own course of conduct. In these previously mentioned reactions to precognized events, we see him doing so—within limits.

VARIATIONS ON THE THEME

ESP impressions of danger to come may not be such that one can consider them instances of precognition. The need to avoid the danger is the same, but the theoretical aspect is different. For one instance, it may be impossible to tell whether a future situation or one already in existence is the cause of the experience. If the latter, it would be a case of clairvoyance, rather than of precognition. For example, a circus clown once had an impression of danger which he felt would occur the next day. However, a defect in the structure of the apparatus could already have been in existence and it, rather than the next day's accident, could have been the basis of his hunch.

"One of the circus numbers is known as the 'Aerial Ladders'" he says. "In this number, twelve girls climb up to individual ladders and to the music of the band are swung back and forth by the clowns. The ladders are swung as high as possible, during which the girls do acrobatic work on them. These ladders are hung on steel rings from the 'quarter-poles' in the tent.

"On the night of April 20, 1955, while we were going through the act, and I was swinging a young girl, Nina, suddenly I saw in a flash a mental picture of her ladder breaking loose from the poles and I *felt* that there would be an accident to my ladder the *next* day. It was a strong mental picture.

"Not wanting to appear foolish or to be laughed at, I said nothing about my warning, but I did not forget it and when on the following day at the matinee Nina climbed up to her ladder, I kept a sharp watch for trouble.

"Sure enough, I had hardly swung her back and forth a minute when a loud crack from above the pole was heard by all who were near. One of the supporting rings gave way, and the next instant the ladder swung crazily on one rope back toward me.

"Being forewarned, I was enabled to pull hard on the net that is used to swing the ladder and I kept the girl clear of the pole in the rear until the momentum had died down a little, otherwise she would have struck this rear pole violently and been either killed or seriously injured. She was helped down and, with the exception of a few bruised ribs, was unharmed.

"But—I feel sure, for whatever reason this warning was given me, it did save this girl from serious injury."

A common kind of ESP experience concerns a future illness or the threat of one. It is usually not possible to know what concealed symptoms may already have been existing, and so in such cases, also, one cannot say that the experience was precognitive. It can only be accounted as an instance of indeterminate or general ESP (GESP). Sometimes, too, such experiences may have to do with the threat or diagnosis of illness, rather than with the illness itself, and as such are not averted, although they may be taken as warnings, and the illness prevented or prepared for.

A family living in a remote area of Australia included three girls and a pair of twin boys, aged two and a half years.

The father says: "I worked from two o'clock in the afternoon until twelve midnight, sometimes an extra hour until one A.M. One night I found my wife sitting up with one of the twins in her lap, rocking him. He had a slight fever. We agreed that it was a touch of malaria. Malaria was not uncommon there and we were always prepared to treat it, usually with success without having to call a doctor. (The nearest one was twenty miles away.) I was satisfied and went to bed and to sleep.

"About daybreak or a little before I had a dream that our family physician came in and examined the boy and said he had diphtheria. I awoke, startled, and tiptoed into the room where my son and his mother were. She was still awake, he was sleeping peacefully, breathing naturally, and his temperature was normal. I went back to my room, but not to sleep. The memory of the dream kept nagging me.

I 'reasoned' with myself that isolated as we were with no contacts between my children and other children, with no case of diphtheria anywhere within many miles reported, it was foolish for me to be disturbed because of the dream.

"After a while I could stand it no longer, but still I did not want to confess the reason for my concern to my wife. I went back to the room and asked my wife if the boy had indicated any pain in his throat. No. He had said he didn't hurt anywhere. Still I wanted to look at his throat. She took him up and, shining a Delco light down his throat, we made a thorough examination and found a tiny white spot about the size of a small pinhead. I phoned the doctor and I asked him if it was possible, in view of our isolation, that the boy might have diphtheria. He said that it sometimes happened that a case would show up apparently from nowhere, and that since it was a long drive and the tiny spot on one side of the throat was ground for suspicion, he would bring along enough antitoxin for all five of the children.

"It was about three hours after the spot was discovered before the doctor arrived. By that time the boy had fever again and the white spot had become a white patch and was on both sides. The doctor was satisfied it was diphtheria—took a smear and injected the antitoxin into all five of the children. The boy was critically ill for two or three days. The other boy and one of the girls had very mild cases, the two others suffered only the customary reaction from the antitoxin. The doctor told me that a few hours later would have been too late for the treatment to have saved his life."

Then again, a precognized scene may not actually portray a disaster, but be closely associated with a possible one. It may, in fact, prevent a catastrophe by calling attention to the danger of one. Some twenty-five years ago, a girl, a young instructor at a normal school, had just learned to drive her first car, an old Model T sedan. A day's outing at a lake eighty miles distant was planned. Several cars were going and this young lady was asked to take four passengers. Although rather nervous about taking that much responsibility, she consented and it was decided she would follow her friend Anne, who knew the way. The night before the picnic the girl awoke from a frightening dream. She thought she had been following Anne's car on a country road which became rougher by the minute. Suddenly the road began descending into a gulley, the descent became steeper and at the foot of the hill she could see a right-angle turn, but directly in front was a wall of rock. In the dream she seemed to smell something burning. The brakes would not hold. Then she awoke.

Before she could eat breakfast the next morning, she told her dream to the others and in spite of their laughter she said that she could not eat until she found out what to do in such a situation. She went to a neighbor's and he told her that if the brakes burned out one should throw the car in reverse.

On the trip all went well for an hour or so, she following Anne's car as agreed. At one point, Anne signaled that she would make a turn, and after that the road became rougher but they went on until there was no longer any possibility of turning back; they were descending a steep hill with a wall of rock at the foot of it and a right-angle turn. All at once, there was the smell of rubber burning and the brakes gave way. After a second's hesitation, she threw the car in reverse and they made the dreaded turn at the foot of the hill in safety.

It turned out that Anne had made the wrong turn and found herself on an old abandoned road. Because of the dream and the precaution it led to, a probable wreck was avoided.

A person who recognizes the setting of a precognized impression—even if it is not an undesirable occurrence—may try to see if he can keep it from coming true, just to test the possibility. Sometimes it seems the "dream wins."

A truck driver's helper for a Sears Roebuck store had the duty every morning of assisting the driver to load up the day's deliveries. But, as he explains, "that driver always managed to arrive when I was about half-finished loading. On a summer morning in 1945 my boss, as usual, came around distributing the day's delivery, and instantly reminded me of a dream I had the night before. In it I had just finished loading the truck. Though it was only half full, that was all for the day. On the right was a water heater in a wooden crate. The driver hadn't arrived yet. Then one of the other helpers happened to stop a moment at my truck. Knowing I couldn't drive, he joked in his Cajun accent that I would have to take the truck out alone, since the driver wasn't in.

"Out of curiosity I went through the receipts to see if there was a water heater scheduled to go. Yes, one of them was on today's agenda. Glancing over at my bin, I was relieved to see that the heater there was not in a crate. However, when it came time to place it on the truck I learned the numbers did not correspond; this was not mine. My ticket matched that attached to one in another bin. Of the four that were to go out that day, this was the only one in a crate. To perhaps break the spell, or whatever it was, I loaded it on the left- instead of the right-hand side of the truck. Soon the last article was placed in the truck, and the driver still wasn't around. It occurred to me then that I had fooled myself in thinking the dream had been jinxed by placing the heater where I did. After all, the left-hand side from outside the truck was the right-hand side from the inside. Suddenly, in Louisiana bayou French tones a voice spoke —it was the same I had heard in my dream all right—'Well, Vic, looks like you'll have to take the truck out alone; the driver isn't in!' "

Summing up, what do these attempts to avoid a coming event tell us? Clearly, any ESP experience, precognitive or otherwise, that alerts a person to danger can be used like a warning from any other source; and if proper preventive measures are taken, they succeed. The difficulty is that often the ESP impression is not sufficiently clear and complete to be the basis for intelligent countermeasures; in such cases, if measures are taken, they well may be inadequate. A second difficulty is that of control. Even if the message is explicit, the person may be unable to exercise sufficient control over the situation. And on this fact the idea of inevitability hinges. If the situation has a wider horizon than a person's own, his efforts may be futile, although just how wide is too wide depends on the individual case.

The theoretical aspect of events foreseen and avoided is very complicated. Even if one considers only cases which seem definitely precognitive, one cannot say for sure that an event *would otherwise have occurred* but was prevented by human will. Perhaps it would not have occurred anyway. Perhaps the setting, the framework of circumstances which did develop, was foreseen by precognition, but the part averted had a different origin. For instance, perhaps the baby would not have been killed by the falling chandelier if it had remained in the crib. Perhaps the child would not have been drowned if he had followed the Scouts. Perhaps the part of the dream that showed a tragic end in each of these events was an imaginative elaboration of foreseen settings. This is theoretically possible, even though the experiences do not give the appearance of being made up of two kinds of mental components.

Whether or not this alternative or any other exists to the idea that events need not occur even if genuinely precognized, one cannot tell. The baby *was* taken out of the crib. The child *was* prevented from getting to the river. And so no evidence remains to show what would have happened without these interventions, and no final evidence can be adduced to say that the prevented event was genuinely precognized.

In 1939 a woman in Detroit had a dream about her brother who lived in East Orange, New Jersey. She dreamed he took a trip to the mountains and that his car turned over, pinning him underneath. The dream was so vivid she placed a call to him at 5:00 A.M.

He answered, and as he did not sound as if just awakened from sleep, she wondered why he had been up so early. He said that he and his wife were going to take a trip up the Jersey Turnpike. She told her dream and he canceled his trip.

Now, what does such a case show? The dream saved a possible wreck, of course, but no evidence remained to show whether it was anything but "just a bad dream." The only detail that could be checked was that a trip had been contemplated. The fact that the trip and the dream occurred so nearly at the same time may have been only a coincidence due to chance.

The case represents the seemingly inherent difficulty which at present prevents experiments from being carried out to test whether precognized items can be averted. Just as a point cannot be proven in law if the evidence is destroyed, so precognition cannot be proven to have occurred if the item precognized is interfered with or destroyed. Formal precognition tests are usually made by having subjects write down the order which they think the cards of a pack will be in later after they have been re-arranged in completely random order. The record of that random order then is the target, and to show precognition the subject's list of calls must check with it to an extent significantly beyond chance. To try to "avert" the hits so made, the target list would have to be interfered with. If it were, one could not tell if the subject's calls had been correct or not. In other words, no one could tell if the predictions showed precognition or were just guesses. Up until the present, no way has been thought of to avoid this impasse in the framing of a suitable experiment to test this question.

However, until experimental tests can be made, the suggestions given by actual experiences are all the more interesting. They cannot give final proof, but they give the best hints presently available.

Those hints do not suggest a fixed and immutable future; at least, not on the practical level. While the universe is firm and not subject to change by human will, the little doings of men glimmer and shift against this stable background and in some manner still as inexplicable as it seems contradictory, his tiny will seems upon occasion to be able to defend him and his own against dangers still hidden in the future.

If the precognitive ability is developed and directed, as in time it is reasonable to expect it will be, its operation, even on a limited basis, could obviously be of untold value to humanity—particularly if with greater understanding of the processes of ESP a way is found to bring it into better focus, so to speak. From present indications, if imperfect ESP impressions, especially those suggesting danger ahead, could be clarified, intelligent preventive action could follow to the untold advantage of mankind.

12

The Problem of Control

People who have had ESP experiences often remark on the fact that they cannot have them at will; they cannot "produce" them, but only take them when they come. One could say that most of the people involved in the cases already given were more or less surprised by their experiences. Whether the message was something they needed and wanted to know, or only a casual one, it seemed to just happen to come and was not the result of an intention to get the information in that way.

In some instances, a person may have had an ESP experience which brought knowledge about some event that did not concern him directly; then he might have no warning when a great personal crisis was looming ahead. Such a person is almost certain to ask, "Why? If I could know that other event, why didn't I know of this, which concerned me so much more deeply?"

For example, take the case of a woman in Minnesota who had several ESP experiences on topics which were not of immediate personal significance. One of them occurred at 2 A.M. and although it was a dream, it was so real, she says, "I shook with dread. I got up, went downstairs to examine my father's old desk beside the stairs. Yes, it was just a desk, but my vision had turned one side of it into a small telephone switchboard and I had been frantically trying to arouse families in the northern part of our state to go to the aid of a poor farm family whose house was in flames. At first I had seen the smoke, and as I watched, the flames came shooting out the windows. The family was trapped. A man jumped out of the second-floor window, breaking his leg and trying to crawl away over the snow to get help in twenty-degree below zero weather. No one would answer my phone calls and I was powerless to help them.

"A few days later the newspaper carried the story. The family had burned to death before help came, and the man in the snow died of burns and exposure."

After giving this example, she asks, *"Why didn't I have a premonition* of what was to happen two years ago when my husband kissed me good-bye and went out and took his own life?"

If ESP were a conscious process like seeing or hearing, then presumably one could govern it and use it when needed, reaping the untold advantages such use would bring. We know, however, that it originates in the deep unconscious, and the information only gets into consciousness if it escapes or overcomes many hazards of which the person is not consciously aware. Because of lack of control over this unconscious process, ESP has never proven to be a reliable way of knowing.

The desire to know about events beyond the range of the senses has doubtless always existed. Such practices as fortune telling, mediumship, prophecy and divination have developed because of it, and with them, their techniques—from the use of crystal balls and playing cards to forked twigs and tea leaves. Though these attempts to *practice ESP* are age-old, and in spite of any local success such attempts may have had or seemed to have, no general reliability of results has developed. In practices such as medicine, engineering, even agriculture, comparatively sure and reliable methods of procedures have been worked out, but not thus far in any area which depends on elusive, spontaneous psi. The situation has always been rather as if a complicated machine were operated by a person with no understanding of machinery. By pushing this lever and pulling that, he might sometimes have limited success, but he is not likely to gain complete control without understanding the principles involved.

Of course, many ESP experiences—as the reader may already have noted—do serve a purpose: the person is able to take advantage of ESP information when it comes. It is like the light of a lightning flash to the wanderer in the dark. For instance, a woman from Oklahoma found that her experience helped her surmount a period of great anxiety. She was expecting a baby in January, 1952. On the night of October 30, 1951, she dreamed, she says, "I was standing outside a nursery window with my husband, parents and some friends, and we were looking inside an incubator at a very tiny, three-pound premature baby girl. She was ours, and although so very tiny she was very bright-eyed and active and perfectly formed, and we were all of the opinion that such a lively baby would come through all right in spite of being premature and so tiny. In my dream the baby had lots of long black hair, very large bright eyes, a tiny red button of a nose and the tiniest mouth I had ever seen. Her unusually small head had lots of long black hair (to her shoulders) and perfect finger and toenails on fingers and toes no bigger than match stems. A baby perfectly formed in miniature. She was waving her arms and kicking her feet as any normal active baby does and even turned over.

"The next morning I told my husband and my parents and another relative who was visiting us at that time. It was such a vivid dream and I shall never forget watching that tiny baby and noticing all the small details about her as only a mother would.

"My family and friends dismissed it as one of the many odd dreams which pregnant women are supposed to have. However, just sixteen days later, they were all truly standing at that nursery window looking into an incubator at our tiny two-pound, fifteen-ounce baby girl. A baby perfectly formed in miniature, and in life the exact duplicate of my dream with only one slight exception. Although she was quite active, as in my dream, it was some time before she was strong enough to turn over.

"Had I not told anyone of my dream before, I'm sure they would have found it difficult to believe after the baby's birth. Also, as in my dream, I heard so many make the remark that such a bright, normal-acting and lively baby would come through just fine. And she has. In a short time she was a fat roly-poly normal baby. I'm sure my dream helped me over those first anxious days after her birth."

Occasionally, a person who has had many ESP experiences comes to think of them as almost a habit, and seems to be able to make fairly reliable use of them. Even if there should be a tendency to forget the failures and to remember only the successes, still the impression these people have of success may well be taken with some seriousness. Not everyone even *thinks* he has used ESP.

A woman in Massachusetts writes that on numerous occasions she and her husband each had "known" the thought of the other: "We live twenty-five miles from the city and my husband often commutes by train. It costs a quarter to make a phone call to tell me which train to meet. He is in the habit of taking the six o'clock but on occasions can make the five-thirty.

"So I said to him one day, 'Just thought-wave to me and I'll pick it up and meet you.' We've been doing it for many months now and his pleased smile when he sees me there meeting the early one is reward enough, to say nothing of the fact that we save many phone calls.

"There is no pattern to the times he takes one train or the other. He rarely comes on the early one. However, it is very seldom I have missed when he sends the message. The few times I did were when I was very tired or when my mind was engrossed with other people. Still, on occasion I have broken away from someone and told them I had to go as my husband was coming on the early train.

"The only other times when I miss are those when I try to apply logic, disregarding the sense which is more infallible than the logic. For instance, the other evening it was pouring, really coming down in torrents. I was sitting on the couch when suddenly I was told to meet the five-thirty. I almost started to obey. Then I said to myself, on such a night as this he wouldn't come early without phoning first because he could be drenched. Also, he said this morning he has too many appointments to be able to get the early train. So I sat down again, putting my coat aside to wait for the six o'clock. Then he phoned from the station to say why didn't I meet him, for he thought-waved like mad. So I learn to obey without question, not trying to use logic, *for logic has nothing to do with it.*"

It is clear, however, that the value of ESP as an instrument or tool for getting needed information would be immeasurably greater if it could be made into a more controllable ability. If a way could be found to use it at will, the practical benefits would be enormous, and research on it would be much more easily and quickly successful. For this reason, one of the main objectives of present-day parapsychological research is to find a way to "control" ESP, to decrease the hazards it runs in getting into consciousness.

Certain kinds of ESP experiences give encouraging hints for this research. Though people cannot now produce ESP at will, occasional spontaneous experiences are such as to suggest that a connection, however imperfect, may exist between the conscious need or desire to know and an ESP experience. These experiences appear to indicate that the unconscious may not be entirely beyond the reach of conscious purpose. Take, for instance, the case of a man in a western state, now a responsible businessman. When a very young man he had gotten himself into prison for a year. He was an only child, and he knew his widowed mother had taken it very seriously. Three months after his term began, she died, and he was notified of her death by his uncle.

As his relatives lived several states away from the place of his confinement, he could only have gone to her funeral attended by a guard and after legal approval from each state. With his return so impracticable, he spent the most miserable time of his life alone in his cell, feeling that he had in a way caused his mother's death, and knowing he could not even attend her funeral.

Exhausted, at last, he fell asleep, and *dreamed* he went home to his dead mother. In the dream, he saw her at his uncle's home, and not her own, where he had every reason to expect the funeral to be held. He saw her in a light gray casket, in a cream-colored crepe dress with her mother sitting weeping by the casket.

A few days later a letter from his uncle came describing the burial. The detail, including the fact that the body lay at his uncle's home, was just as in the dream. He felt that somehow he had gone to his mother, in spite of physical barriers. It was as if his intense need had been answered in some unconscious way and an ESP experience had resulted.

The effect of strong need in producing an ESP experience sometimes seems also to be shown when the need is another person's, rather than that of the individual himself. A secretary to a Florida state senator had among her duties the making out of the weekly paychecks for the office help. Among these people was the old Negro janitor, who was also the minister of his church. His check was regularly made out and delivered every Saturday noon.

She says: "Over a period of three years I have never once paid him except at that particular time. Two weeks ago I was working at my desk on Friday morning when I suddenly went to the safe, took out the checkbook, wrote Jack's check and took it to the Senator to sign. He did not question me, as all bookwork is in my hands, and I frankly did not realize what I had done until I found myself back in my office with the signed check in my hands.

"Then I realized that it was Friday and that I had done a thing that I had never done before. I opened my desk and put the check away. An hour later Jack walked into the office. He said, 'I hate to bother you, and I never have before, but I want to ask if you could please get me my check today.' I opened the desk and handed him a signed check. He stood very still. 'Did you hear me? Did you hear me this morning?' he asked. 'Hear you?' I questioned. 'Yes, M'am. I have to go to my church conference in Winter Park tomorrow at four A.M., and neither my wife nor I had the money for me to go, so at breakfast she asked what I was going to do and I told her we would ask God to let Miss G get the check for us today instead of tomorrow. We folded our hands and prayed, and that is what I asked for. I guess you must know how I felt when you opened that desk and took out the signed check.' "

In that particular instance, need had been expressed in the definite form of a prayer. But the need of another—particularly if it is a very strong and real one—is apparently sometimes effective, even though it takes some other form. An English woman who regularly went to work in the same office as her husband, stayed at home one morning, slightly indisposed with a cold; however, she became violently ill in a few hours with the onset of pneumonia, one symptom of which was an unquenchable thirst. As she had no telephone, and knew that her husband would not return until night, she began to concentrate for help on her mother, who lived nearby. Though her mother too would have every reason to think her well and at work, they had had telepathic experiences before and she felt that possibly in her "dire distress," she could reach her. Within half an hour her mother came—bringing two lemons with her. She admitted she did not know why she had brought them or even why she came, for as she said, "By rights, you should be at work."

The impression that ESP does sometimes respond, however imperfectly, to strong need or motive has been suggested not only by spontaneous experiences like these, but also in laboratory tests. In fact, one of the conditions now thought to be necessary to get evidence of ESP in the laboratory is that the person tested have a strong motive to succeed.

The difficulty is, however, that "dire distress" or any other of the strong emotional drives of real-life situations cannot easily be reproduced under controlled laboratory conditions. The recognized approach now, therefore, is somehow to "motivate"—as research workers say—the person who acts as subject. For this, different devices have been tried: praise and approbation, of course, and sometimes competition, with prizes and rewards selected according to the interests of the subject.

One experimenter in ESP, a young psychologist, Mrs. Olivia Rivers, was able to test the power of motivation in a rather striking way. Her situation did not make possible the strict conditions of the laboratory, but did, nevertheless, demonstrate that strong need can have a dramatic effect.

She had a young nephew, Franklin, eleven years old, and the attachment between the two was strong. When she was visiting at his home, he had "guessed" through several decks of ESP cards for her. He had scored fairly well, though not spectacularly, the highest for a single run being nine correct in twenty-five (five is the average for pure chance). But since she felt convinced he could do much better than he had, she set to work to prove it, and reports the result as follows:

"I was *determined* to make him give me some high scores. I knew if two people could work together, he and I could. And so, when I took him to his room that Wednesday night (in October, 1948) I gave him a pep talk. I made him feel that he was the one person in the world who could help me most on this. We talked and talked. I convinced him he could *see* those cards, if he really tried, and I would give him something very nice if he got some high scores.

"I got his interest: the moment came. He said, 'Go on, I'm ready.' I went across the room and sat on a chair by the wall. He sat relaxed on his bed. We were perfectly contented. We knew we were extraordinary peoople! No one else in the world might ever think it, but we knew it and set out to prove it. Nothing was between us once we began.

"On the first run he got eleven. He said he guessed he really could make high scores if he tried. I told him I had known all along he could. Next he made seventeen. I was amazed; I suppose I had been assuring him of something that I myself was in doubt about. 'I could tell!' he cried, 'I could see them!'

"He was very excited, breathing fast, his face red, his forehead damp with perspiration.

"Then I said I wanted him to get a score of twenty. He looked crushed. 'Twenty?'

" 'Yes, you get twenty, then I'll give you a very good prize.'

" 'If I get twenty will you get me some train switches?' I knew nothing about train switches and I agreed readily. My husband said afterward it's a good thing he didn't ask for the B & O Railroad. I probably would have promised it. He looked at me for a moment and said,

"'I'll get twenty for you.' And I replied 'And I'll get you those train switches, too.'

"Then the minute he started calling, he again became excited and tense. He was soon panting with excitement. He chewed his lips, he wrung his hands, he made all sorts of facial grimaces. At the end he ran over to me to see if he had made his mark. He had made nineteen. When he saw he had missed by one, he flew back to his bed and demanded that we do it again, *quick*. It was as if he had something for a minute that he was afraid he was going to lose before he got those switches.

"He went very fast, making the same wild mannerisms as before. I was sitting on the edge of my chair *making* him get twenty.

"He made twenty-two!

"He ran out to tell his brother. They jumped up and down. (I learned the switches cost twenty dollars! I'll have to get them for him.)"

One can notice another condition besides his strong will and desire to make a high score. In this experience the boy evidently fell into a very special state of mind, one not easy to define. His complete concentration on the task of "knowing" those card symbols was the visible part of it.

In the laboratory, however, there have been many indications that strain, effort, strong motivation to get high scores may inhibit rather than induce ESP. Strain of any kind, which could include strong need, may introduce inhibitions instead of concentration. In addition, it seems quite possible that in spontaneous situations also, tensions such as those of personal anxiety may inhibit extrasensory experiences. Certain people who may experience ESP about subject matter which is not personally very important to them, may very well be inhibited when their personal involvement is greater. This could explain cases such as the one of the woman who had an ESP experience involving the crisis of strangers and yet had no warning of her own husband's suicide. It is clear that need *alone* is not enough, and is no guarantee that an ESP experience will result. A special state of mind, too, may be necessary, one of detachment from the irrelevant, permitting concentration only on the event concerned.

In line with this, different devices seem at times to work for different people. As a child, a woman in California was good at finding lost articles, so that the family usually turned to her when something was missing. She says: "In the course of time I discovered that if I took the time to reason about the probable location of the article, I could do no better than my sisters did. But if I stood still and thought intently of the object itself, unrelated to any location and said to myself, 'I'll find it in a moment,' and then turned to do something else, suspending all thought about the article, I would suddenly dart toward the object and find it. It was important to *suspend all conscious thought* on the subject."

Once when her mother lost her glasses early in the morning, the girl found them *in the blackberry patch* by this method, and without knowing that her mother had risen early and picked berries for breakfast.

The method this woman described, of not concentrating consciously, seems to fit the idea of the train-meeting woman cited earlier who said, "Logic has nothing to do with it." But at the same time, it seems to contradict the method of the boy who won his train switches. He got the cards by concentrating. These others seem to have achieved their objectives by abandoning conscious effort. The contradiction, however, is probably only a superficial one. In neither case did the individual try to reason, remember or perceive sensorially. Each, in effect, and in different ways, tried to prevent conscious thought from obstructing the emergence of the impressions from the subconscious. Apparently the same effect can be created in different ways by different persons.

In some, as we have already seen, the proper mental state may be acquired by prayer which, whatever else it may be, is a method of inducing concentration with a minimum of conscious strain. A young woman secretary in a dye-house firm tried that method. "We had a storage vault, two stories high, with filing drawers piled high, containing bills, orders, correspondence, personnel records, etc. Prior to this day, I had *never* been in this vault. Our office manager had suffered a stroke, so was absent. One of our engines broke down and the company engineer and his helper rushed up from New Jersey to fix it. But before starting on the engine, they had to know the details. Time had erased all the markings but the name. No one knew what year it was bought, what price, what guarantee, what parts, names or numbers to order, etc. The manager asked me to 'drop everything and look for some information on this, if it takes two weeks.' I felt sick. My regular clerical duties kept me quite busy. I

suffice; therefore, perhaps, in the long, slow evolutionary process the extrasensory ability fell into disuse. Now, perhaps, for most persons, it is only the faint flicker of an earlier possession, operating sporadically as occasion happens to permit. The senses have been developed instead. They bring us the immediate, the present, with comparative reliability. In modern times, with the aid of instruments, the senses make extrasensory awareness of far events and future ones largely unnecessary to human existence.

However true this evolutionary conjecture may be, the two methods of knowing about the world—the sensory and the extrasensory—are alike in one way, though different in another: the eyes and ears in sensory perception register casual as well as significant items, and we have seen the same range in the topics of ESP. The difference between the two is that we can to a great extent control sensory, but not as yet extrasensory, perception. We can open and close our eyes, give or not give attention to sounds around us, but few of us can reliably decide when to have or not have an ESP experience.

And so, ESP occurs sporadically and spontaneously and sometimes serves, sometimes fails to serve, desired ends. It may work imperfectly and its value be reduced; it may seem sometimes to operate quite aimlessly, as might be expected of an involuntary process. The problem of finding a way to bring it into conscious and voluntary control, then, seems to be that of finding a method of tapping the deep unconscious and preventing its content from becoming "contaminated."

One method which has already been used and which has been thought to be efficacious is that of hypnosis. Hypnosis seems to be, in effect, a way of concentrating the subject's attention so as to exclude much of the conscious experience that ordinarily engages it. It seems as if it should be a means of allowing ESP to bypass some of the barriers and hazards. But it has not generally proven so.

Although it has seemed to help to clear away the conscious obstructions and induce a stronger drive in some subjects, others do no better when hypnotized than when not. Either hypnosis fails to remove the obstructions for these people, or else the structure of their personalities is such that a special and different technique of hypnosis is necessary. Just what that technique might be is still a question. It seems that the understanding of one unknown, as ESP itself still is, is not achieved by working on it with another unknown, like hypnosis. But proper research may perhaps shed new light on both.

That research, however, looks long and difficult to parapsychologists. Thus far, man has done better at solving the puzzle of nuclear energy than at understanding his own inner nature. But when he has given the latter the concerted attention the former has already had, the results may be comparably spectacular. But for the present the usefulness of ESP is limited to its spontaneous manifestations, and to those semi-spontaneous effects captured in experimental research.

13

The Telepathy Impasse

Telepathy is probably the most familiar type of ESP, the one which has most captured popular interest and imagination—yet the mental process that produces it is still the most debated of any. It has a special complication not shared by clairvoyance or precognition. This is because of the exceptional source of telepathic messages. Each of the three types of ESP brings information from its own specific kind of source; but telepathic messages are the *only* ones that come from other living persons, persons who also think and who sometimes try to "send" their thought.

What effect does this thinking and sending have? The question is whether the *active* sending of a thought plays a necessary initiating part in telepathic transfers. If it does, then the process of telepathy has an aspect lacking in clairvoyance or precognition. In each of the latter, the only person involved is the one who has the experience. The initiative for it must therefore come from him. Only in telepathy is the situation complicated by a second person who also could have an active role.

We have been content thus far to describe telepathy quite superficially and say only that it *looks* like a simple mind-to-mind contact. It could be so characterized because no sign was visible of any process intervening between the minds of the two people. In many of the instances already given, one person seemed to get a thought when the other had had no intention of sending it. This was especially noticeable in some of the instances of childhood telepathy.

A young woman one night was asked by an acquaintance about her four-year-old daughter at home. The mother took from her purse a small picture of the little girl, which the friend looked at with interest, and then remarked: "That child should have a musical education. It would be to her a book of gold with notes of silver for her, in it."

Surprised by her friend's seriousness, the mother thought again and again of the suggestion. When she got home the little girl was asleep, but the child awoke next morning, sat up in bed, turned the pillow over and searched among the covers. She then climbed out of bed and went to the dresser where she moved the articles about, hunting something.

Her mother asked her what she was looking for.

"I want the book of gold with something in it for me."

We are ready now to ask what really goes on when ideas are transferred. One can say a "mind-to-mind" contact was made, but that phrase actually tells nothing. After all, what is a mind? Psychologists have had much difficulty trying to define mind; many prefer not to use the word. In any event, in both technical and popular usage its meaning is changing. According to Webster, it once meant "an entity residing within an individual," but today its popular meaning more nearly coincides with the psychological definition, "the organized totality of conscious experience." Common as well as technical usage, however, has come to include in the definition *unconscious* as well as conscious activities.

The issue here is the relationship of thought to the brain. But this relationship represents a truly great question mark in scientific knowledge. Some now think that the answer will be found in a correlation of nerve impulses and thought—but that such an explanation could ever be the complete one seems unlikely, especially because it would have to explain precognition as well as all other thought categories. The gap in knowledge of the thought-brain relationship is so broad today as to leave *mind* basically a still unexplained concept; accordingly, the phrase *mind-to-mind* contact can have no exact meaning. Until neurologists and psychologists can bridge this gap, it seems that the puzzle of telepathy must remain. In the meantime, the most one can say about it and be safe no matter what the relationship turns out to be, is that telepathy represents a *person-to-person* contact. But that idea does not help one to understand the process.

As it happens, in the long history of telepathy, pre-suppositions were made about the part played by each of the two people involved and before ESP had been scientifically proven, they had been given distinguishing names. The names were given on the assumption that the person who had the thought first sent it to the other. Accordingly, the former was named the sender or *agent;* the latter, the receiver, or *percipient.* It was assumed when these names were given that the thought was transferred because the agent sent it—the kind of transfer implied in cases like that of a young man in California. One weekend he had a busy Saturday planned. It did not include a trip to Richmond to see his sisters. He had work to do on his car, a man to see on business, and a date with a girl. But he found himself thinking about Richmond and his sisters and he got the feeling he should drive to see them. He dismissed the idea but it refused to stay dismissed. Finally, having started to see the man he wanted to see, he found he was headed for Richmond without having intended it.

Annoyed at himself, he nonetheless decided to go on and get it off his mind. Arriving in Richmond, he went first to the home of his sister Shirley but felt immediately that the answer was not there. He refused even to sit down, and after talking a few minutes, drove across town to his sister Sally. He opened the door and said, "What the heck do you want?"

Sally said she was never so glad to see anyone. She had been hoping he would come, for the baby was sick and they were "flat broke" over the weekend. She remembered that her mother had had telepathic exchanges, so she had tried to send him a message to come.

If we examine other examples of telepathic transfer, however, we find that it often occurs in situations when no agent deliberately sends his thought. In some of these, however, the agent may need or want the other person, even be calling aloud for him, without the definite idea of making a telepathic transfer.

In a California hospital some ten miles from his home, a man lay critically ill. His wife, who had been attending him constantly, had been persuaded to go home for the night and had asked her sister to go along with her. Worn out with worry and anxiety, they had lain down, and she was dozing when suddenly she heard her husband's voice calling her, "Irene, Irene." She asked her sister if she too had heard the call, but she had not. In a few minutes the phone rang. It was the hospital calling to say her husband was dying and that he was calling her name.

Then, too, people sometimes respond to another's strong need to send a message, though it may be quite inarticulate. A woman in

New Brunswick, Canada, had gone to town with a friend for an afternoon of pre-Christmas shopping. Suddenly, and long before she had finished, she knew she had to go home, and did so at once despite her friend's annoyance.

She arrived home to find her husband lying unconscious in his car, his face purple. He had recharged the battery and was replacing it in the car. A blizzard had come up and he had closed the garage door, thinking there would be ample air, but the carbon monoxide fumes overcame him. When he tried to adjust something, his hands would not move. He thought of his wife; his last memory was of an urgent call to her for help. In spite of his 172 pounds, she managed to get him outside on the snow, to call a neighbor and a doctor and get him carried indoors, where four hours later he recovered consciousness.

The strong need felt by the sender in such an instance, and in the preceding one, might seem to be a factor just as effective (and necessary) as the conscious attempt to send a thought, as in the case of Sally above. But one must remember instances like that of the mother whose little girl wanted the book of gold. She simply had the thought, but had no idea of sending it.

One factor in all these cases that might seem important is that a close and positive emotional relationship existed. In contrast to situations with such "postive" relationships, however, one finds occasionally that telepathic transfers of thought occur when the relationship is a negative one. A woman from California writes, "It was proven that my husband had been intimate with a woman I supposed was a friend of mine. When I learned the true facts I told her I would forgive her, but I would never accept her in my life again as a friend. She later married another man. I forgave my husband and we were getting along nicely, when about five or six years after this incident, one night I dreamed she called me and said she was happily married now and why couldn't we all be friends and pal around again together like she and her former husband had done with us. The next morning at nine my phone rang and the very identical conversation took place, word for word just as it did in the dream. I said, 'Effie, I am not surprised at this conversation, for I dreamed it last night exactly word for word.' She said, 'I am not surprised either, for I have thought of you so much and would start to call you up and then I would think that you wouldn't talk to me, but this morning something just urged me to call you.' Needless to say, I never took her back into my friendship, but this is as it actually happened."

Whether people like or dislike each other, however, one can still say they are at least interested and emotionally involved to some extent. But numerous experiences are reported between people either slightly or not at all connected by emotional bonds. For this reason, there is a strong tendency to think of such occurrences only as odd coincidences when they could very well be instances of telepathy.

An Illinois businessman was returning to his office after lunch. He noticed an acquaintance, a state politician, standing in the doorway of another office, apparently in deep concentration. "Then," said the businessman, "as he looked up and recognized me, a thought entered my mind and I went across the hall and told him a little story, how as a youngster I had visited in New Hampshire and had been shown a tree on a small mountain on which our guide said were cut the initials of Daniel Webster, placed there in the late 1830's. There were indeed the initials D. W. on the tree, deeply cut in the bark and evidently very old. As a boy and later I often recalled this experience, but had completely forgotten it for years until this particular time. The Illinois legislator looked at me and said, 'This must be what you call mental telepathy or something.' Then, picking a card from his desk, he ran off the words of Daniel Webster spoken years ago which he had been trying to memorize to quote at a Democratic rally that day."

Similar experiences may involve complete strangers. Considering the unlikelihood of the occurrence being recognized, more instances when this is the case are reported than might be expected. They strongly suggest a telepathic transfer.

A man, now living in Ohio, was in 1944 a soldier returning to his army base in the Canal Zone. He boarded his plane about one o'clock in the morning. The hostess told the passengers that the ship was not fireproof, and she collected all the smoking paraphernalia to keep until they arrived at Colon later. Everyone was soon asleep, and this man dreamed, he said, "that my desire to smoke was so great I looked around and, making sure that everyone else was sleeping, I took from my pocket one cigarette which I had held back and lighted it. The embarrassment of my act and the sudden chilling fear that came over me woke me up. Needless to say, I was not smoking but the horrible feeling of guilt that came over me caused me to search the deck around my feet, but there was no sign of a stamped-out cigarette butt or a lighted match.

"After we landed at Colon in Panama, our personal items were returned to us and I proceeded to the waiting platform for passengers who were going across the Isthmus to Panama City. While on the plane, the seat across from me had been occupied by a young lady who now was standing at my side and offering me a cigarette, smiling, and saying, 'I dreamed about you last night.' Never having known the girl before and only having nodded in the fashion that fellow travelers have of nodding at one another when they are seated face to face over the Caribbean Sea, I guess I showed surprise in my face, for she then added, 'Yes, I dreamed you were smoking a cigarette and when I awoke I had to look around to make sure there were no signs of a cigarette or a match.'"

And so we find people "getting" someone else's thought in a wide variety of emotional relationships, needs or impulses to transfer thought. In all the above instances the transfer was a one-way affair. But cases are occasionally reported, though rarely, when the transfer is reciprocal. In these one can scarcely say that one person rather than the other was responsible for starting the exchange.

A woman in Michigan dreamed one night that she was sitting high up in the branches of an enormous pine tree. Then she heard the sound of someone approaching through the woods. Presently she saw it was a man, and by his wanderings and general bearing, she knew at once he was lost. As he came closer, she saw he was her son, the one who was attending a distant university. His face was scratched, his clothing torn by bushes. In a rush of pity she cried out to him, "Clarence, go this way. Here is the path you must take." He turned a gray-looking face to her, smiled and took the path she had indicated.

Later in the week she had a letter from her son in which he told her about a dream that had made a great impression on him. He thought he was lost and confused and wandering in a wood full of dense underbrush which tore at him from every side. When he became fearful that he would never find his way out he suddenly heard a voice, but could see no one. The voice said, "Clarence, go this way." It seemed to come from high above him. He took the path indicated and soon found his way out of the woods. When he came home for his vacation soon after, his mother's first words of greeting were, "Clarence, that was I. I was up in the tree."

Whatever such instances of mental interaction mean, they do not seem to help in solving the puzzle of telepathy. Rather, they add to the difficulty of doing so!

We must recall, too, that a number of cases of clairvoyance (in which no possible sender exists) bear a strong resemblance to some telepathy cases. The resemblance comes in experiences in which a sender has urgent need to get a message to the receiver, and the receiver seems to get it, for he acts accordingly. In some of these clairvoyance cases, a danger exists and a receiver responds to it *when no person is aware of the danger,* and hence no message could have been sent. The resulting impulse of the receiver may be just the same as if a telepathic message had been received, yet the information could only come clairvoyantly.

A woman in New Jersey went to town to shop, leaving her husband and two-year-old daughter at home. Then, as she says, "I was almost at the center of Paterson when I knew—but I cannot explain how I knew—that I had to get home very quickly. I simply was filled with panic. I got off the bus and immediately took a return bus home. I found that my husband and daughter had decided to nap on the sofa in the living room and the house was filling with gas. My daughter had played at the stove and had turned on all the gas jets while my husband napped. Then she had lain down beside him and fallen asleep, too. I can remember nothing more than the feeling of panic and the need to forget shopping and return home."

The inescapable point of comparison between this experience and the earlier telepathy case involving escaping gas is that the messages were the same, even though the situation regarding the sender was significantly different. One was aware of his danger and "called," the other knew nothing of it. But the receivers in both instances got the message. Whether the situations were telepathic or clairvoyant made no detectable difference.

What about the receivers in all these cases? Their role, of course, was to get the thought. But their degree of interest in it, their need for the message, varied. In some instances it was much stronger than in others. When the relationships were close, the receivers were very much concerned about the needs and crises of the relative or friend involved. When the relationships were casual, the receivers were also presumably as much concerned as the senders. We can say, then, that the messages received were all of some interest to the receivers.

If ESP, as has been suggested, scans the horizon of each person's interest like a searchlight, it is within the scope of these receivers' ESP ability to become aware of situations regardless of whether or not the agent is taking any action or initiative in sending a message. In the cases of telepathy in small children, the lack of initiative taken by the adult "senders" was obvious. The child seemed simply to "know" the thought.

And so one is, as it were, forced to shift the emphasis from the sender to the receiver. It does not necessarily mean that the sender never plays an essential role. One cannot say that. It does mean that we see telepathy occurring regardless of the sender's initiating action. What effect he exerts, whether his action facilitates the transfer (or does so for certain people at least), and if so how far, one cannot tell.

We are still waiting for experimental research to furnish evidence indicating just what part the sender plays. In most of the telepathy experiments so far performed, the sender was either concentrating on having the other receive the thought (as in the case of Sally and her brother); or if not actually concentrating on "sending," he was at least supposed to be holding the thought in mind (like the estranged friend who made the phone call). The results of the experiments have not been particularly different, despite the difference in mental condition. And no experimental procedure has yet been devised to show if the receiver could get the sender's thought when the sender was not aware of the test, was not sending or even carrying the thought in mind. The test would have to be one of "pure telepathy," of course, with all possibility of clairvoyance excluded, a difficult experiment to arrange. But it seems as if only such a test could tell just what the role of the sender is.

It is necessary to give detailed attention to the sender's possible role in telepathy, not only because of the need to get a better understanding of the telepathy process, but also because a quirk of history gives telepathic "senders" special interest.

In England as early as the 1880's an idea of the telepathic process, already mentioned as an assumption, was more or less expressly formulated—the idea that the sender is a necessary activating party in thought exchanges. The time was well before the occurrence of clairvoyance had been established or thought to have any relation to telepathy, still longer before precognition had been recognized. It was a period when materialistic ways of thought were gaining prevalence, and those who reacted against them were trying to find evidence that human beings are not wholly mechanistic systems. Such evidence seemed to be indicated by the transference of thought by nonsensory means. If that transference were one initiated by the sender's mental effort, the argument seemed particularly effective, because in some of the most striking cases, the person who seemed to communicate with the other, and to send a thought or message of warning, was someone no longer living. Such occurrences seemed to imply not only a nonmaterialistic aspect in life, but also to suggest that the spirit survives death and can communicate with the living. This seemed at once to promise a final blow to materialism and to satisfy the great need of humanity to know with certainty about the reality of a future life.

Telepathy, then, particularly telepathy in which the transfer was made because one person sent his thought to the other, was of transcendent importance. The sender was especially important because on him devolved the proof that the deceased could communicate with the living: if his initiative caused the experience, while the one who got the thought was only a more or less passive receiver, then proof of telepathy furnished the support of strong plausibility for belief in spirit survival.

The general effectiveness of the argument was all the stronger because the *form* of telepathy experience that seemed most convincing was that which here we have been calling the hallucinatory. Hallucinatory experiences seemed obviously to mean that the sender was actually there as seen or heard. Telepathic experiences in other forms, and without the connotation that the message came from the deceased, received no emphasis. Thus, if a dying person was "seen" or "heard" at a significant time, it was scarcely to be doubted that that person had actually in some spiritual sense been there; he seemed to be bringing the news of his departure and saying farewell. Today, since we know that ESP can bring information about distant events, such an experience need not necessarily mean that the dying person brought the message. Neither does the fact that he was "seen" or "heard" necessarily imply that he was there, because we now know that one of the ways of expressing information received by ESP is by means of an hallucinatory effect.

Experiences involving persons already dead, rather than just dying, were even more convincing. When a person known to be deceased was seen or heard, the reasonable interpretation seemed to be that he was actually there; often informing or warning the living person about some threat or danger. Such would have been the interpretation of an experience like that of a woman in New York. She was awakened one night by hearing her dead grandmother call her. She recalls the incident thus: "Grandma had been dead for a number of years. I jumped up and did not even glance at the baby sleeping on two chairs and a soft pillow at the side of our bed. I rushed down the hall to the room where my mother was sleeping.

" 'Did you call me? Someone did. It sounded like Grandma.' My mother answered sleepily, 'No, no, I didn't call.'

"I went back to my room. There I discovered to my horror that the baby, pillow and all had slipped off the chairs and lay under a heap of bed clothes on the floor. In another few minutes he would have smothered."

The explanation, that earlier seemed so convincing, of course cannot today be taken as conclusive. Even though the grandmother *seemed* to be sending the warning message, we now know that that explanation is not the only one possible. We know that the living person could have known of the danger by clairvoyance, and expressed it in the form of an unrealistic dream or auditory hallucination. One cannot say for a certainty that this was the explanation, since the older interpretation has not been excluded. We now know only that we must look farther before we can be certain of the answer. The great importance that was once given to the sender in a telepathy exchange can be appreciated and also the fact that with greater knowledge, the possible perspective covering the range of ESP has widened. The advance in knowledge of the field has been a little like the exploration of a mountain range. The importance of a foothill in the foreground may be lessened by the peaks that come in view beyond it. In this instance, of course, the highest peak of all concerns the basic nature of psi, and its place and meaning in the personality. A view from its summit still lies ahead, still in the misty distance. And the puzzle of telepathy is one of the remaining obstacles to that perspective.

14

Puzzling Physical Effects

At last the time has come to turn back to the "leftovers" that did not fit into any of the three categories of ESP. They did not fit, it will be recalled, because they involved physical happenings primarily, and not, as in ESP, ideas or at least cognitive effects of some kind.

These leftover cases traditionally might have been called "signs," for they include such effects as clocks that stop and pictures that fall, when someone dies. In each case an objective event occurs for which observers find no ordinary cause, and which they therefore interpret as having a hidden one.

Accounts of such occurrences have seldom been taken seriously by the educated public, and by scientists even less so. Tales of "signs" have generally been considered as so much poppycock indulged in by the credulous, and explainable as bad observation and coincidence.

Here, we can pause and examine the evidence a bit before passing judgment. We can do so because a trace of "mind-over-matter" effect has been found by the same order of carefully controlled laboratory research that established the case for ESP. This effect is usually called psychokinesis, or PK for short. As we all know, old beliefs and superstitions have sometimes been found to have a nucleus of truth, however deeply imbedded in extraneous accretions. That thought leads to the question whether any of these puzzling occurrences could be the result of PK operating spontaneously in life situations.

Turning to the "evidence," one finds that on the basis of the interpretations that have been given the occurrences, some have been considered to come from dying persons, some from those already dead, and also some from living individuals.

FROM THE DYING

Among the various kinds of objective occurrences which observers have interpreted as bringing a message from a dying person, the most common is the stopping of a clock. But the circumstances vary. Sometimes it is said, "never to run again," as if irreparable damage (usually of unspecified kind) had been done to it. A group of Duke University students were sitting around a campfire one night when the conversation drifted to odd experiences. Quietly and seriously a New England girl said, "I never could explain this. When my father died the clock was found to have stopped just at the same time. Later when I took it to the jeweler, because it would not run, he said it was beyond repair. It was a Swiss clock and had been a wedding gift to my parents; Dad had always kept it going, but we never got it to run again." In the cases reported, however, lasting damage to the clock is not always mentioned, so one may assume that some timepieces later run as usual.

Occasionally the point is made that the watch or clock had not simply "run down." A man in Canada was given a gold watch by one of his brothers, and then several years later, when this brother was dying of cancer, he was called to the bed side. As he says, "I took leave from my job and sat up nights to help my sister-in-law during the last two days of my brother's terminal illness. He breathed his last at six-twenty-five in the morning. I called the family immediately and we phoned for the doctor and the undertakers. At about seven-thirty we were sitting around a rush breakfast—my two brothers, the widow and the nurse.

"Arrangements had previously been made to be at the undertaking parlors at nine-thirty, so as the wall clock neared nine o'clock, I suggested it was about time the widow and my other brothers made arrangements to get started for the funeral parlors. Someone asked how much time we had, and I took out the pocket watch mentioned above, when, lo and behold, it had stopped at the exact minute of his death. I called the attention of those gathered around the table to this phenomenon and, in order to show that it was no common occurrence, asked my brother to wind the watch to make sure it had not run down. It was three quarters wound."

More than one timepiece may be involved. A man from Wisconsin says his father died in the easy chair in the living room. The watch in his vest pocket was stopped and the large clock in the same room also, both just after midnight, the time the death occurred. In the upset, and the moves and changes that followed, no attention was paid to either the watch or the clock for nearly a year; but when rewound then, both started and ran as before.

Not all clocks and watches found to have stopped at the time of a death are in the room where death occurred. A person may die miles away in a hospital, perhaps, when the timepiece is at home. Usually, but not always, it is one that has a special meaning to or connection with the person dying.

On October 3, 1953, at 9:35 P.M., a man died in an Indiana hospital seven miles from his home. His daughter writes, "We came home from the hospital and started making arrangements, telegrams, phone calls, etc., and when we looked up at Father's favorite clock, a cuckoo clock, which Mother had given him as a gift that year, it was stopped at exactly nine-thirty-five, the same time Father died. We were all awe-struck and it took a long time before anyone could muster up courage to start it again."

In a few instances, a striking clock has been reported to strike aberrantly, (Clocks that strike are somewhat uncommon, of course, which may explain why reports of unusual striking are less frequent than those of unaccountable stopping.) A women in New York State recalls, "A spring evening about twenty-eight years ago in our home in Massachusetts my dad, mother and I were reading aloud when suddenly at twenty minutes after seven, the clock struck once —a clock which struck only the hours and had been doing so for years. This striking was so unusual we all noticed it and about five minutes later a telephone call told us my mother's favorite sister had died suddenly of a heart attack—at seven-twenty. The clock never struck out of turn again."

Accounts like these show little uniformity of particulars. The time-piece may be near the dying person, or at a distance from him; it frequently is one he owned and cared for, but sometimes it has no special significance for him, and may have belonged to someone else. The one constant feature seems to be that the people who observe the occurrence are close friends or relatives of the one who died; persons who are affected by the death. The stopping of the clocks seems to them to be a message.

Although not quite as frequently as clocks, pictures also are involved in occurrences that are interpreted as bringing death messages. A man in New York, for instance, had a picture of an old classmate, then living in Honolulu, in a little silver frame standing on his dresser. After midnight, January 28, 1949, he heard something fall and found the picture lying on the floor. Surprised because he had not been aware of any wind or vibration which might have caused it to fall, he picked it up and replaced it, saying aloud to himself, "I hope nothing has happened to John." Within a day or two he got a cable saying his friend had died in his sleep that very night.

Other kinds of objects, usually significant, may sometimes be involved. In a home in Detroit, the evening of August 13, 1957, a woman was alone in the house when the noise of something falling startled her. A crucifix that had hung on the wall for years had fallen to the floor. It was one that had been given her by a priest, Father F, a special friend with whom she had once been associated in some work connected with the parish. Later he had been transferred to another parish, and in the nine years after, she had seen him only rarely. But the crucifix had hung on the wall over all these years. She found the nail intact, the wire in the back of the crucifix apparently the same as when put in.

The next day's paper reported the death that night at 10:30 P.M. of Father F at his parish across the city. There was a discrepancy in the time, since the crucifix fell at 6:15 P.M. Father F died of a heart attack. It is not recorded whether he was stricken hours before his death.

Sometimes it is the breaking of a fragile object that seems to convey the message. A woman in Nevada tells of an experience which centered on her elder brother Frank. He was an especially thoughtful boy who did many little things to please his mother, to whom he was very close. She says: "One day he came home with a beautiful cut-glass dish. Mom thought it was just about the most wonderful thing that ever happened to her and put it on our sideboard.

"When the rest of us had chicken pox, my brother Frank was sent down to my grandmother's in Grand Haven, Michigan, which was about forty miles from where we lived, although Mother was reluctant to have him go. Two days after Frank left, Mom and our neighbor were having their morning coffee and talking, and we children were told to be quiet. All of a sudden, this cut-glass dish that Frank had given Mother popped and broke right in two. It was just sitting on the sideboard. Mother screamed and said, 'My God! Frank has been killed.' Everyone tried to quiet Mother, but she said she just knew.

"About an hour after, or a little more, we received a telegram from Grandpa which said to come right away, something had happened to Frank. Mom said, 'I know.' She cried all the way going to Grand Haven, and Grandpa met us at the train. Before Grandpa could tell us what happened, Mom cried, 'At what funeral parlor is he?' Grandpa just stood with his mouth open and Mom ran right up the street and went to the place where Frank was without being told. They wouldn't let her see him because a terrible thing had happened.

"The boy next door to Grandfather was home from school and his parents were not at home, so he started playing with his father's shotgun, and came outside, showing it to Frank. The boy, not knowing it was loaded, pulled the trigger and killed my brother. The strange thing—Frank was shot at the same time the dish broke."

In addition to such occurrences as these, which are definitely physical, various kinds of sounds, most frequently knocks or raps, are reported as coinciding with the time of a death. In 1944 one member of a family in New Jersey was a young soldier fighting then in Holland. Before he left home he had the habit, when visiting his aunt who lived nearby, of tapping three times on the door so she would know beforehand who was there.

On a particular night she and two of his sisters were sitting in her parlor and her own sister was in the bathroom. All were talking when suddenly three taps on the door were heard. They knew he could not be home and all sat dumbfounded. The sister in the bathroom called out, "I'll be out in a minute." She had heard the taps and thought they came from one of those in the living room.

There was no one at the door. Soon after, his parents got the word that he had been killed in action the day they heard the taps.

All cases like this one, in which the effect is an auditory one only, raise the question of whether it was actually physical or whether it might have been a psychological effect, or, in other words, if it was an hallucination. Arguing against the latter possibility, but not finally excluding it, is the fact that usually such sounds (as in the above instance) are heard by all who are present.

From this incomplete but assorted list of unusual sounds and physical effects, one can see that the association with the dying person was made partly because no ordinary physical cause seemed to exist. The clocks stopped when not run down. The pictures fell without an obvious cause. And besides that, all the effects occurred at times which seemed to be significant. The question is: Was the time significant or coincidental? Was the occurrence the result of an unusual force, or an undetected ordinary one?

FROM THE DEAD

Every person who has lost a close relative or friend is likely to find certain occasions very acutely reminiscent of that person or very closely associated with his memory. At such times, some individuals have become aware of the occurrence of a physical effect for which they find no ordinary explanation. Clocks again are frequently affected, but in this association are less often reported simply to have stopped. More likely a stopped clock will be said to start to tick, or a striking clock to strike erratically.

A Florida man, with his wife and daughter, had gone on a business trip to a city a hundred miles or so from home. He was suddenly taken acutely ill, rushed to a hospital at 11:00 that night, and died the following morning at 10:20. "Afterwards," his wife writes, "my daughter accompanied me home. The following morning, as we went about tidying up the house, we were suddenly conscious that an old clock (silent for years) was ticking loudly. Neither of us had been near it and we were alone in the house and had been all morning.

"We rushed over to it, not believing it could be possible. As we stood there with tears streaming down our faces, the pendulum was swaying in full motion. We stood there motionless for at least two minutes, unable to move. I glanced at my watch. It was 10:20, the exact time of his death the previous day. When I realized the time, I knew what it meant. Until this happened I had that small doubt about such things, but now I knew that my loved one was assuring us of his presence.

"Slowly I reached up and stopped the swinging pendulum. It had been going four or five minutes."

Besides the unaccountable behavior of clocks and other objects at significant times, a miscellaneous assortment of occurrences are reported. In these odd physical effects the specific phenomenon may be unusual in that it may be unlike others reported by other people, but it occurs *at an appropriate moment* and so is in line with the clock effects, the objects that fall, etc.

A woman in Massachusetts recalls: "In late November, 1952, I was in the beginning of my second pregnancy and I was quite ill. One day in the early afternoon I was lying in my bedroom, which was right off the kitchen. I was alone; my husband and small son were upstairs in my sister's apartment on the second floor.

"At the time, I was in danger of losing my baby, which I had greatly desired, and was in great anxiety. I started to pray to God to save my baby. Then I started to pray to my father, who was dead. I said to him, 'Please, Pa, intercede for me to God and save this baby because I wanted so much to name him after you, please save him.' As the words left my lips, I heard a rushing noise and, glancing into the kitchen, I saw both faucets on my sink turned on and pouring water in the sink at full force. Because I was not supposed to get out of bed on doctor's orders, I lay there watching. About five minutes later my husband came in and witnessed it. He asked me why I did a thing like that. I replied I had not left the bed. The outcome of the story is that I successfully completed the pregnancy and a fine, healthy boy was born and I named him after my father as I had promised him.

"My faucets are of modern type and have to be operated manually by turning them. They both came on at once, but turned to their full capacity. I had lived in the house for three years. This was the first time the faucets behaved in this fashion. They were in good condition, didn't drip, and were tightly connected as far as I could see."

The occurrence of sounds, too, is associated with communication from someone deceased. Among these, as in the cases coinciding with deaths, unexplained knocks and raps probably are reported most frequently, but a variety of other sounds also are included. Even when a potential physical source is present, the possibility of an auditory hallucination cannot be excluded. But sometimes no object is present from which the sound could come. One can scarcely question, then, that it had a psychological origin. A woman in Florida was alerted in a strange way on the night after her father's death. She explains it thus: "To understand what I'm going to tell, you will almost have to listen through a hearing aid. My father wore one, the kind in which the batteries were worn in a harness on the chest. There is a lever on it that controls volume and he used to run the volume up and down to amuse the children with the odd noise it made. It had a sound as distinctive as a violin or piano. That sound couldn't be mistaken for any other. He had had an operation and was in the hospital and was doing very well. He died so suddenly that I hardly knew what was happening, and I was with him at the time. My mother and father were very close and she was terribly upset. I stayed with her that night.

"I lay quite still, hoping she would cry herself to sleep and wondering if I should call the doctor to give her a hypo. It must have been about twelve o'clock when I heard this sound. I thought surely I was just imagining things, so I didn't even glance at Mother, but she stopped crying in a few seconds. I heard it again, this time louder, and Mom said, 'Do you hear what I do?' And I said, 'Yes.' She said, 'It's Dad's hearing aid,' and the sound grew louder until it filled the room and sounded almost like code, as if trying to get a message to us. The unusual thing about it was it didn't stop. It continued for an hour or more, until it lulled us both to sleep. It calmed my mother as nothing else could have done. I never heard it again. The hearing aid wasn't in the house at the time. I told my brother about it and he just laughed and said it must have been the wind, but it was a clear still night in July and not even a leaf was stirring. If someone else had told me it happened to them, I don't suppose I would have believed it, but it did happen."

These effects were noticed at times which seemed to give them relevance to a *particular* deceased person. It was not a time of crisis for the deceased as were the incidents associated with the dying, but one significant *for the living observer.*

In the above experiences, the persons involved were well known to each other. Unusual effects, usually sounds rather than manifestations more definitely physical, are sometimes associated with the *unknown* dead; in other words, with someone deceased whom the living person had never known, perhaps never even known of. Most, but not all, such sounds (which include knocks, raps, the sound of footsteps, etc.) are repeated, and not single episodes like these which concern us here. They are effects usually included under the general term "haunting." They make a topic of discussion and investigation in themselves, and one which cannot be undertaken here.

FROM THE LIVING

Instances in which an inexplicable occurrence in the environment is associated with someone living are less frequently reported than those that are interpreted as involving the dying or the dead. One reason could be that this association is less likely to be noticed or thought significant. The kinds of occurrences reported in this group are familiar, however, for many are similar to those associated with the dying and the dead. Clocks, for instance, are sometimes involved here, too, and again, exact effects vary. It was a little after 1 A.M. March 16, 1958, when a woman in Connecticut wakened with a start. As she recalls, "I didn't know what had wakened me. I got out of bed and went to the room where my two sons sleep, and was surprised to see they were not in bed. They had gone out together. They always returned early. I glanced at the clock in my room. It had stopped at one-ten. I went to the kitchen and saw it was one-twenty. I thought then it must have been the sudden silence of the clock that wakened me.

"Then the phone rang. It was a hospital nurse asking permission to take care of my son. It was explained only one boy was there, not hurt badly. I later found out my other son was in another hospital, hurt very badly and needing an emergency operation to keep him alive. As far as the police and the boys knew, the accident happened about one-ten A.M.

"When I noticed that the clock had stopped, I picked it up and it started ticking. It did not need winding, as I had wound it that evening. The same clock, a cheap alarm clock, is still working fine and has never stopped since. I wind it at the same time each night when I go to bed."

Along with clocks that stop are others that start to tick. During World War I a clock belonging to a soldier in General Pershing's army in France stood on a shelf in the dining room of his home in New Jersey. But in October, 1918, a terrific explosion in a nearby powder plant shook it down, and it would not run again. The soldier's wife tells of the subsequent history of the clock.

"We moved from that house in February and I put the little clock on the kitchen shelf. Well, on April eighth, my sister and I were sitting in the kitchen when the little Ben *started to tick*. My sister turned white and said, 'Something has happened to Leon.'

"By then we knew he had moved into Germany with the Army of Occupation. One month later he arrived home and his papers were dated Germany, April 8, 1919. He left almost the minute the little clock started to tick on our kitchen shelf."

In other cases a dish may fall or break, in a manner quite similar to the effects frequently associated with a death. In September, 1953, a woman in Ohio was much engrossed in the job of washing and putting away a new set of dishes she had just received. She knew her sister-in-law was having an operation that morning, but there was no cause for alarm about that, for as she says, "My sister-in-law was in good health, about forty-two, a nurse, and my brother a doctor. The operation was more or less routine. I remember thinking it was about time for Ruth to be going into the operating room.

"Then the dishes came and I was almost as entranced as a woman with a new hat. I began stacking them on the counter by the sink. I did all the smaller pieces first. There remained the stack of eight large plates directly under the cupboard above. Suddenly a celery dish which was on the next to the top shelf just waltzed right out of the cupboard and came crashing down on my stack of new plates. It was an old antique one that I prized. It had stood on that shelf for almost ten years. I didn't use the dishes up there often, for the shelf is too high for me to reach, and I was not working with nor touching in any way anything up there.

"I noticed it had chipped two plates. Then the strangest feeling came over me. My knees just turned to water. I held on to the sink, and Ruth flashed into my mind. I started to cry, standing there all by myself, and then I started to pray. I can remember saying, 'God, you can't take her. Her children need her so. What will happen to them?' I noticed it was almost eleven o'clock.

"There I was with my hands in the dish water, crying and praying. I washed the plates and put the dishes away. Then I had to get lunch for the children and get them back to school.

"About one-fifteen the phone rang. It was my sister Grace calling from the hospital.

" 'I thought I'd call and let you know Ruth is okay.'

" 'Well, I'm so glad because I was so worried about her.'

"Then my sister said, and her voice broke. She could hardly go on—

" 'We almost lost her. They had to take her back to the operating room, and she was about gone. It was—'

"And I broke in—

" 'I can tell you when it was. It was about eleven o'clock.'

"Grace wondered how I knew, for she had glanced at the clock as they wheeled Ruth down the corridor. It was almost eleven.

"Ruth had had a hysterectomy and then had hemorrhaged. By the time it was discovered she was in shock, her pulse and blood pressure were very low. The surgeon had gone to the golf club, my brother to his office fourteen miles away; and to make matters worse there was no blood in the hospital of Ruth's type. Just by chance a young nurse's aide was of the type. She gave the transfusion."

Still other inexplicable occurrences may seem to bring a message. One night in Arkansas the light bulb in the floor lamp exploded in the bedroom in which a man and his wife were sleeping, the wife says, ". . . with a noise that brought us wide awake. It had been cold for hours and we could see no reason for it. I said, 'Something bad happened to some of the folks.' I felt sure of it. My sister lives across the street and when I saw her I told her about it. We did not hear anything that day. Nor the next—and she and my husband began to laugh at me. When we didn't hear anything the next day I too began to doubt. Then we heard. *That night, at that time,* my brother's big farm home had burned to the ground. The family had barely escaped. The cause—defective wiring. They had all been too torn up to tell us."

As one might expect, even the kinds of electrical effects involved vary. A young woman, the wife of a linesman, was alone at home with the children one night in 1945. Her husband was out of town. "The children had been asleep for hours," she says. "After a while I decided I would go to bed, too. I had only been there for a few minutes when the lamp *went on* in the front room. Naturally I was petrified, and wondered if somehow someone could have slipped into the house without me hearing them. I made the rounds of the house. The children were still asleep, no one was in the house. So I went back to inspect the lamp for a mechanical defect. I shook it, the cord and the globes, but nothing happened. And the only way the lamp could be turned off was by turning the switch the way I had done when I first went to bed. I repeated the procedure several times, but it was always the same. Then I began to worry that there must be something wrong with my mother or something had happened to my husband. Since there was no way of checking, I had to convince myself that there was nothing I could do but wait to see what would turn up.

"I didn't have too long to wait, for at five in the morning the bell rang and there was my husband at the door with all his 'linesman's equipment' in his hand—and no truck. He had been on his way home when the air brakes had given out and he had run into another car. He had been en route all night, managing as best he could by hitch-hiking until he could make connections with the streetcar.

"Incidentally, the lamp is still here in use, has never done that again. Everything is intact as it was then with the exception, of course, of the lampshade and an occasional change of light globes. Explain it if you can. It has puzzled me all these years."

Unexplainable knocks and raps figure in this group, too. On May 25, 1952, a young woman learned that her husband's brother had been critically injured in an automobile accident and was in the hospital. As she says: "During the next day or two my husband and I were naturally at the hospital as much of the time as we could be.

"My husband stayed the first night and I was there part of the next day. He was, too, but came home early to get some rest. I came in that night and wakened him. He went to the bathroom to shave. I went right to bed. In what seemed like just a few seconds I heard three taps that startled me and I got up and ran downstairs to my husband, who asked what was wrong, and I told him. It was about 10 P.M.

"He assured me everything was all right and said maybe it was a shingle flapping on the roof, or maybe I was asleep and dreamed it. This satisfied me, and being worn out I went back to bed and to sleep. And about ten-fifteen he went to the hospital. He didn't tell me until he came home between one and two o'clock that he had heard the taps, too. He said that as he stood at the mirror shaving, three taps came on the bathroom window.

"When he got to the hospital at approximately ten-twenty the nurse told him that his brother had taken a turn for the worse, some fifteen to twenty minutes before, exactly the time we heard the three taps. His brother died the next evening at ten o'clock.

"There is a porch on the back of the house and the roof of it goes over the bathroom, so nothing could blow or fly against that window. Our house is insulated and very little noise is heard from first to second floor, so I scarcely think we could have heard the same taps.

"If it had just been I who heard the taps, I would have passed it off because I was so tired and might have dozed off, but my husband was wide awake and had the same experience.

"My brother-in-law was never actually conscious after he was hurt, at least not enough to carry on a conversation. Most of the time he was praying, or calling his wife, or just mumbling. At the time we heard the taps he was not conscious, but probably more in delirium than coma, I think."

In reviewing these three groups, one sees no sharp line of demarcation between cases involving the dying and the dead on the one hand, and the living on the other. Rather, one can find a common denominator among them: namely, crisis. More than that, a line of difference in the circumstances of the crises in the three groups separates the dead from the living and dying rather than the dying and dead from the living. For in the dying and living groups the crisis, whether it be death or something else, is one *shared* by emotionally connected persons. While one of them is affected primarily, the fact must not be missed that the observer is also very much concerned. The other person's crisis is his, too.

In the deceased group, however, as we have noted, the event occurs at a critical time for the living observer who is still emotionally attached to the deceased. We do not know, of course, that the time is critical for the deceased, or that his former emotional relation with the living observer still persists. The common denominator one can be sure of, then, is not only a crisis, but a *crisis of the observer.*

The observer is, of course, the one who associates the event with the other person, who usually is someone within the circle of his close personal relationships. As already observed, he does so for two reasons. First, because he finds no ordinary explanation for the occurrence: the clock was not run down, the nail did not pull out when the picture fell. Second, it happened at a time that seemed to him to be significant.

The skeptical view is, of course, that an ordinary cause was there but overlooked, the occurrence just happening to coincide with the time of a distant crisis. However, if it should be a fact that familiar and ordinary causes were really lacking, then the occurrences were caused by some other force or influence. If that operated meaningfully so as to bring a message, then the occurrence helped the person to get significant information about the world. On that supposition, these occurrences would be bringing information, just as ESP experiences do, only these would come in an *objective* way, those of ESP by *subjective* methods.

How well does the research mentioned before, that on "mind-over-matter," or PK, back up this possibility? It is suggestive, but still at too early a stage to do much more than that. PK has been observed thus far only on objects already in motion. Six-sided cubes (usually playing dice) have been used the most, but in several researches an effect was secured using discs and spheres (coins and marbles).

The results secured have shown in general that the "will" of the human subject could produce an effect on these objects as they moved. In terms of total energy involved, the effects secured have been small, but definitely measurable. For that matter, the sparks from Franklin's electric machine were small too, compared to the power of electricity in a thunderstorm. Today the PK tests are perhaps only comparable to Franklin's, but so many different researches have been made that the reality of the effect can be taken as established.

It is not easy to see just how PK could be the basis of the effects observed in cases of clocks that stop and pictures that fall at times of crisis. We do know at least, however, that in a PK test an objective physical effect is not the only one produced. A subjective, mental influence is also involved, or at least the effect has a subjective aspect. In the physical world each face of the die is the same. It is merely a cube, and cubes know no numbers 1, 2, 3, 4, 5, 6. The numbers are mental concepts and somehow in the PK process the mental and physical must have combined to produce the desired result, as when that was to have a specific face come up. Similarly, to produce any of the physical effects coincident with crises, taken as reported, a combination of intelligence and physical force would be necessary.

Much more, and more far-reaching research on PK is needed. As yet, for example, we do not know the effect of distance on PK. We know that distance does not limit ESP (and PK and ESP are closely related phenomena). A number of PK experiments have covered distances up to twenty-five yards and suggest that distance as such may not be inhibiting here either, but a much more extensive inquiry is needed to make sure.

It is also still unknown whether PK can occur without the *conscious* volition of the person exercising it. Although we know that ESP is an unconscious operation, in all the PK tests so far, the subject or person responsible for the effect is not only aware of the falling dice but he deliberately sets out to will that they fall in a specified way. Although he is unaware of whether or not his effort is successful until the result is observed, no one knows if an effect would be produced without his conscious willing.

In the cases under consideration, a question comparable to the unsolved one in telepathy comes up. Here, too, two persons are involved. The question is, if PK is involved, which person exercises it: the one who observes the occurrence and is rather close to it, or the distant one, usually undergoing a crisis? He is the one who traditionally has been assumed to be the agent. On *a priori* grounds, however, either of the two, or both, could exert the PK effect.

Since we found the emphasis here more regularly on the observer than the other, it is to be noted, that if he is the one responsible he plays his part entirely unconsciously and unsuspectingly. When the event coincides with a crisis in the experience of someone living or dying, usually the observer could only know the crisis by ESP. As we know, however, the crises of close friends and relatives seem particularly likely to be picked up by ESP, although in cases of ESP they are expressed in dreams, intuitions and ESP hallucinations. We thus come to the suggestion that these physical or *motor* effects could be simply another way besides those of ESP of expressing or registering a psi message.

Suppositions so far out as this one seem at first almost fantastic; they do go beyond established facts. But only time can tell whether they go unreasonably far. The knowledge that could support them can only be obtained by careful, reliable experiment, repeated and confirmed as have been the facts now established about ESP.

· 15

Communications from Beyond?

One of man's oldest and greatest questions is raised anew by some of the psi experiences. It is the question of the destiny of the human personality. Does some part of man live on after death? Certain psi experiences suggest that the answer is "yes." Indeed, the idea of an afterlife has surely been strengthened by "psychic" occurrences that suggest the agency of persons deceased. The idea today is most familiar as a part of orthodox religion: the doctrine of immortality.

As a religious doctrine, immortality has been widely accepted on authority alone. Comparatively little scientific attention has been given it, in spite of the advance of knowledge in other areas of human affairs. In this modern age of scientific standards and ways of thought, evidence that seems to bear on the question needs to be weighed carefully and critically just as that on other topics of importance to mankind is weighed. Of the several lines of such evidence, only one concerns us here—the one made up of ESP experiences.

Many personal experiences that have been taken to imply the post-mortem survival of personality, however, do not afford objective evidence, the only kind that can be used as data in a scientific investigation. Such experiences may be very vivid and convincing to the person to whom they occur, but give no evidence that is not possibly explicable in terms of the person's own psychological processes. Under the stress of bereavement and personal need, an individual may feel the presence of the deceased, dream vividly of him or see him in a "vision." But if the experience brings him no *objective in-*

formation; in other words, if it does not qualify as involving psi, it is not of interest here.

Psi experiences that are relevant here are those in which the dead appear to bring objective information. The question such cases raise is whether the messages are what they appear to be: communications from a world beyond. A "yes" on this would be a "yes" on the larger question of the survival of death. A "no" would not necessarily answer it.

A young American in the Air Force during World War II had an experience that brought him objective evidence. He had entered the service several years after his mother's death, and was now a tail gunner in a B-29. He had been flying on missions over Europe, and one night he and his crew were returning to their base after completing a bombing mission. All the crew except the pilots were asleep when in a dream the gunner saw his mother standing on the tip of one wing of his plane. She was dressed in white flowing robes and calling his name, warning him of danger. She begged him to awake, that danger was very near. Her voice was far away and echoed in his dream—yet it was so realistic he awoke . . . to find a German fighter plane flying directly above their B-29 and out of vision of the pilot or copilot. With the rest of the crew asleep, no one had known the enemy was there. The gunner wakened his companions and they were able to fight off the plane before any damage was done. He felt that had it not been for his mother's warning, neither he nor his crew members would have escaped.

Experiences like this, if taken seriously, seem to mean that the deceased was in some sense "there." But the discovery of psi ability has complicated the question of interpreting such experiences. It has also removed some of the evidence that once was thought to have bearing on the question. This evidence includes experiences that occur *at* or *before* the time of death, as in the case of a woman in Pennsylvania. She awoke one night from a simple but disturbing dream. It was only 4 A.M. when she awoke, but the dream was so vivid and so upset her that she could not go back to sleep. The dream, she says, was only that "My cousin Lucille had appeared and told me she was going away.

" 'Why, Lucille, you mean you are leaving your husband and the children?'

"She said she was. I asked her where she was going, but she just disappeared out the door. It was as if someone had awakened me and I got up, wide awake.

"Later that morning they called me to say that Lucille, who as far as I knew was in perfect health, had had some kind of an attack and was unconscious. She remained so until she died that same day.

"I felt as though I had been talking with the dead. I went all to pieces. I am positive my cousin was trying to let me know she was dying."

However meaningful experiences like that may be, one must recognize that they cannot tell us what happens *after* death, for the person, even if in the death crisis, was still living. For definitive evidence it is necessary, therefore, to look to cases involving those already dead.

Experiences in which someone dead appears are comparatively rare, but they are reported often enough to make data for study. They come in various forms. Unrealistic dreams like that of the tail gunner above are perhaps the most frequent. As we saw in the preceding chapter, sometimes physical occurrences are associated with a deceased person. The hallucinatory form, too, is occasionally involved, either as an auditory or a visual experience. Although the former is more frequent, the latter (in recent times very seldom reported) is nevertheless the most often mentioned.

A possible instance of a visual hallucination occurred in a family in Ohio some years ago. Several young daughters slept in one room in different beds. One night ten-year-old Mary wakened her mother in an adjoining room to complain that her older sister Nancy was standing by her bed and wouldn't go away. The mother went to the girls' room, and saw that Nancy was asleep in her own bed, and she thought Mary was just imagining things. Before long Mary again disturbed her mother. Nancy was standing by her bed, she said, but she wouldn't answer when spoken to. Again the mother went to the girls' room and again found Nancy asleep. Throughout the night at intervals Mary kept talking to Nancy, asking her to please go over to her own bed.

The next morning, as was their custom, the family arose, leaving Nancy asleep, for she was not a strong child and needed extra rest. Later, at bed-making time, her mother called her and getting no response, came closer and discovered that Nancy was dead. The doctor's opinion was that she must have died soon after retiring.

Over the years, visual hallucinations of the dead have become notorious. Referred to as ghosts, spectres or apparitions, they have accumulated a quite exaggerated aura of mystery. Their psychological origin has been so much debated, and science has so firmly relegated them to the realm of pure imagination or superstition, as to make them the natural subject matter for wild and woolly fiction. In the hands of imaginative authors, the idea of ghosts and apparitions has often led to such unrestrained flights of fancy as to give the words connotations that do not fit well in an objective and matter-of-fact discussion, such as this one. Unlike the lurid ghosts of fiction, the figures "seen" in visual psi hallucinations are, as in cases already given, quite realistic. They seldom show the fantasy or the dramatization that often characterizes dream experiences. The deceased person is likely to appear as he was known in life and in the garb he might have been expected to wear.

No matter what the form in these cases involving the dead, they are no different from those that do *not* imply spirit survival. On that account, it is clear that forms *as such* do not distinguish or tell one whether a deceased person actually had a part. As far as it is a matter of the form, the living person presumably could have produced it himself, just as in any other instance of ESP.

If form, then, is not the answer, one must look beyond it to various other aspects of the experiences from which one might hope to get a basis for a judgment. One such might be in the imagery used. In some forms—dreams in particular—it is detailed and profuse. Can one here find evidence of the influence of the discarnate?

All dreams significant to this inquiry are in the unrealistic category because someone dead appears in them, someone no longer part of "real life." One finds, however, that the imagery used varies just as in other unrealistic dreams. In some instances, it is unreal and fantasy-like, as in the case of the tail gunner whose mother appeared on the wing-tip of his plane dressed in white flowing robes. In other experiences, one may find a much more mundane and realistic form of imagery, which still, of course, is not true realism. A woman in Pennsylvania had such an experience. Five years before, her father had died while visiting a relative, Howard, to whom he had been much attached. One night she dreamed that the telephone rang and that she jumped out of bed to answer it. She says: "A voice I instantly recognized as Father's said, 'Hello, is that you, Alice?'

" 'Yes, Father! Where are you?'

"In a voice so happy and light, he answered, 'Here. I called to tell you we are looking for Howard at any time now. We will be glad to see him but sorry for the ones he left there.'

"Then changing, he said, 'How are Billie and Jane?' (My two children.) The connection was broken, but I woke up and was very much disturbed. It seemed it couldn't be a dream. So I wrote and told my brother about it, and as he and his wife were reading my letter they got a phone call telling them that Howard had just passed away at a Pittsburgh hospital. I hadn't known he was sick."

Among unrealistic ESP dreams in general, it is not unusual that an individual be dramatized even as if present, and dream conversations that bring information to the dreamer are not unusual.

When the person pictured as present and conversing is someone alive, however, the dream dramatization is unmistakable, and the person is clearly not an actual participant, no matter how convincing the experience may have seemed to the dreamer at the time.

A woman in London knew that her husband, a machine gunner, was dangerously ill in a hospital in Italy. As she says: "One night I had gone to bed, which I shared with my sister, and my last thought was a prayer for my loved one. How long I slept I cannot say, but suddenly I seemed to be wide awake, and to my amazement I saw my husband sitting beside my bed. He looked desperately ill but he seemed to be swaying as though he was in a bus or some fast-going vehicle. Also he had his hat on with a peak at one side and looked as if he were too weak to put it straight, and had been hurriedly dressed. He gave me such a look, no words can explain, and called me by a pet name he used. I called to my sister, 'Eva, Eva, Arthur is dead. I have seen him.'

"She tried to comfort me and some days later I had news that he had been moved to France and was not expected to live. Well, he did. When he came home I asked him the time he was moved and if he had been dressed as I described. He said, 'Yes. Exactly.' They had been badly bombed and had had to evacuate camp very hurriedly. I said, 'What were you thinking?' He said, 'I thanked God that I would be nearer you.' As those thoughts were formed, I actually saw him as he was, even to only having one shirt button left and no tie. That, too, he said was correct. My sister can vouch for this."

One must conclude, then, that the varied imagery in which the roles of the deceased are expressed in these unrealistic dreams does not go beyond the bounds of ordinary dream imagery when the dead are not involved. One cannot assume that the dead were involved because of it, whether it be unrealism, as in the tail gunner's dream, or a simulated realism, as in the telephone conversation.

On the other hand, however, one cannot say that the deceased had no part in these experiences. Perhaps in some obscure way he caused the dreamer to have the dream. After all, its content was something he presumably would have wanted the dreamer to know.

When we turn attention specifically to the content of these experiences, whether dreams or any of the other forms, it is of several main kinds. One of the more common could be called general information. Such was the message of the telephone conversation above. In that case, the information came unsolicited, as one might say, but even if it comes as if in response to direct request or need, the deceased seems no less to be playing an active role. A young man in Los Angeles after his mother's death found he had inherited not only her objective belongings but also some of her human obligations. Among these was an unfortunate dipsomaniac acquaintance to whom his mother had given help and advice, as he says, "any number of times after I had long since lost patience with her drinking and other weaknesses. Now she had disappeared after being discharged for drunkenness by the wealthy family for whom she had been working.

"Late at night, after notifying the rather listless police, I was at my wits' end and stood resting for a minute on the rail outside the lawn surrounding City Hall. Without thinking, I said aloud, 'Well, Mom, I've done my best to find her and now I don't know where else to look. I am very much afraid she will commit suicide, thinking all her friends have left her now that you are gone.' Quite clearly and at once, I heard my mother say, "'Why, Dick, she is right over there in that little old hotel.'

"I wasn't particularly shocked or afraid. Looking over, I saw the little hotel about a block away. I asked at the desk for Mrs. B. She was registered there and came out at once, her face white, and she had been crying. I knew she was about to take her life. 'Dick, how did you ever find out in time I was here?' she asked. I told her that Mother had told me and she smiled and nodded as if she might have known that. You see, she had attempted to drop out of sight from everyone and no one could possibly have known where she had gone after she left the house upon the mountain where she had been discharged."

Messages from the deceased often bring warnings of danger

and/or information to the living person, as in the case of the tail gunner's mother. Often the presence of the deceased seems very real and details may be noticed, which far from being items in consciousness, are on the mental level of "forgotten memories." An overwrought businesswoman-housewife in California one night found she needed a quiet place of refuge away from the distractions and interruptions of home. She says:

"I had a good book, and for peace and quiet I went back to the office in the plant. After about an hour I suddenly had an intense sense of my father's nearness, though he had been dead ten years. I even 'saw' his expressive hands and, of all things, his watch fob—an old-fashioned one he had not worn for many years before his death. I also heard his voice using my childhood nickname say, 'Girlie, leave here at once.' Quickly I left and was in the car going home before I realized with what immediate obedience I had acted.

"The next morning when I opened the plant along with the others, we found that the place had been entered and someone with the big axe used for splitting beef carcasses had opened a number of possible places where money might have been. The place was wantonly damaged as well. According to the night watchman, who had seen me come and also leave, the entrance of the intruder was between my departure and his next round, when he saw a car pull away from the back entrance.

"In retrospect, I could remember nothing which would have made my father definitely on my mind that night, nor account for the very positive feeling that he was warning me in person."

It is noteworthy that such warnings usually come from some deceased person like a parent to whom the living one had looked in the past for help and protection. It is again quite possible that on unconscious levels the old orientation persists, that this authoritative person might be the dramatic symbol of a clairvoyant or precognitive impression, rather than a communication from the dead.

I was reminded of this possibility recently because of an experience, not involving psi, of my own. In the grip of a nightmare—evidently close to, but not quite at, the level of wakefulness—I was presented with a terrible menace and I struggled to call for help. Eventually I found a voice and woke myself by crying out my childhood name *for my father,* who died fifteen years ago, and from whose protecting presence I have now been separated for over forty years.

The old habit, certainly now far below my conscious level, still asserted itself.

However, if the dangers in these cases were perceived extrasensorially by the living persons themselves, the method of projecting them *as if* coming from a deceased protector seems very round-about. If, on the other hand, the deceased were still aware of the life situation, he would be the very person who would give a warning, and that would seem to be a more direct explanation. But questions such as these are not solved by saying "it seems to be." One must recognize that in estimates like these of what seems more direct, or less, he may be influenced by the cultural hangover of pre-ESP days. As yet it is too early to say whether or not the apparent "roundabout" aspect of an interpretation is an argument against it.

Closely similar to warning cases are those in which the deceased seems to bring help of one kind or another to someone for whom in life he felt responsibility. In 1947 in California, a young man died suddenly of pneumonia, only seven weeks after his marriage. His young wife was left almost prostrated, not only by the shock of his death but by attendant financial worries with which she had not had the experience to deal. Among other things, his death had occurred so soon after their marriage that he had not gotten around to having his life insurance transferred to her; she was worried about hospital and funeral expenses and did not know whether his mother, who would collect on two large policies, would pay the bills or not.

After the funeral she packed and put in storage all household goods. During the packing she ran across a small black bag that she had not seen before. She thought she would go through it when she had more time.

About six weeks later she awakened one morning early—just enough to hear vaguely the traffic in the street. Suddenly she thought she was standing on the top step of her front porch. Her husband was leaning against the trunk of a tree a few feet away. Without a word he pointed to the lower step: there was the small black bag. That was all of the dream.

She tried to forget the dream, but it stayed in her mind until finally she decided to look for the bag. She found it and it was full of insurance policies on her husband that had all lapsed as long as five years before. There must have been a dozen. She was discarding them, as she examined them, until she came to a certain one. The instant she touched this one she knew it was significant. It had been five years since the last payment on it had lapsed, but somehow she just had to investigate further. She called the insurance office and learned the policy was still payable after death; and since it did not name a beneficiary, it would be paid to her. She collected it with interest. If the death had occurred eighteen days later, it would have been worthless. It would have been months before she would have discovered this policy, without the dream, since she did not take her belongings out of storage for almost a year. In cases like this, just as in warnings, the relationship of the deceased and living is reciprocal: The deceased would have wanted to help the living person, and he was one of those to whom the living would turn in times of need.

We come now to a group of cases in which the messages are quite different. Instead of giving warnings or aid to the living person, the deceased seems to be sending assurance of his continued existence. These could be called "identification messages." A woman in Pennsylvania tells of something that happened the night after the death of her grandfather. As she says: "He was a coffee fiend. He lived on coffee. When he came to anyone's house they knew they must put the coffee pot on or he would.

"In our family we entertain the family in the kitchen, for we love to sit around the table and gab. That night, people came and went, but gathered around the kitchen table with coffee cups sat the daughters and sons. Just automatically Aunt Lois started to make coffee. Papa made coffee in this pot for years; it's a drip with a pottery bottom. When she poured the boiling water in the top, the drip part of the pot jumped out of the bottom part and blew apart with a loud bang. Everyone looked as if slapped in the face. Lois got it together to make it over again, and it happened again and again. They could not make coffee in that pot until after my grandfather was buried."

The unspoken interpretation in cases such as that is that the deceased is indicating to the living that he has survived. But if a psi element is involved, in this instance PK, the question of whether the living or the dead exerted it would come up. We know that while the deceased may be interested in assuring the living they still survive, the living are also interested in the assurance.

All in all, no matter what the content of the experience, then, we find no unquestionable indications that the deceased have had a part in producing these experiences. We still have to say that a living person certainly shaped each experience in accordance with his capacity for ESP, and that thus far we cannot tell whether the living one was the sole author of it. But if either one *could* have been responsible, one could still ask which one *would* have been. The motives of each party thus came under scrutiny. Motives can give clues. Detectives use them constantly to try to decide between suspects. Let us see what they show in a mystery like this one.

WHOSE MOTIVE?

Detectives have to establish a motive in their suspects, or to show that the motive of one was greater than that of another. Here, the question is: would the living person himself have produced this experience? In most instances we can suppose to begin with that both of the two, the living and the deceased persons, might have had some interest in the message. The question really is whether that of the living person can be presumed strong enough to account for his experience. One cannot, of course, use presumptions about the deceased as arguments, because his part is the point to be established.

Many of these experiences, as we have seen, involve two persons closely related, and who presumably would be equally interested in a topic such as the survival of the deceased one, after death. A girl in New York State was involved in such a case, in an experience in which ordinary explanations seemed unsatisfactory, and which therefore appeared to be a message from her deceased father, a PK experience. Her story goes like this:

"My father died in 1946, at the age of seventy. I have always hoped that there is life after death, but there has always been a slight doubt in my mind when I asked myself how it could possibly be. However, something happened two years ago last summer which leaves no doubt in my mind now, about eternal life.

"My mother and I have lived together since my father's death, and we take in roomers to supplement our income. One morning, my mother and I were alone in the house, and we were sitting at the kitchen table. The cellar door, which is off a small entryway out of the kitchen toward the front hall, was open and pushed all the way back toward the front hall. No windows at the front of the house downstairs were open, and the front door at the end of the hall was closed.

"My mother and I were discussing a serious problem one of my older sisters had at the time, and I had it in mind to say, 'If Dad were alive, I wonder what he'd say.' I spoke the words 'If Dad were alive,' and before I could speak another word, the cellar door slammed shut with such a tremendous bang that my mother and I literally jumped out of our chairs.

"We were very much frightened at first, because we have to push fairly hard to close the cellar door in the summer, when dampness gets into the house. There was no noticeable wind that day, and there would have had to have been practically a hurricane force to have closed the door from the upstairs windows which were open, as the stairway is at the right of the hall, parallel with the hall. Halfway up, the stairs turn and run perpendicular, towards the hall, but blocked off by a wall from the downstairs hall. Also, any wind coming from the pantry or cellar windows which were open would have pushed at the door the other way, instead of closing it. Since there was no through draft, we couldn't figure out how the door could have slammed shut by itself. Then suddenly I realized the words I had spoken in reference to my father, and my mother and I felt he must be near us, and we were no longer frightened.

"A few minutes later, we started talking about my sister again, and inadvertently, without consciously realizing it, I started to repeat the same phrase again concerning my father. A split second after I had said, 'If Dad were alive,' down came the kitchen curtain. Of course, the curtain could have fallen by itself, but it happened right after the door had slammed, and after I had said the same words about my father. I think it was Dad's way of telling us he lives."

Obviously, when relationships are reciprocal, the motivations of the two cannot be thought of as decisively different. They sometimes seem about even, too, when the two people are only casual acquaintances: If, for instance, they both have a similar background of interest. Such was the situation in the case of a man in England, a personal acquaintance of mine. He had a friend, Mr. D., who like him was interested in scientific subjects, and they sometimes exchanged books. My acquaintance, Mr. W., loaned Mr. D. one on psychic research. It contained the story of two friends who made a compact that whichever died first would attempt to let the other know by any means possible. One of the two in the story one night noticed the chandelier over his desk swinging and he was later informed that the other died at that time.

As Mr. W. tells the story, "On Sunday, May 29, 1932, I attended morning services and on leaving the church my friend came up and said, 'I've brought your book back, Herbert.' I asked him what he thought of it. He said, 'Well, I thought it was rather good.' To which I replied, 'Yes, but that story of the swinging chandelier takes some swallowing,' for although I was interested in psychic science I had difficulty in believing that psychic forces could move physical objects."

Mr. D. died suddenly within the next twenty-four hours. Mr. W. had been notified of the death only about one hour before, when, on the evening of May 30, he relates:

"I was standing in front of my dressing table (about six P.M.) when I heard a sharp click and, looking around, saw the two wooden pear-shaped switches hanging over the middle of the bedstead swinging to and fro and now and then hitting each other with a clicking sound as they swung.

"At rest these two switches hung about six inches apart. I tried to get a natural explanation by slamming doors, etc., but nothing I could do gave them more than an almost imperceptible tremor. All my bias is against a psychic explanation, but it seems to be the only one that will meet the facts of this occurrence."

What about the comparable motives, or interest of the two men, in thus having a "sign" from the beyond? On that basis one must assume the interest of the living one to have been no less than that of the deceased.

Sometimes a third person is involved, one who is ostensibly the individual most directly concerned in the message. This third person may be someone equally related to the other two, or more significantly in our present quest, someone to whom the deceased had been closer than was the living observer.

A young couple in New York, Larry and Violet, had been sweethearts for several years. Larry fell ill and died. There had been no formal engagement and although Larry's mother had met Violet at his funeral, she was absorbed in her own grief and did not see or hear from the girl until one night some three months later when she had a strange experience.

At 3 A.M. one Sunday morning she thought her son, Larry, stood in the doorway of her room and called to her to help Violet, that Violet was in trouble.

In great perturbation the mother, Mrs. M., waited till morning, and then at seven o'clock she phoned the girl, saying that she was "Mother M," and she wondered if Violet was all right? Violet did not answer, so Mother M told her to let her know if she ever could be of help, and thinking it strange she got no answer, she hung up.

Some weeks later, Violet's mother phoned saying she and Violet would like to call. They came and told her what had happened. Violet had fainted at the phone that Sunday morning.

When Larry was courting her, he always brought her home right to her apartment door, but it seemed that after his death, she began to keep late hours, and to get home after the elevator in her apartment building stopped running (twelve o'clock).

The night of the trouble she came home about 3 A.M., the time of Larry's appearance to his mother. The elevator was not running and she had to walk up. On the second floor she was attacked and raped. The phone call from Mother M that morning was too much and she fainted. But she still did not tell her parents what had happened to her. Now—long enough later that the result was certain—she had told her mother of the occurrence. They called because Violet needed help and did not know which way to turn. Mother M felt that a message from those who have passed on was not to be ignored. She took Violet to a midwife. And thus she helped her as her son had asked.

Naturally, the decision as to the source of the message in cases like this is difficult. The weight of the motive seems to lie strongly on the side of the deceased. But the living person too would surely have had a degree of concern. Was it strong enough?

Occasionally the relationship is such that the living receiver is quite unrelated and apparently unattached to a third person to whom the message is directed. It, therefore, comes in an indirect way, in which at least any motivation the living person would have would not be the obvious one of emotional attachment.

A man who in 1912 was a Columbia law student says, "I was then nearly broke. I wrote my father for a loan. He was expanding his business and, as it happened, also broke. But he sent me a collection of ancient coins he had inherited from his father, saying I might be able to borrow and use them as security.

"I needed thirty-five dollars and located an old coin shop in the city. I showed my box of coins, which were twice fingered, and obtained my thirty-five dollars. The numismatist wrapped and sealed the box, gave me no receipt and I parted from him and the coins, never to see either again. When I returned to redeem the coins, he was not there, no one knew of him and my letters were returned.

"My father wrote suggesting that I not mention the loss to my family and said that he had not. I married, was practicing law, and did not discuss this with anyone. But I was deeply worried and had in mind a fund for distribution to my sisters on my father's death, which occurred in 1924.

"Very soon after his funeral I received a letter from a woman in Washington State who had served as temporary stenographer for me months before. She said she did not understand but would tell me of an incident. The night before, in a dream, an elderly gentleman had appeared before her, saying he was my father. He was rather short and stocky, bald with a wide sweeping mustache, and very like me. He begged her to listen, said he had tried to give me a message and could not. He knew she knew me and asked her to tell me from him, 'Not to worry about the coins,' that I would understand.

"My father always wore a wide-spreading mustache. He was about five feet, six inches tall, broad and strong. His message meant a great deal to me in my obligation to my mother and sisters on a problem I did not know how to solve, but must solve if I was to rest easy in mind and conscience.

"How could this woman have described my father, written the admonition against worrying about the coins? The only written record was the name and address of the place I left them."

Pursuing this line further, it sometimes happens that the relationship is even more remote, for the person getting the message may not even have had any direct connection whatever with the deceased.

A woman in California who had a couple of pure-bred dogs sometimes sent puppies to a kennel some distance away in the southern part of the state. Although she had corresponded occasionally with the owners of the kennel, she had never met them. Then one night she says she dreamed: "I was wandering in a crowd of very happy people when a man came up to me and took my hand. He was laughing and seemed so pleased to see me. He said, 'I've always wanted to meet you as I do so enjoy your letters.' I said, 'I don't know you, do I?' He said, 'Yes, you do, because of the little dogs. Remember that? Because of the little dogs.' I said, 'I don't know what you mean about the dogs.' He said, 'Remember about the little dogs and you must tell her you saw me, as it will comfort her.'

"I awoke and told my dream to several people and my husband. The dream was so vivid I could not shake it and so I told it several times. After two weeks I got a letter from the wife of the kennel owner telling me that when her husband had gone to pick up my puppies he had died from a heart attack while in the station. Before he left the house he hadn't felt well, but had told her he must go to get the little dogs. I wrote her of my dream, describing the man who spoke to me. Both she and her son wrote back telling me that the man in my dream was their husband and father beyond a doubt."

Beyond a doubt, too, the deceased in that instance would have had a stronger more immediate motive in getting that message across than the dreamer would have had. The question is, would hers have been just strong enough to have caused her to have this unrealistic dream?

In the preceding cases, the strength of the personal motives of the living can be seen to vary greatly. It is never quite possible to say that a person had *no* motive for his experience, though in some instances it seems clear that he did not have a strong one. But remembering the "free-ranging" tendency of some minds in getting ESP information, it is evident that at least some persons have ESP experiences without strong motivation, and also that they may upon occasion draw information from a practically unlimited range of sources. On that account, in these cases of obviously low motive on the part of the living person, one still cannot finally say that he could not himself have obtained this information and dramatized it into the form it took in his experience. He need not have, and the influence of the deceased could have been a factor. But—no matter how much the influence of spirit agency appears to have been the important factor in some of the cases—the comparison of motives leaves the question unsettled, for in *no* experience is it possible to say that *only* the deceased would have had any motive in transferring the information.

A few cases are reported in which some special circumstance seems to add weight to the likelihood that the deceased was the active party. One such instance involved a Canadian woman of my acquaintance and her twenty-one-year-old son, Ned, who had been instantly killed in an accident. For some time after his death his mother had dreams in which he appeared. And then his sister Ethel too began to have vivid and lifelike dreams of him. One night his mother, lying awake, was thinking of him and of the possibility of sending him a message "by telepathy" as she thought *he* might have been doing to *them* in the dreams of him she and her daughter had been having. She tried to think what message she could send that would be vital enough to penetrate the "great silence."

Suddenly she knew just what it should be. She had longed to tell him after he was gone how she had regretted that she could not even kiss him good-bye.

"I decided to try to concentrate on this and to send him that last kiss, so with my mind a blank to all else I tried to send the message. Then in a moment of hopeful enthusiasm I asked him to send me back a kiss if he received my message.

"Once it was done I thought it was a pretty foolish request. The only way he could send me a kiss would be in a dream and then I would think I had cooked it up in my own subconscious. I had asked the impossible, so I dismissed it from my mind, thinking, 'That is that.'

"Several days later, but within a week, Ethel called me up to tell me that she had had another dream in her series. Incidentally, I had not mentioned my experiment to anyone, and in fact had not thought further about it. So imagine my surprise when Ethel said, 'It is a funny thing. Always before when I have dreamed of Ned he has come at once and put his arms around me and kissed me. But this time he turned his back on me and kissed you instead. I was rather hurt and said, "Why, Ned, aren't you going to kiss me?" He laughed like anything and came over right away and kissed me, too.'

"Naturally I was struck forcibly by this answer coming out of the blue. It was such a clever way around the difficulty. She did not know she was getting a special message for me, and furthermore, the time interval of several days made it appear that she had not received the message telepathically from me, but that it had traveled by a more round-about way through other intermediaries.

"There was another interesting thing about it. Ethel had mentioned being puzzled by Ned's laughter, and was hurt, for she didn't see anything funny about his having neglected to greet her. In my mind, his laughter was about the most pointed part of the dream. If she had been receiving the material for her dream from my mind, this part which was so clear to me should not have been so obscure to her. That seems fairly obvious. Furthermore, she recognized the dream as one of her series because it carried, too, reassurance to her over an immediate problem of her own. It did not occur to her that it contained any special import for me until I told her. I have never undertaken any further experiments of this sort, for the only message I felt a real need of getting across had gone."

In this case, although one cannot distinguish between the strength of motive of mother and son, or of daughter and son, the process by which the living persons could have produced the effect is complicated by the introduction of the third person, the sister of the deceased. This tends to tip the balance toward him, without absolutely excluding the living.

Another kind of circumstance which can tip an otherwise balanced situation is the introduction into the message of some item with which the living person is, or thinks he is, quite unfamiliar. Such items, if "good" enough, would add another aspect by which one could try to distinguish between the parts played by the living and the dead.

A woman in Connecticut had a very realistic dream about her father, who had died the week before. In fact, it was so real she could not believe afterward it was a dream. At least, at the end of it, she was sitting up in bed and was very cold. She thought she had been up and down stairs and that her father had been there. As she recalls:

"It seemed as if I had just come back. I woke my husband and asked him, 'Have I been out of bed?' He answered, 'I don't know.' Then I said, 'Well, Father came and told me something to tell Mother and he said I would forget about it before morning. I am afraid I will forget it, so will you remember this word? It is a word I have never heard before. My father told me to tell my mother something about the furnace and that if she would look she would find a ——— on the pipe. Now don't forget it, for it would be awful if I can't remember the word to tell my mother." My husband repeated the word after me, but forgot it by morning and so did I. The word is the object on the pipe on the furnace, but here is what happened in the dream.

"I seemed to have been downstairs in my kitchen. It was night; it was very cold and I was standing with my back to the stove, which was banked and had little heat. I was shivering. I heard a clattering coming toward the front door like chains dragging and shuffling feet. I opened the door and my father came in. He had his big overcoat on that he wore to work and he was very cold. I was terrified with fright but tried not to show it. I said to him, 'You frightened me, but I am glad to see you. You look so cold. Are you all right? Please forgive me for being frightened.' He looked at me in a sad, but annoyed way and said, 'I have been trying to get something over to your mother but can't seem to, so I came to you. She is having trouble with the furnace. I want you to tell her something and don't forget. I want you to tell her that I rigged up something on the back of the pipe.' He called it something like a generator or some name I am not familiar with. I said, 'How could I forget a thing you came back from the other side to tell me?' He said, 'Well, you will forget it. You are always forgetting something, leaving your pocketbooks around everyplace, never remembering anything.' Then he said, 'I can't stay here long. They allowed me to come here to tell you that and I must be getting back.'

"Next morning I tried and tried to remember the word and my husband did too, but we could not. I hated to tell my mother for fear she would take it lightly, but the next night I went to see her and told her about it. She said, 'Isn't that strange? I almost burned the house down last night. You see your father had always tended to the furnace and he had rigged up some contraption on the pipe he never told me about. The furnace was overheating and I was almost ready to call the fire department when I finally got your brother out of bed by phoning him. I thought he would not answer the phone but he did. Just in time we found this gadget that you father had rigged up.'"

If the word had been remembered and found to be one the person had never known in connection with its specific application as her father used it, then the case might illustrate knowledge which would seem more likely to have come from the deceased. Unfortunately, the word was not remembered. Perhaps it was not such an unusual word after all; not one rarely used in this connection and not one this person had never heard. Without being certain, therefore, that the missing word was an actual datum, one cannot tell whether perhaps the daughter had—instead of a "message from beyond"—an unrealistic dream stimulated by ESP knowledge of the crisis concerning the furnace. A technical term like that, however, could add to the case for the agency of the deceased.

A few, though a very few, incidents are on record in which a child seems to get a message from someone deceased. If a very young child is involved, however, it may be necessary to *assume* the agency of the deceased from its actions. This, of course, detracts from the certainty of interpretation of the episode. A situation of this kind is reported by a woman from New York. In the summer of 1945 she and her husband rented, "sight unseen," through an agent, a beach cottage on the New Jersey coast.

After their arrival their two-year-old son was put in one of the bedrooms for his afternoon nap. His mother heard him saying "See man. See man." She peeped in the room and he was standing up in his crib, smiling and pointing upward. On succeeding days it happened again and again, the baby sometimes urging the parents into the room with great insistence. He would toddle out of the room, take the hand of some member of the family, make that person return to the room, and point with smiling recognition, saying, "See man." At times they would peek into the room without his knowing and watch him smile, offer toys, etc., to this invisible man. He had never before appeared to see things they could not see, and this time they could find no shadow, furniture shape or anything remotely resembling a man where he pointed.

This behavior continued over the entire month of their stay at the cottage. The day they were leaving, the owner, of whom they had known nothing, called. When she entered she became very upset and close to tears. She explained that it was her first time back since her husband's death the previous year. He had loved the place and had died in the bedroom the baby had used.

When she saw the little boy, she remarked that her husband would have "loved this adorable baby. He was so fond of children."

In a few instances, an incident involving a young person able to remember and himself report it, seems impressive because the content or implication of the episode seems to have been beyond his full comprehension at the time.

In 1919 in Oklahoma, a fifteen-year-old girl had a dream in which it seemed that her deceased stepfather gave her a warning message about her mother. She and stepfather had been very close. As she says: "Mother was a very sweet person, a Christian who had always walked the straight and narrow. After Dad's death we rented a small house and the people from whom we rented were, as far as I then knew, an ideal couple.

"One night I was sleeping with Mother, and I had hardly thought about Dad all day, when all of a sudden about ten minutes after we had gone to bed and I had not been asleep . . . I heard Dad's voice as plain as I ever heard it while he was alive. It seemed to be coming from the other side of the mountains and the voice said, 'Sis,' (his pet name for me) 'your mother is getting into some serious trouble. There will be a lot of gossip, but you stay with her through it all; she is a good woman and I love her.'

"I touched Mother as soon as the voice was gone and told word for word what Dad's voice had said. She said she knew of nothing that would cause him to say a thing like that and that I was probably dreaming.

"The voice also said, 'There is a gulf between us, so you stay with her through what is going to happen, for I cannot come to her.' With that the voice died away.

"In less than a year the man we were renting from had convinced Mother that he had not lived with his wife for six years, and that he wanted Mother to marry him. Actually, he was still living with wife number one, but he got her to get a divorce. There was a scandal and until this day poor Mother is still paying for her mistake. His relationship with her proved to be a bad one in every way. He wasn't ever good to her. Why did she go on and get into all that trouble, lose her good name and almost her life?

"Why did that voice come to me? At the time I did not know anything about the man. But it all happened as Father said. I stayed with her just as he asked me to and I've never been sorry I did."

Granted that the girl would have had a strong motive to help her mother, could she at fifteen sufficiently have understood the situation to have foreseen the consequences and recognized the danger? The deceased husband, of course, would have fully understood.

In these different cases, one can see the issues and something of the difficulty of judgment they present. In a few instances, the motives seem unequal, and definitely much weaker on the part of the living, than the deceased. In a few other cases, some added factor or complication seems to increase still more the likelihood that the living person himself was not the unaided author of his experience. But in each individual case, individual weaknesses can be adduced, just as is true of practically any ESP experience, if taken alone. As pointed out in the beginning, the strength of ESP experiences in life, as treated in this book, lies in the large number of them, against the background of experimental laboratory proof of psi. On the question of the influence of the deceased, both elements of strength are lacking. For in the first place, the number of experiences which bear on the topic is comparatively small. In contrast to the multitude of cases that bear witness to telepathy or precognition, these are almost negligible. Only the special interest of the problem they present, not their weight of numbers, singles them out for attention.

In the second place, experimental results proving the survival of some element of personality are lacking. The nearest approach that has ever been made to experimental treatment of the survival question has been in studies of mediums, the individuals who seem to bring communications from the dead by automatic writing, by trance utterances, or otherwise. Studies of several mediums under strict control have been made and deserve to be called experimental, for they were so conducted that it was possible to rule out the medium's sensory knowledge, her shrewdness of reasoning, and the possibility of unguarded disclosures by the person who sought communication through her. Yet material received under these conditions still had to be judged correct or incorrect by the persons for whom it was intended, and in this judgment was a possible source of error.

In a study at Duke University by J. B. Rhine and J. G. Pratt, an added safeguard was used for the first time, in that the person for whom the material was intended did not know which of the medium's utterances—presented in form of typed records which the person was asked to check—was meant for him. By this method it was shown that the medium tested (Mrs. Eileen Garrett) had given correct information to a statistically significant degree.

In spite of all this refinement of technique, however, the experiment still left the important question unanswered. Did the information the medium gave come from the deceased persons who had purported to bring it or did the medium produce it via her own (well-documented) ESP ability, unconsciously dramatized into the form of a message from the deceased? The inquiry still rests there, with the same question unanswered that hangs unanswered over the individual experiences.

The scientific development of any line of inquiry usually proceeds from the noting of spontaneous natural occurrences to final pinning down by experiment. On this question the decisive experimentation still remains to be done. The process of experimentation would no doubt be stimulated by an increased number of reported experiences whose bearing seemed as strong as some of these above. The need is not necessarily for tremendous numbers, but only for a sufficient number to give suggestive variety and a degree of reassurance that here really are data that call for investigation. It well may be that many more such experiences can be found if their value and significance comes to be more generally appreciated. It is reasonable to suppose that if there are discarnate personalities and if they can ever influence and communicate with the living, they may do so with some degree of frequency. Possibly the evidence is available, once eyes are opened to see it.

At the same time as one follows that line of reasoning, the opposite one must also be kept in mind. In making the present study we have seen the changed interpretation that must be given many experiences involving the dead, simply because of the establishment of ESP. A number of occurrences particularly most of the "death coincidences," that once quite reasonably were considered evidence of survival have now lost their weight since they can equally well be seen as indications of the psi powers of the living.

With this balancing thought in mind we can still recognize the meaning of the establishment of psi on the question of survival. Psi, whether expressed in personal experiences or occurring in the confines of laboratory experiments, shows the human being possessed of abilities transcending those of his purely physical and sensory make-up. Those abilities or qualities in themselves are of the order of the spiritual, if by that is meant extra-physical. They may be the first clear evidence of it the age of science has produced.

The scientific approach to this great area—that is, to the unusual abilities of the human being and to the ultimate destiny of personality—is a relatively new one. Whatever the value of the older ways of dealing with this area has been—and we must be grateful for all they have brought and conserved for civilization—this scientific approach has now been introduced and been shown to be a fruitful way of gaining wider knowledge and understanding of man's inner nature. Even though still in its early stages, it is an approach which promises to open new vistas if the world wants the answers enough to make the effort to find them out.

The Larger Perspective

We have now surveyed the field of spontaneous experiences that could be the result of psi. Although the cases come from many different persons widely separated by time and space, similarities can be glimpsed that suggest that in the background lawful processes are operating however great the foreground differences appear.

In all these separate occurrences we see people finding out about their world, getting information from sources not tapped by sensory channels, sources so diverse and seemingly inaccessible as thoughts, things, and the future. Moreover, the information comes not only from these diverse sources separately but also from them in combination. The line separating telepathy and clairvoyance, for instance, is seen to be hazy. Often in the experiences labeled ESP it cannot be distinguished, sometimes because of lack of information but sometimes also because the source of the experience, the event itself, seems to include both thought and thing. In the area of precognition, too, distinctions are not always clear-cut. The division between present and future is often blurred; the past and future are perceived as if they are the present. The extrasensory perception of these various situations seems simply to encompass all, as if in a timeless, spaceless purview.

The perspective given is such, in fact, that the lines of distinction laid down between the types seem to be only superficial markings necessary at first to help make "sense." One can see now that they are chalk marks only, like those of preliminary or scouting stages of map-making, and do not necessarily mark fundamental divisions of reality.

What can all this mean about the extended universe, the world which is the source of all our information, whether it comes through sense perception or more hidden channels?

It seems to mean that basically the different dimensions of reality are not divided as our senses show them. It seems as if perception by the senses has superimposed these distinctions on reality, and that in some ultimate way these differences of thought and thing, near and far, present and future, are only superficial, the creations of the human mind. Scholars trying to comprehend the universe have recognized that back of the world as we perceive it must lie a reality quite different from the psychological concept of it with which we are familiar. The implications of psi experiences fit in with the idea of a less limited reality and they add to it the data of observation. The meaning could be that the reality glimpsed through psi is a truer representation than the one the senses picture.

A concept of reality without the familiar distinctions, however, is almost incomprehensible to the sense-conditioned mortals we all are. A few of us may be able to escape to a degree the blinders of this conditioning. But many of us are unable to do so and no doubt will long remain uncomprehending before the mystery of the reality suggested by psi. We will continue to be unable to conceive how it can be possible to know another person's thought or perceive a hidden or future event; unable to imagine how precognition, intervention, and free will could all be facts, if such they are. This inability to "imagine" is and will be our limitation—just as it is a limitation for most of us to be unable to feel the reality of atomic structure, so that a table remains a table; a rock a rock; and neither becomes a system of minute particles surrounded by vast space, no matter how well or ill we know our physical theory.

Nevertheless, we have finally come to accept the theory of atomic structure as an idea, even though it never seems real to us. In a similar way, in time, with information about and familiarity with the concept, we may also come to recognize the universe as glimpsed by ESP. We will come to know about it whether or not we are able to reconcile it with the universe our senses present to us.

The world will go on just the same in any case. We shall have no more, no less freedom because we know that some dreams come true, that sometimes the distant is nearer than the near, that sometimes the future is foreseen. We shall live with these unknowns and whether we like it or not we shall even use them, when we can, to smooth our paths a bit and to avoid our little personal calamities.

As we realize more and more that the world is larger than it seems, and that we are more than the sense-bound mortals a mechanistic stage of science tends to make us think we are, we shall like the expanded universe. We shall see that if people have this potential, the universe is greater than it seemed. We shall realize that, *logically* at least, there is room enough for the continuation of something of personality after the senses have ceased to function. Whether or not such continuation is a fact, or just what the form or *modus operandi* of it could be, is and long may remain an unsettled question. But at least from this perspective, one can see that *it could be.*

This glimpse of a more vast universe is the climax of the survey of psi experiences. It is a climax, really, that goes beyond the topic of survival of personality after death. It is a climax that could only be arrived at with a degree of objectivity today by the particular kind of exploration pictured herein—a scouting trip. For much of the area is still unexplored territory. But the study of experiences in the raw, like a preliminary exploration, can give a perspective not yet accessible by more firmly marked pathways. Even from this vantage point, one can see that many of the outlines and patterns glimpsed are not yet co-ordinated. We can see that it is still too early to expect all initial misdirections, inevitable in pioneer explorations, to have been corrected. Nevertheless, these experiences, in conjunction with the experimentally established facts in the background, seem to show distinctly that the human spirit is not to be confined within its sensory limits. This much of the project of exploring the wider reaches of personality is now on firm and solid ground.

Suggested Readings

GENERAL BACKGROUND

Murphy, Gardner, *Challenge of Psychical Research*. New York: Harper & Brothers, 1961.

Rhine, J. B., *The Reach of the Mind*. New York: William Sloane Associates, 1947. (A non-technical review of the main experimental researches on the types of psi.)

Rhine, J. B., and Pratt, J. G., *Parapsychology*. Springfield, Ill.: Chas. C. Thomas, 1957. (An introduction to parapsychology intended for the student or professional man needing a textbook or handbook of available test methods, general results, lists of references.)

Journal of Parapsychology. A quarterly founded in 1937, Durham, N.C.: Duke University Press. (Reports original research, discussions, book reviews, abstracts of current research in other periodicals.)

SPECIAL EMPHASIS

EVIDENCE FOR ESP.

Rhine, J. B., and others, *Extra Sensory Perception After Sixty Years*. New York: Henry Holt, 1940. (Out of print.) (A survey of the experimental research to 1940 with criticisms and replies.)

Soal, S. G. and Bateman, F., *Modern Experiments in Telepathy*. New Haven: Yale University Press, 1954. (A survey of English research, especially.)

Rhine, J. B., *New World of the Mind*. New York: William Sloane Associates, 1953. (Chapter 2. Claims, Challenges and Confirmations. An outline of the types of evidence.)

Schmeidler, G. R. and McConnell, R. A., *ESP and Personality Patterns*. New Haven: Yale University Press, 1958. (Chapter 2. Evidence that ESP occurs. A joint account by a psychologist and a physicist.)

Eysenck, H. J., *Sense and Nonsense in Psychology*. Baltimore, Md.: Penguin Books, Ltd., 1957. (Chapter 3. Telepathy and Clairvoyance. A detached evaluation by a competent psychologist.)

POST MORTEM SURVIVAL.

Hart, Hornell, *The Enigma of Survival*. Springfield, Ill.: Chas. C. Thomas, 1959. (A presentation of arguments pro and con.)

Heywood, Rosalind, *Beyond the Reach of the Sense*. New York: E. P. Dutton & Co., 1961. (Eight chapters on mediumistic material. Historical.)

West, D. J., *Psychical Research Today*. New York: Macmillan & Co., 1953. (Four chapters on mediumistic research.)

Library of Congress Cataloging-in-Publication Data

Rhine, Louisa E., 1891-Hidden channels of the mind / Louisa E. Rhine : foreword by
J.B. Rhine.
p. cm. — (Collector's library of the unknown)
Reprint. Originally published: New York : Morrow, 1961.
Includes bibliographical references.
ISBN 0-8094-8050-6. — ISBN 0-8094-8051-4 (lib. bdg.)
1. Extrasensory perception—Case studies. I. Title. II. Series.
BF1321.R553 1989   133.8—dc20   89-27208 CIP